SWAMPWALKER'S
JOURNAL

Books by David Carroll

THE YEAR OF THE TURTLE

TROUT REFLECTIONS

SWAMPWALKER'S JOURNAL

DAVID M. CARROLL

....

SWAMPWALKER'S JOURNAL

A WETLANDS YEAR

A Mariner Book

HOUGHTON MIFFLIN COMPANY

BOSTON · NEW YORK

First Mariner Books edition 2001

Visit our Web site: www.houghtonmifflinbooks.com.

Library of Congress Cataloging-in-Publication Data
Carroll, David M.
Swampwalker's journal : a wetlands year / David M. Carroll.
    p.   cm.
ISBN 0-395-64725-8
ISBN 0-618-12737-2 (pbk.)
1. Wetlands — New Hampshire. I. Title.
QH105.N4C27 1999
333.91'8'09742 — dc21   99-27342 CIP

Printed in the United States of America

Book design by Robert Overholtzer

QUM 10 9 8 7 6 5 4 3 2

For Laurette, Sean, Riana, and Rebecca

ACKNOWLEDGMENTS

This book came to entail more time, pages, and turns in the road than I ever could have foreseen. I am grateful for the gracious patience of my editor, Harry Foster, and Houghton Mifflin Company. I especially thank Harry for his long-term commitment and, in the final stages, his editorial suggestions, which did much to clarify a manuscript in which the author himself became lost on more than one occasion. Peg Anderson's attentive, perceptive copy editing greatly assisted the final phase.

I am especially indebted to Brian Butler and Annie Burke for constant and generous soundings as I wrestled with this project and for deep information and perspectives on wetland ecology, evolution, and (of course) turtles. Sheila Tuttle, Margaret Liszka, Todd Aubertin, Edie Hentcy, Sy Montgomery, Gordon Ultsch, Michael Klemens, Carl Ernst, Jim Harding, and Scott Warren have been extremely supportive and have shared sites and/or insights as well as specific information that has been central to my knowledge of turtles and wetlands. A continuing inspiration in my work has come from David Holden, who died at an early age, early in the formation of this book.

I have been fortunate to come to know and benefit tremendously from other outstanding field workers and wetlands advocates, and I deeply appreciate what they have done for habitat preservation as well as for the evolution of my own project: Margaret Watkins, Jamie Fosburgh, Mark Kern, Judith Spang, Kitty Miller, Joan McKibben, Trudy Loy, Laura Eaton, Anne Tappan, Sara Callaghan, Kim Babbitt, Sally Turtle, Jim Taylor, Barry Wicklow, Jaime Haskins, Alison Whitlock, Joan

Milam, Tom Akre, Bill Brown, Nancy Bell, David Mauger, Bern Tryon, Tom Tyning, Brett Stearns, Carol Foss, Amanda Lindley Stone, David Brown, Barry Paterno, David Allan, Heather Behrens, Bill Niering, Laura Deming, Toni McLellan, Gordon Russell, John Kanter, and Rich Cook. Norman Stevens provided unflagging encouragement.

A knowledge of aquatic botany is fundamental to any understanding of wetlands; I have been greatly assisted in this realm by Mary Perry, Dan Sperduto, Rick Van de Poll, and Don Padgett and also helped by Liz Harvey and Frankie Brackley.

During the book years, access to certain lands expanded my range of familiarization with wetlands: special thanks to the Courser and Bates families; to Tupper Hill, Norcross Wildlife Sanctuary; to Fran and Paul Verrette; to the Blickels, Larsons, Fisks, Plumleys, and Chapins; and to Camp Hedding and Tilton Woods.

I also want to thank agencies that provided funding and/or logistical support that helped to keep me in the wetlands and often provided me with valuable new venues as I worked on the book: the National Park Service, the United States Environmental Protection Agency, the Norcross Wildlife Foundation, the Lamprey River Watershed Advisory Committee, the Lamprey River Watershed Association, the Great Bay Partnership, the New England Interstate Water Pollution Control Commission, The Nature Conservancy, and the New Hampshire Department of Environmental Services.

Much appreciation goes to my agent, Meredith Bernstein. And I want to remember here, and thank, some people who go back to the days of my first wet sneakers: Julia Chase, Gordon Ultsch, and Herb Clement.

A final note of deepest appreciation goes out to those researchers I do not know personally but whose work is an ongoing invaluable legacy, freely given, and to all who have labored with great dedication in the exceedingly difficult arena of habitat protection.

Any errors herein are the sole responsibility of the author.

CONTENTS

INTRODUCTION

It is my delight and good fortune to have spent a large measure of my life in wetlands. For close to five decades now, from an intuitive boyhood bonding to a more scientific perspective in later years, I have moved among vernal pools, marshes, swamps, floodplains, and peatlands. Later science has done nothing to diminish earlier poetry: answers only unlock questions, and specific knowledge only deepens the mystery of the earth's landscape and life. As a boy, I knew ponds and swamps and streams; if the word "wetland" had been coined, it was of rare or specialized usage, and I never heard it. Today one can hardly glance at a newspaper or a television program without encountering the term. Magnificent even in their present broken and besieged state, wetlands have become arenas of intense human debate.

My focus has always been freshwater wetlands, and that focus has led to this book. Each year I head out to the pools, marshes, and swamps at thaw, always with a particular eye out for turtles, and I stay there for as many hours of as many days as possible, until the ice returns. This long, wonderful season generally extends from late March to late November or into December in my home wetlands in New Hampshire. My intent in this book is to take the reader through some of my rounds and to convey aspects of what I see and experience over the cycle of the seasons. There is so much to be seen, even in a little vernal pool, let alone in a river's great floodplain, that any account is necessarily limited. I introduce the hydrology and structure of various wetland types and a range of the plants and animals typical of each.

The wetlands I describe are in the glaciated Northeast, though I do refer to other parts of the United States and Canada. In each chapter I enter a different kind of wetland and attempt to describe something of its defining essence, mindful that marshes, swamps, fens, and the like are elusive entities, that they mingle among and shade into one another as well as into the surrounding uplands. My hope is that the reader will gain a feeling of familiarity with these habitats that will engender a deeper, more personal appreciation and awareness of them and perhaps inspire work toward their preservation, which is so critically needed.

The foundation of my writing and drawing is personal experience, my "being there," and what I have learned from having been there through so many epochs of my life. Over the past decade this experience has been greatly augmented by readings of the literature and by dialogues with other field workers, to whom I am much indebted. But my greatest debt is to the wetlands and to the turtles who first led me there and who keep me there today. Though all wetlands are tragically diminished and under incredible pressure in the human-serving modern landscape, what they hold can still be found, often surprisingly close at hand. Moments outside of the human world in the shallows of a marsh, with red-winged blackbirds calling and the wind rustling in cattails or reedgrass, or a solitary spell at the edge of a swamp on the edge of winter — these will bring intimations of the spirit that moves with the water, the light, and the life of the marsh.

Gray treefrog (*Hyla versicolor*) and swamp azalea (*Rhododendron viscosum*)

1 VERNAL POOLS

Finds tongues in trees, books in the running brooks,
Sermons in stone, and good in every thing.

— William Shakespeare

The Reedgrass Pool

September 24, first full day of autumn, 4:47 P.M. Reed canary grass rustles momentarily on a slight dance of evening air that quickly dies away. High above, long trails of cloud race eastward on the winds streaming over the near-breathless layer of air close to earth. Not a single blade of the long dry curls of grass stirs now. The steady pulse and drill of insects becomes an evening raga. Light has begun to fade from the alder thickets behind me, though it lingers in the open, grassy, shrub-scattered hollow before me, a topographical depression set among rounded knolls to the west and north and a high, steeply ascending ridge to the east. Slipping through a screen of reed canary grass on the low ridge of the hollow's southern rim, I step down into it.

From time to time, unseen sparrows punctuate the intensifying insect drone with their final furtive soundings of the day. There is something outward-bound about their shadowy movements, their brief, almost whispered calls. Swamp and song sparrows arrive in spring, animated in flight and exuberant in song, and settle in around and above the water that fills this basin in the earth to overflowing at that season, as though they have come to stay forever. But, like the water, they are seasonal. Most years they depart just before the water starts to return to the pool. But the water and birds are perennial as well as seasonal: in the course of the year they always come back. They will continue to do so every year unless the landscape and the cycles of its water are disrupted.

The open hollow I have stepped into looks like an unmown pasture.

The footing is firm and dry, the earth strewn with the straw of the past years' growth. The matted floor-weavings of stems and blades form artful arrangements: over the seasons the tall grasses die, dry, and lie down under their own weight, or are toppled by wind and rain, pressed by snow and ice and the weight of standing water. Scanning the drapings and carpetings of reed canary grass, I see a more deliberately designed structure, a carefully wrought casing nearly an inch and a half long, built from the same grassy materials in which it lies. This is not the work of the elements or a form created by plant growth but the construct of an animal, a small insect larva. This house made of straw, fashioned from cut pieces of reed canary grass and sedge, adhered to an interior tube of spun silk, served as protection for a caddis fly larva. Until its metamorphosis into mothlike, winged adult, the larva had lived an entirely aquatic life, molting through a series of five encasings like this, making a larger one each time as it grew. In what now seems to be a grassy upland field in which meadow grasshoppers, crickets, and katydids sing and feed, an insect larva that can live only in water completed the subadult phases of its life.

Lifting a decaying section of alder stem that has become partially embedded in the turf of the basin floor, I find an even more readily recognizable indication of an aquatic environment, the shells of half a dozen tiny fingernail clams, ranging in size from an eighth to three-eighths of an inch. The shells are huddled where the last of the season's water collected as summer came on. Fingernail clams inhabit a wide variety of permanent wetland habitats, but they are also able to live in pools that dry up every year. Adults and young burrow into the substrate during the dry season and emerge when their pools refill.

The casing of the larval caddis fly and the shells of the fingernail clams lie close to the base of a tussock of grasslike growth. A number of symmetrical mounds of inflated sedge have colonized a deeper pocket of the two-acre basin. They look like a village of straw huts settled into a small clearing in a forest of grass four feet tall. The reed canary grass, growing on rises a foot or so above the pits in which the sedge grows, towers all the higher. Slight differences in elevation in a wetland can affect the depth of the water and its duration at any given site; those factors in turn dictate what plants are able to grow there.

Inflated sedge can grow only in wetlands. Like the caddis fly casing and fingernail clamshells, it indicates an environment that is, over the long term, ruled by water. Reed canary grass is also virtually confined to wetlands. Its luxuriant growth dominates this seasonally ponded hollow, which I call the Reedgrass Pool. On the sloping rim of the basin, swordlike leaves of blue flag iris thrust from sedgy tangles. Beyond these grow brushy stands of sweet gale, thickets of taller winterberry holly, and alders. The native iris and sweet gale are obligate wetland plants, and winterberry and speckled alder rarely grow outside of wetlands. Even if I had never been here before, never seen this pool at the height of its flood season in spring, the plants and the signs of aquatic animal life would tell me that this currently waterless, grassy place is in fact a wetland, more specifically a vernal pool, which every year alternates between being flooded and drying up.

Earlier in the year, at spring thaw, this pool is filled to overflowing, and even before its central block of ice and the surrounding snowbanks have completely melted, a tumultuous evocation of the changing season begins. First comes the ructious cacophony of wood frogs, quickly followed and joined by the shrill piping of spring peepers. In a week or two, after breeding in the water, the wood frogs depart to a terrestrial life of silence in surrounding upland woods. The peepers pipe on and are joined in time by the high-pitched, drawn-out, sweetly descending trills of American toads, and then by the echoing trills of gray treefrogs, punctuated at times by the clamorous twangs of green frogs.

I come wading here during the season of water, from thaw in early April

Swamp sparrow
(*Melospiza georgiana*)

until the drying up that occurs sometime between the summer solstice and the end of July, depending on the year's rainfall. This is the time of mosquito, mayfly, and caddis fly larvae, early-breeding wood frogs, spring peepers, and spotted salamanders. These are followed by insect-hunting green frogs and bullfrogs, who breed in more permanent waters, and later-breeding gray treefrogs and American toads, who come to trill and mate. It is the time of other annual migrants: spotted turtles, young Blanding's turtles, occasional wood and painted turtles, juvenile snapping turtles, and northern water snakes, all drawn to the rich foraging waters where so many amphibians and insects breed. These reptilian predators are accompanied by wading hunters who wing in and out while the water is here — American bittern, spotted sandpiper, sora, Virginia rail — and the furred hunters of the night, raccoon and mink. Swamp sparrows come early in spring to work the water lines, deftly snaring mosquito larvae and other aquatic insects and at times tadpoles, I think, from the pool. These dark, musically trilling sparrows stay on to nest and, as the pool dries up to become a field again, hunt crickets and grasshoppers where spotted turtles swam in pursuit of tadpoles.

Although vernal pools are not permanent wetlands like swamps, marshes, and peatlands, the only plants that can persist in them are those adapted for life in water or in soils that are periodically flooded or saturated and thus deprived of oxygen into the rooting zone through all or much of the growing season. Such plants are called hydrophytes — literally, water plants. All of the plants around me, the reed canary grass, sedges, blue flag, alder, and winterberry, are hydrophytes.

During cycles of drought, some wetlands may be dry for several seasons, even years. If water does not stand on the surface or if the water table — the upper level of water in the ground — does not rise into the rooting zone during the growing season, seeds of upland plants will germinate. Soil areas formerly deprived of oxygen through flooding or the persistence of water become aerated. Oxygen filters into spaces in the soil, and burrowing animals go to work. Upland annuals move in and may live their full cycle, from germination to seeding. Upland perennials, from grasses to trees, begin to infiltrate and replace entrenched wetland vegetation. But unless a major transformation occurs in the topography, by way of natural causes or human engineering, or a profound shift in climate takes place, the water will return, saturating the root zone and drowning out upland plants, all of which require well-drained, oxygenated soil. Then wetland plants will return.

Two dead pine trees, standing in reed canary grass behind a hedge of winterberry, are testament to such a cycle in this vernal pool basin. During a succession of drier years, the white pines, upland trees that can tolerate some degree of wet footing, germinated on a shelf of land abutting the trough in which the winterberry grows. Though struggling in the seasonally soggy environment, the pines grew to a height of fifteen feet or so, until years of more abundant rainfall restored the hydrology of the pool. They stand skeletal now, surrounded by northern arrowwood, maleberry, silky willow, and the ubiquitous alders. In death, the pines provide hunting perches for eastern kingbirds, seasonal birds who take insects over the seasonal waters here, as well as nesting and hunting places for year-round chickadees, who seem able to find food in the dead branches and beneath the last shinglings of sloughing bark during every season.

As dusk nears, the cadence of crickets grows louder. Light lingers here, as it does in many wetlands, after the surrounding upland forests have darkened beneath their dense canopies. Wetlands, with the exception of low-light cedar, spruce, and hemlock swamps or shadowy forested wetlands crowned with red maples in leaf, lie open to the sky. Even when this hollow holds no sky-reflecting pool, it remains an arena of light in the twilight landscape. It may be the light, as well as the water, that draws me to wetlands.

I thread my way among the tussocks of inflated sedge. Not far from where I found the casing of the caddis fly larva, I come upon rabbit droppings under arching blades of sedge: the husk of a completely aquatic life adjacent to the droppings of an animal as terrestrial as I. I think back three and a half months or so, when I waded here as thousands of wood frog tadpoles swam through the grasses and sedges that snowshoe hares nibble now without so much as getting their namesake feet wet. Where hares dine, foxes hunt. From late summer into winter, and at times on winter's frozen water, foxes track hares here; from early spring to early summer, the hunters are bitterns stalking frogs.

Being dry for most of the year, vernal pools are uninhabitable by fish and are critical breeding places for a small group of invertebrates

Blue-spotted salamander
(*Ambystoma laterale*)

and amphibians: fairy shrimp, wood frogs, and spotted, Jefferson, blue-spotted, and marbled salamanders. While many other animals make significant use of vernal pools, the life cycles of these six species make them dependent upon seasonal wetlands. They are considered indicator species; the presence of any one of them in a seasonal wetland identifies it as a vernal pool habitat.

The specialized wetlands known as vernal pools are extremely variable, ranging from broad, heavily vegetated lowland depressions of over two acres in extent, like the Reedgrass Pool, to unvegetated, water-filled clefts a few feet in diameter in hemlock-shrouded ledges of mountain forests. Although typically associated with wooded areas, vernal pools can be situated in open meadows, sandy washouts, and river floodplains. Some feature rank growth of grass and sedge, some are crowded with emerald-mossed islands of highbush blueberry and swamp azalea, encircled by a high canopy of red maple; many are bowls of dark water with sunken black-leaf floorings in which no plants grow, ringed by a narrow band of wetland trees like swamp white oak and black gum, or surrounded by upland trees like pignut hickory and white oak. They may be set within an extensive wetlands complex or, more typically, entirely isolated from other wetlands in an upland forest setting. Within this bewildering array of physiographic settings and plant associations, vernal pool habitats are defined by a common key set of ecological parameters: they lie within confined depressions that lack a permanent outlet stream; have seasonal, impermanent flood periods that generally last from two to five months; dry out completely most years, usually by late summer; are free of fish; and, most significantly, support the life cycles of animals that are utterly dependent upon this habitat for the perpetuation of their species. The pools define these animals, and these animals in turn define the pools.

Although the term vernal pools comes from the Latin *vernus,* "belonging to spring," most of these pools refill over the course of autumn's transition to winter and could be thought of as autumnal pools. But it is at snowmelt and ice-out, the last sleets, first rains, and earliest warming breaths of spring that they beckon wood frogs, salamanders, and spring peepers from surrounding upland woods, where they have passed the winter in rotted-out tree roots, under layers of bark and litter, in small mammal tunnels and other hibernacula in the earth. The vernal pools summon spotted and Blanding's turtles from wetlands near and far and birds from thousands of miles away.

6:23 P.M. Strange, unsettling cries break the deep silence surrounding the low swishing sound I make as I brush my way through difficult meadowsweet thickets at the north end of the Reedgrass Pool. Two eerie calls, silence, then two more calls. The pattern continues. The repeated drawn-out cries sound like the downscaled bleating of a lamb. I have never heard anything like them, but they seem to express the epitome of distress. I cannot even decide whether the animal who cries out is a bird or a mammal; I can only determine that it is not very big. I begin to track the sounds around a high shrub-and-sweetfern knoll, drawn to them yet at the same time put on edge, touched by a feeling that I would just as soon not see what they are all about. My naturalist's curiosity is compelling, but there are some fates I would as soon not witness. The cycle of two long, drawn-out calls followed by an interval of silence continues. I trace their source to heavy sweetfern cover at the base of the knoll. The cries become even more penetrating. I search the brush hesitantly, knowing that I am virtually on top of whatever utters them. I still cannot guess what kind of animal I am hearing. I sweep aside the low sweetfern with my walking stick, allowing enough twilight to enter and reveal the scene: a wood frog, caught in the teeth of a young garter snake, cries out. Of all the possibilities that went through my mind as I searched for the source of these wails, I never imagined a frog. The snake has one of the frog's hind legs in his mouth, and, winding backward, is dragging him up the slope. This maneuvering takes considerable effort. The snake is not much bigger around than my little finger. I do not see how he could have captured a full-grown frog in the first place, but he has managed to latch on to the frog's foot and steadily work his grip to midthigh, having no more to work with than his jaws and teeth. The frog continues to cry out. The snake coils and uncoils, flexing his belly plates, resolutely seeking traction in soft, plush haircap moss. He has twisted his tail around a sweetfern stem to gain more leverage.

I am not given to interfering with nature, but I find myself unable to walk away from this scene. Snakes have legendary capacity for swallowing prey that seems impossibly large, but the wood frog is in fact well beyond swallowable size for jaws that are already almost completely unhinged in the effort to encompass one hind leg. My human perception that no good can come of this for prey or predator moves me to gently tap the garter snake with my walking stick. The tenacious young hunter lets go of the frog's hind leg at once. He curls back into the sweetfern and is gone. It surprises me to see the snake disengage so quickly. I had expected the release of such an engulfing hold from a mouth full of recurved teeth to be arduous, an additional struggle for both parties, perhaps not even possible. The wood frog pulls his bleeding leg back under himself and settles into a familiar crouching position, completely still. He may well fear that any move he makes will have the teeth of an unseen predator fastened upon him again.

I continue on my way. Snake and frog will soon be entering their separate hibernacula in the uplands around the vernal pool basin to wait out the long winter. The male wood frog, certainly one of last spring's chorusing revelers, is silent now that he has been released from his distress. (I could not tell if the young snake was a male or a female; it is hard for me to refer to any animal as "it," so I resort to the convention of using the masculine pronoun except where I know the animal to be a female.) He will not give voice again until he emerges in the spring and migrates back to the Reedgrass Pool, the site of his metamorphosis from a pool-swimming tadpole to a land-dwelling frog. Wood frogs are silent throughout their approximately three-year lifespans, except for the eruptive vocalizations of breeding males. These are confined to their mating season in vernal pools, which generally lasts no more than two weeks. Following this, they return to land and live in the forest in silence.

Some frog species have distress calls, but other than the prolonged, loud, almost childlike wailings of a struggling bullfrog, they are seldom heard. It is thought that such cries may startle a predator and facilitate an escape. I have captured and observed many wood frogs in their upland haunts, and I have never heard one of them make a sound. The terror, or whatever response the frog felt, of being caught in the teeth of a snake brought forth a rare utterance. The wood frog's nerve-jarring expressions of distress fell on literal and figurative deaf ears in the case of the young garter snake. His was truly a voice crying out in the wilderness. The frog's calls, like the rest of his history, go back hundreds of millions of years farther than the history of my own species. How could such a primordial crying-out ever imagine ears and a sensibility that might interpret it as an appeal for intervention? Neither protest nor imploration would seem to have a place in the natural world, yet their embodied evocations can be sensed in such dramatic existential voicings as the wood frog's distress call. It is hard for a human perception, with its own evolution of cries, to ignore such an expression, even from the nonhuman world. One could well wonder about the possibility of plea and protest, and how far back they might go in the history of living forms. I have seen birds wing to a scene of distress in response to piercing alarm calls of their own kind. No band of wood frogs rushed in here. None ever will. And yet, in the face of an unfathomable unhearing, life cries out at times.

Salamander Rains

April 4, 8 P.M. I set out in darkness on a salamander run to the Hemlock Pool. I celebrate the vernal equinox, but it is ice turning into water that signals the most profound change in the season for me, the end of hibernation and the beginning of the great opening up of the wetlands. My first excursions at thaw come by day, in warming sunlight, to a shrub swamp in which the earliest ice-out takes place and in which spotted turtles begin to move in the first open water of the wetlands year. This irreversible yielding of winter usually comes between March 26 and April 6 in the region of my home wetlands. My second sequence of searches takes place in darkest night, with the earliest rains that hold the promise of setting salamanders on the move in their annual pilgrimages to the breeding waters of vernal pools. Most years, the salamander rains come a week or so after the first stirrings of the spotted turtles, although in seasons with sudden early thaws, these signal turnings of spring can arrive in close succession.

Having already kept my first appointment of the season eight days ago, with a spotted turtle just up from overwintering in the Shrub Swamp, I continue my quest for my traditional second appointment: this with the first salamander in the midst of migration or, suddenly, startlingly, already settled in place in the pellucid meltwater of a vernal pool. Tonight I return to an intermittent stream and its nearby hemlock-shrouded pool in a high forest expanse, wetland traces that are all but lost among the wooded ridges above the Reedgrass Pool and its neighboring vernal pools, permanent stream, and great wetland complex. Even where the earth's restless shiftings and the inexorable work of the glaciers have shaped high and steep terrain, piling up mountainous jumbles of unsorted rock fragments and baring bedrock in places, there are scorings in the topography where water can run and isolated gouges where it collects and stands for a time.

I rushed the season even more five days ago, coming here on a mild night of heavy, snow-eating mist and ice-eroding showers. It was my first time here since the Hemlock Pool dried up last summer. The intermittent stream, a running thread of water that, like the Hemlock Pool, has its essential season at thaw and spring rains and then dries up, was still motionless, a silent vein of ice in deep woods. The forest floor was rock-hard beneath sodden leaves. The drisk and drizzle of that dark night, with clouds of fog curling from receding snowbanks and a steady, metronomic dripping from the hemlocks, did not prove to be the salamander rain I had been waiting for.

Nor is it likely that tonight's chill rain, which has turned to quickly accumulating wet snow, will draw out the salamanders. Large flakes of snow cling to all the bare branches and bend the hemlock boughs, closing the forest in all the more, so that I have to stoop to follow the thread of water that has been set to flowing, indicating at least some progress in the season since the other night, and has begun to run through the ice and frozen earth. This plastering of snow a few days into spring is all water to the waiting wetlands and the abundant life about to awaken within them or to return from winter's waiting places. My lantern beam finds its way through snow tunnels in the transformed, unrecognizable woods. I must follow the intermittent stream now; without its readable pathway, I'd soon become disoriented. As I struggle through white-coated branches and boughs, snow cascades to my neck and wrists, and melts. Encased in snow, the night quiet seems even more silent. In the silence upon silence, I can hear my heart beating. Only the water trickling over ice here and there in the quickening brooklet has an occasional voice.

Although I have twice seen my first salamander of the year on nights much like this, when I arrive at the Hemlock Pool, I see that I am clearly too early for my appointment this season. The pool is an ice shape under a contour-following mantle of fresh, wet snow. While shivering through this onion-snow, I had in mind catching sight of an eager, season-pressing male spotted or Jefferson salamander carrying snow on his back, nosing along the edge of an ice sheet, seeking a meltwater entrance into the pool. But tonight the only being shouldered with snow, looking for water along rims of ice, is me.

April 5, 8:17 P.M. Still seeking the first salamander, I take to the lowlands bordering the upper run of Alder Brook, a strikingly different setting from last night's. Seasonal ponds here are set in depressions in sand and gravel deposits, in basins scoured out by shiftings of glacial ice, or in hollows left in mounded alluvial deposits by the melting of chunks of glacial ice. These vernal pools have become fringed with wetland growth. Red maple and speckled alder encircle their high-water marks. Emergent shrubs — winterberry, black chokeberry, and sweet gale — ring the shorelines out to depths of about a foot and a half. There are also dense, brushy stands of meadowsweet, a shrub that can be at home in flooded wetlands as well as in dry pastures and woodland clearings. Snowmelt comes earlier here than it does in the hills. On the northern sides of the pools, warming sun from the south has melted back some snow cover on sparser shores to reveal edgings of sphagnum moss in wetter hollows and haircap moss on drier mounds. Both of these perennial greens are laced with maroon-leaved vines of large cranberry, some still bearing their crimson fruits of last fall.

My shadow from the three-quarter moon is sharply etched before me as I crunch across the glowing blue-white sheets of crusted end-of-winter snow. The deep, clear sky is made milky by moonlight, but Orion is visible well to the west. The Pleiades have set. Bud swell is noticeable,

Large cranberry
(*Vaccinium macrocarpon*)

especially in the red maple branches silhouetted against the moonlit sky. It is a little below freezing, but salamanders would not move on a clear, moonlit night like this even if it were well above freezing. I have come to see if any might have already moved in these less snowy lowlands, which are quicker to warm than the hemlock- and pine-cloaked ridges, and entered the water while I was looking in on the Hemlock Pool last night. Ice has begun to recede from the margins of the three vernal pools set in a chain along the floodplain of the permanent stream. With sweeps of my lantern, I search the narrow band of clear water between shore and the great ice sheet of the largest pool. Nothing stirs. I wade into the 40-degree water, press my neoprened knees against the ice float and give it a thrust, so that it glides back another two feet or so. Still I see nothing. The water that seems so expectant, and will soon embrace so much vernal life, is empty, waiting.

I walk down an old logging road to the Reedgrass Pool, about five hundred yards away. There is only stillness here as well, save the wintry crunching of my footsteps and the faint tinkling of thin ice breaking as I wade into the pool. I find some open water in the beds of fallen reed canary grass and, shining my flashlight into it, I see the first life moving in the meltwater—hovering clouds of mosquito larvae and hundreds of lumbering caddis fly larvae carrying their straw cases as they work their way through submarine mazes of grass and sedge. Amphipods and isopods, their bioenergetics geared to icewater, zip in and out of leaf layers in the willow and alder shallows at the edge of the pool. There are myriad invertebrates here that cannot be seen without a microscope.

Vernal pool habitats hold a galaxy of small things that come to life the instant ice and snow turn back into water. Spring-fed pools, and those that are deep enough not to freeze to the bottom, may have something astir even in the heart of winter, alive beneath the ice, ready to move on and proliferate at the first warming touch of April's sun.

I shut off my light and wade back to the dark screen of the alders. I don't mind being too early for the salamanders. I do not grow impatient with the reluctance of winter to release its hold. Soon enough the season will break, and not long afterward will take up the quickening rush that makes me feel, until ice and snow return to quiet things down again, that I cannot keep up with any part of it. Reflected stars glow softly on ice so thin it flexes with the gentle undulations in the wake of my wading. The Reedgrass Pool may well freeze over from shore to shore again tonight, but its waters will reopen in April sun tomorrow. Even the denser, glacial strongholds of the ice float and the enduring snowbanks on the north side of white pine stands will be further eroded. I feel certain the next night rains will be salamander rains.

April 9, 7:43 P.M. As soon as it is dark I go out into the rain, which started as midday drizzle, became a downpour in the late afternoon, then leveled off to steady, light rain as day gave way to night. I walk a sodden world as I near the Reedgrass Pool and turn along the alder thickets of its flooded margins at the base of the high eastern hill. It is 47 degrees, a night rain on the verge of mildness. I have every expectation that I will meet a salamander tonight. I manage to take on the patience of the season as I walk and sweep my light for an hour and a half, seeing nothing but wet, black earth, glistening leaf litter, and gray-white lingering snowpack. Now and again, peripheral glimpses of rain-black twigs with specklings of white lenticels or pale patterns of lichen, and dark curls of old white-pine cones, their scales tipped with light-reflecting pitch, have me do sudden double-takes and take a closer look with my light, for they mimic my salamander search-image.

Perhaps the mode I settle into, as inevitable chill moves in and rain runs off my poncho, is more one of endurance than of patience. But I have learned from my years of swampwalking that spring is spring; it is ice sheets and snowbanks, sleet storms, biting winds, and icy water, late snow and killing frosts, as well as the spotted turtles emerging to bask on sun-warmed tussock sedge, the first salamander migrations, wood frog calls, budbreak, unfurling ferns, and the return of migratory birds. For life, spring is in good measure a time of waiting within a constant, incremental advance. With our tendency to think that the world turns for us, or at least revolves in the direction of our wishes and aims, we humans easily become impatient with its turnings; but of course the earth simply spins and tilts toward the sun, away from the sun, with utterly impartial, cyclical wheelings, to which life on earth has become so well attuned. It is hard to see, as melted pools freeze over again, that the turning in time and space, the planetary inclination toward light and warmth, is as inexorable as the coming of winter.

Suddenly (or, after nearly three hours, is it at last?), I am startled by the very thing I have been looking for, surprised somehow by discovering the living embodiment of a search-image I carry from spring to spring: a glistening, impressively sturdy jet-black salamander over eight inches long, brilliantly decorated with two slightly staggered rows of stunning yellow spots. As in the past, the meeting of my expectant search-image with reality is a striking revelation, undiminished by remembrance or repetition. To see these living things anew is to know them anew. With each spring's rebirth there comes a necessary reacquainting.

The salamander does not move. He is stunned, not by chill earth or remnant snow he has crossed but by the sudden intrusion of bright light into his nocturnal world, a brilliant island of light in a sea of darkness. Like the first spotted turtle, he is spring incarnate. In meeting these animals, I meet ice and water, earth, air, and sunlight; the day and the night and the season itself. There is a deep reassurance for me in these meetings. Am I somehow unsure of the seasons, of their landscapes, cyclings, and life? Do I hold some deeply buried apprehension that a time will come when there will be some other progression, when spring will not follow winter? I will not outlive the seasons. They will outlast, by an incalculable measure, my own final turning in planetary time. I know that some of my uncertainty, set aside for now by my finding these signal animals of mine once again making their seasonal rounds in their intact world, stems from the fact that I have outlived too many wetlands, and all of the life and meaning they held.

The spotted salamander faces downslope toward his destination. I am struck by the confidence of his stance, shoulders raised, legs set, neck erect, his head angled sharply parallel with the earth. His mission and manifestation give him a Carboniferous bearing, as though he were one of his immensely larger — three to fifteen feet long — amphibian ancestors. I think of the conflicting forces of waiting and eagerness (equally compelling, no less than obligatory), worked out over great time, that reside within this salamander and his vernal pool kin. They cannot move too soon; they must not move too late. Their individual lives and the reason they exist, the continuance of their kind, are timed to the duration of water in their seasonal breeding pools. His progeny's race against the drying up of the Reedgrass Pool begins with this migration. The chill, edge-of-spring night with abundant rain, final snowmelt, saturated earth, and an overflowing vernal pool is measured against the inevitable day of blazing sun, great heat, and desiccating winds in July or August, when the last film of water in the deepest pool depression becomes transformed into windborne vapor. If the pool has not lasted long enough to allow the metamorphosis of the aquatic, gill-breathing young into terrestrial salamanders, those that come to breed here will have lost their progeny for the entire year.

The salamander and I are on the very edge of the amphibian season. If the day had been warmer, or if this were the second night of a warmer rain, with temperatures in the mid-fifties or better, I'd have encountered scores of salamanders by now, perhaps hundreds of mingled salamanders, wood frogs, and spring peepers. Such explosive movement may occur on the next rainy night. Some years a succession of warm days and rainy nights triggers mass migrations of vernal pool amphibians. The soil's thermal profile reverses, with the earth becoming warmer at its surface than at a depth of a foot or so, and this reversal amplifies the movements. Streams of frogs and salamanders can be seen crossing rain-slick roads. But with the northern spring's tendency to make small advances, then retreat, hold in place for days, and even turn back toward winter, it is more common for these amphibians to move in successive waves or pulses, rather than en masse. Whatever the numbers, the migration routes of these amphibians have been traced out far back in time, predating by thousands of years the ever-expanding, landscape-fragmenting grid of roadways and chemicaled wastelands of lawns and parking lots that has been superimposed upon their once-unhindered world. These seasonal migrations subject frogs and salamanders to enormous roadkill and, in some situations, chemical death.

April 5, 8:30 P.M. A second night of salamander rains. I return to the Hemlock Pool in the hills. Even on the hemlock ridges, where the active season commonly arrives a week or more later than it does in the lowlands, the warm mist and drizzling rain of this 56-degree night must have the first salamanders on the move. In many years, islands of wood frog eggs and the first spotted salamander egg masses have appeared in the Reedgrass Pool before the first arrivals have made their way to the Hemlock Pool. There have even been seasons when, on the same night the first wood frogs and salamanders moved in silence among the lingering snow mounds on their way to this pool, deafening choruses of spring peepers already filled the air over the great wetland mosaic of the Reedgrass Pool, only five miles away. But in springs like the current one, delayed thaw followed by a bursting forth of sudden warmth can even out the progression from lower to higher elevations and from more exposed to conifer-shaded pools, so there is little time lapse in the amphibians' initial migrations.

The intermittent stream has a louder voice than it had my last time here. Warm, wet nights have loosened its tongue. But all along its course there is still more ice than water. The quickened little current slides over smooth, silvery ice, cuts a race beneath it, bores tunnels through it. Awakening water retraces its ancient streambed in earth and stone.

The hemlocks keep some snow yet, within the deep-shaded enclosures their dense, drooping branches form. The mild mist and rain take on a chill in these evergreen winterholds. Set almost entirely in stone, the Hemlock Pool is, at twenty by thirty yards, only a fraction of the size of the Reedgrass Pool. This vernal pool is no bowl of light but a deeply shaded black-water pocket even on the brightest spring day. No vegetation grows within the depression even when the water is gone. Its plant shelter, and the source of its food chain, is provided by fallen leaves and hemlock needles, occasional branches and twigs, bits of bark and finer plant material, such as spent tree flowers, bud scales, and pollen. The larvae of one species of caddis fly in this seasonal forest catchment construct their cases from hemlock needles; another species employs bits of twig and bark. This pool, which could seem some woodland spirit's watering trough, serves as the cradle for the developing young of wood frogs, spotted salamanders, and Jefferson salamanders. These are the forest spirits who come to this bowl of water, not to drink but to procreate.

I go to the deepest pocket in the pool, where Jefferson salamanders congregate. They are found in only a few of the vernal pools where the related spotted salamanders breed, and in far fewer numbers. The Jefferson salamanders tend to breed on a slope that descends to the pool's deepest hollow, where the water is about thirty-four inches deep now. Spotted salamanders and wood frogs share a breeding niche in a shallow extension at the far end of the pool, where water lies eight to ten inches deep at thaw. My first sweep of light in the meltwater moat surrounding the thick, persevering central ice float catches the dusky brown shape of a Jefferson salamander at rest on a submarine ice shelf. Hoping to get a closer look, I attempt to net this one, but with sudden serpentine thrusts he is off his ice perch and out of sight in the deep leaf pack on the pool bottom. As he disappears, another emerges from the same cover. A little quicker this time, I catch the salamander. He is large for his species, a little over seven inches long, deep maroon brown, generously flecked with tiny blue-white spots along his lower sides and legs.

Throughout much of its range, including the glaciated Northeast, the Jefferson salamander hybridizes with the closely related blue-spotted salamander, producing individuals that are sometimes difficult to assign precisely to either species. Hybrids are often referred to as the "blue-spotted group." The distinct blue-spotted salamander, a more northern species that ranges well into Canada, is smaller, at four to five and a half inches, with considerably more elaborate patterning, spotted and flecked with sharp white and dazzling blue on a blue-black ground. In coloring, these salamanders bear a striking resemblance to old-fashioned enamelware. The spring-breeding spotted, Jefferson, and blue-spotted salamanders, along with the late-summer-to-autumn-breeding marbled salamander, belong to a group referred to as mole salamanders, because of their subterranean lives. Except in their aquatic larval period and during their brief annual mating rites in vernal pools, they are completely terrestrial, inhabitants of upland woods. These fossorial amphibians dig and tunnel beneath fallen trees and forest litter, burrow deep into decaying logs, snake their way into the earth along networks of rotted-out tree roots, and follow endless mineshaft mazes created by burrowing mammals such as moles and voles. But in the icy waters of dark-night vernal pools, they become elegant swimmers. If I did not know the life history of the animal I have netted, I could easily take him to be thoroughly aquatic, more akin to a fish than a mole, with his moist, glistening skin and, when I set him free, his adept eellike glide as he disappears in the leaf litter. Several Jefferson salamanders perform their routine of trick mirrors and sliding glass doors in my beam of light, alternately appearing and disappearing, in and out of sunken leaves.

I don't know of another vernal pool nearby; I have circled around for perhaps half a mile in all directions without having found one. Jefferson salamanders have been discovered as far as a mile from any temporary or permanent wetland habitat. Any of the vernal pool–breeding amphibians may travel eight hundred to a thousand yards on their migrations to breeding sites. Vernal pools, which are typically wetland oases set in terrestrial landscapes, enhance the diversity and abundance of species in an area. In addition to their critical role as breeding sites, these unique habitats serve as watering and foraging places and, in some cases, refuges for resident upland as well as wandering wetland species. Some give wetland plants a place in the forest. In many of the landscapes shaped by the last glaciers, chains of vernal pools provide vital corridors for animals moving through upland terrain. Temporary in terms of water-holding capacity, they are enduring habitats over the years, archipelagos in reverse, wetland islands in a sea of land.

Vernal pools are particularly vulnerable to eradication through the wholesale fragmentation and development characteristic of the modern landscape; enormous numbers of them are lost every year. The amphibians who depend on these pools simply cannot persist in highly fragmented habitats; many colonies or populations have been extirpated within the past three decades or so. Recent efforts to identify and even certify vernal pool habitats, while commendable in intent, fail to protect them as viable, persistent habitats integrated into their larger systems. "No-build, no-touch" buffer zones of twenty-five to forty feet along streams and around wetlands fail to protect vernal pools. Even the absolute protection of the natural vegetation and the hydrology—the movement and distribution of water—in a one-hundred-foot swath around these pools, a rarely implemented preservation standard, would not assure success over time. Roughly one half of the salamanders who breed in a vernal pool shift to woodland habitats that are over five hundred feet from the pool for the remainder of the year. Even if the Reedgrass Pool and the Hemlock Pool had an enforced buffer zone of one hundred feet (something on the order of thirty-three paces), encircled by roads, driveways, lawns, parking lots, and the like, they would still be doomed to ecological extinction. Yet even this modest buffering measure would be considered unthinkable by most development interests. Faced with the inevitable prospects of lawsuits, it is a rare regulatory body or community that will stand firm on even this inadequate degree of protection. More dramatically than many habitats, vernal pools become lost when they are cut off from their larger systems. Where filling, draining, and pollution are regulated, the seasonal ponds may still be present, and the water quality may possibly be reasonably high, but they cease to exist as habitats. Their animal life dies out with the death of their ecological integrity. Leaving a narrow band of buffering vegetation around an encircled vernal pool has been likened to protecting a bird's nest and the tree it is in, while eliminating the surrounding field and forest habitat required by those who fledge from the nest. Where are a vernal pool's transformed tadpoles and salamander larvae to go after they have become land dwellers?

Our economy demands that we maximize human use of the land. In particular, the heavy dependence on new housing starts and the automobile, with their attendant road building, consumes the natural environment. These factors are compounded by cultural, economic, and legal traditions that one has the right to do whatever one pleases with one's land. We appear to believe that this right is incontrovertible, even God-given, however large or small the parcel, however it came into our hands, whatever impact that use may have on the natural landscape. Overshadowing these impacts are the pressures of devastating increases in global population. Against these overwhelming forces, the remaining vernal pool salamanders advance at each winter's end with evolutionary confidence and guidance. They will move to their pools even when the migration has become a death march.

Liebesspiel

April 8, 9:17 P.M. The rain had the surface of the Reedgrass Pool fairly boiling for a time, then slackened to a confusion of ripplings that continued to prevent my looking in. Now it has abated enough that I can begin to see into the water spaces, sunken grass tangles, and sedge mounds. During the time I was unable to see, I searched for later-arriving salamanders in the difficult meadowsweet thickets and the more open cranberry edging of the northwest corner of the pool. I found only a solitary female. At just over nine inches long, egg-laden and looking quite swollen, she is one of this population's matriarchs and no doubt the mother of many salamanders over her lifetime, which could span twenty years or more. She was just about to slip into the pool among the cranberry vines, which now lie under about a foot of water. Evidently most of the spotted salamanders are in the pool by now. When the critical factors of precipitation and temperature, which decide whether migratory amphibians advance or hold in place, line up favorably, there is no time for lingering. The interconnected abiotic and biotic events of the breeding season are tightly compressed, commonly with two weeks or less for mating and two or three months for metamorphosis of the young.

This compression in time and space is embodied in a stunning scene revealed by my sweep of light into a sedge pocket where abundant spotted salamander egg masses are deposited each year. It seems that all of the salamanders I have been looking for this spring are here, and have all become one, in a mesmerizing black mass of interweaving sun-yellow spots. On many occasions over the years I have seen dozens of artfully posed and intermittently moving spotted salamanders crowded together into a small section of a pool bottom, some touching, occasionally clasping, in premating aggregations known as congresses. But I have never before witnessed this *liebesspiel*, as it is called, this loveplay, a great communal congress of salamanders continually weaving among themselves in a dense, nearly spherical mass. It is a dizzying, fluid flow. Limbs tucked against their sides, one main stream of salamanders slips from one pole of the rough globe to the other, while others slide around in all directions. The integrated mass seems solid salamander, with no spaces anywhere. Now and then individuals emerge from the whole without leaving a space, swim eellike to the surface to take a gulp of air, then dive to reimmerse themselves in the liebesspiel. The entire swiftly flowing company turns its collective outer curves in an undecipherable doubling back that is pure legerdemain. I watch, transfixed, unable to make out any one salamander or discern how they wheel back toward the center. Adding to the magic, the *perpetuum mobile* of the entire living orb remains stationary in the water.

Oblivious to the spotlight that has come to illuminate their theater-in-the-dark, the salamanders weave on and on. A congress generally starts out with all males, as few as four or five at first, their numbers swelling as others join in. Even a full-fledged liebesspiel commonly begins with all males, in time joined by females. A vernal pool may host two or more congresses in separate niches. As females join the waiting males, a communal congress of the dimensions of this one, numbering a hundred or more, may form. Shifting my beam of light from the hypnotic swarm, I find that several pairs and threesomes have separated out, or perhaps never joined in. The purpose of the communal loveplay is evidently to stimulate the later stages of the courtship and finally mating. One of the separate pairs is engaged in a courtship dance, circling around each other and nudging heads under each other's bodies, each paying particular attention to the base of the other's tail. The male rides up over the female and rubs his chin along her back. My searchlight also reveals a bed of spermatophores clustered on the grass-strewn bottom and lined along some shafts of the sedge. The males may begin to deposit spermatophores several days before mating and egg-laying. The tiny, bluish white, irregularly shaped stalks of gelatinous material resemble spits of pine pitch. They are crowned with tinier packets of sperm.

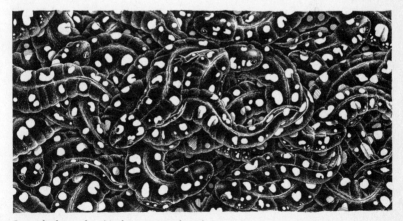

Spotted salamanders (*Ambystoma maculatum*)

After a courtship that may include a closeness of the magnitude of the liebesspiel, the actual transferral of sperm to receptive females is a curiously distanced transaction. Following bouts of the courtship dance, the male walks in front of his intended female slowly, wriggling his tail, signaling an invitation to another dance, one that takes on the air of a procession. The courting male endeavors to lead his prospective mate to where he has placed his spermatophores. If all of the group and individual preliminaries, as well as the timing and the ambient aquatic conditions, have been stimulating enough to render the female receptive, she will follow him and finally straddle one of the spermatophores. With her cloaca, she will take up the male's sperm packet, which will fertilize her eggs internally. This is generally the culmination of the mating ritual for the female, who will show little or no further interest in her mate or any other male, although she may take up sperm packets from more than one suitor. The male may move on to another congress and find another mate.

Within a day or two I will find egg masses here. Unlike female wood frogs, who lay their eggs while in the tight embrace of mates who have mounted their backs, a union known as amplexus, female salamanders move off alone to deposit their eggs. They may do this directly on the pool bottom, be it leaf pack, peat, or mud; but more commonly they ascend grass or sedge stems or fallen branches in the water, take a grip with their hind feet, and extrude and affix their eggs near the surface, sometimes with the upper dome of the mass showing above the water. Salamander eggs, like those of wood frogs, are tightly compacted when first laid but swell greatly as their jellylike matrix expands. The average number of eggs is 100 to 125, but older, larger spotted salamanders may lay 250 or more, sometimes in a single clutch, sometimes in two. Younger females tend to lay their eggs in several clusters of a few dozen each. Depending on water temperatures, the eggs take one to two months to hatch. The globular egg masses from which the larvae emerge may persist for weeks beyond that, providing highly visible proof that a vernal pool supports breeding by spotted salamanders.

Before wading out of the Reedgrass Pool, I shine my light on the liebesspiel again. The ceremony looks as if it could go on all night. Although it takes place under water and is the dance of voiceless animals, I find the total silence of this unceasing choreography somehow baffling. With all this resurgent life, all this energetic movement and consummate grace, I feel I should be hearing some accompanying music, or at least some rhythmic beat, calls, or steps. A flock of birds wheeling in air without calls at least makes the sound of wingbeats. But this magnificant primordial ceremony of boldly patterned amphibians takes place in total darkness and utter silence. It is a dance unseen and unheard by the dancers themselves, but the touching and feeling, so prolonged and ever in motion, and perhaps amplified by ambient darkness and silence, must be profoundly felt by these sensitive-skinned ones. After their few nights of loveplay are over and mating consummated, they will leave the pool and separate out widely over the upland landscape to become solitary, subterranean animals for the rest of their active season.

Fairy Shrimp

April 12, 7:53 P.M. As the day's light fades, I set out to locate a vernal pool, new to me, that I was alerted to by a rollicking chorus of wood frogs in the afternoon. I heard the frogs calling upslope, to the west, as I explored a stream running through a red maple swamp. Their vocalizations do not carry nearly as far as those of spring peepers, who can be heard from half a mile away. When I detect the ducklike calls of wood frogs, I know I am within two hundred yards or so of their pool. These vociferous frogs have led me to the breeding places of the silent salamanders, who never betray their presence with sound and can be seen only by night.

The day is giving way to a clear, cold night, with winds astir. I make my way along the upland border of the red maple swamp to a trailing of surveyor's tape I tied to a branch to mark the point where I should turn uphill to get to the pool. Most vernal pools are relatively minute in relation to the acres of forested terrain in which they are set. Finding one's way to such a pool on a darker night can be a challenge, especially in mist or rain.

I ascend an oak-studded slope to its high, narrow crest, brushy with an understory of low-growing black huckleberry. As is common in places not traveled by people, a well-worn trail, etched into the land by centuries of passing deer, runs along the spine of this huckleberry ridge.

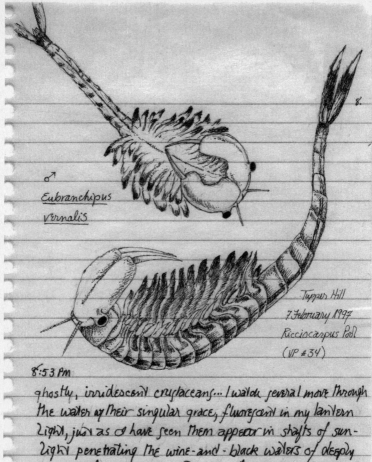

8.

♂
Eubranchipus
vernalis

Tupper Hill
7 February 1997
Ricciocarpus Pool
(VP #34)

8:53 PM

ghostly, irridescent crustaceans... I watch several move through
the water w/ their singular grace, fluorescent in my lantern
light, just as I have seen them appear in shafts of sunlight penetrating the wine-and-black waters of deeply
shaded forest vernal pools... They hover and glide w/
rhythmic, wavelike pulses of their legs, ascending and
descending, as if by magic, in the water column. Subtle
neon creatures in the night, pale blue-white, tipped at
times w/ bronze, a slash of red toward their conspicuously forked green-white tails; they have a quality
of starlight about them. Their watery dancing turns

Swamp notebook page with fairy shrimp (*Eubranchipus vernalis*)

Looking down, I see the pool, a broad oval of diminishing silvery sky light lying in a deep, dark hollow. Descending and pacing it off, I find it to be relatively large, about forty by twenty-five yards. By lantern light it seems to be mostly open water at this point in the season, with several red maple islands and highbush blueberry mounds. The stars are brighter now. Entering the dark water, I wade among their reflections, heading toward the Big Dipper. There is no sound but the wind, lulling away. The temperature has fallen sharply, to about 40 degrees, too cold for wood frogs to be calling.

The first line of light I cast into black water catches the glimmerings of ghostly, iridescent crustaceans, barely an inch long. I watch several of the fairy shrimp move through the water with their singular grace, fluorescent in the slant of my lantern light, just as I have seen them appear in shafts of sunlight penetrating the wine and black waters of deeply shaded forest pools. Swimming on their backs, slowly drifting, they dart occasionally, spasmodic tail-flicks giving them surprising bursts of speed. They hover and glide with rhythmic, wavelike pulses of their legs, ascending and descending as if by magic in the water column. Subtle neon creatures in the night, pale blue-white, tipped at times with bronze, with a brilliant slash of red, their own bright blood, toward their conspicuously forked blue-white, green-white tails, they have a quality of starlight about them. Their watery dancing turns my lantern beam into a fairy wand. Their eleven pairs of gill-feet, broad, leaflike appendages, not only propel them but serve as gills and help manipulate their food, microscopic protozoans, floating diatoms, and other algae that abound in vernal pools. Delicate, ephemeral, elusive animals, somehow they are at once dark and transparent. Fairy shrimp may appear in a pool for years, then fail to show up for a number of years, then reappear. When their pools dry up in the summer, the adults die and their eggs lie dormant before hatching out in icy midwinter waters. If the pools do not become recharged, the eggs can remain viable through waterless periods of a decade or more.

Fairy shrimp go beyond being edge-of-winter animals, appearing in the very heart of winter to drift and dart beneath the ice cover. By hatching, growing, mating, and laying their eggs during the time of coldest water, fairy shrimp avoid the more intense predation that comes with the warming of the pool. But there is no time of complete sanctuary. My shifting lance of light reveals another aquatic animal who swims on his back, an insect known as a backswimmer, who has captured a fairy shrimp almost twice his size. This predator strokes about the pool with great difficulty, his prey in tow. With their long, oarlike back feet and keeled backs that slice through the water, these predatory water bugs could be models for racing shells. Backswimmers belong to one of several aquatic insect families that can inflict painful, often long-lasting, fiery stings. They are among the reasons I no longer wade, as I did as a boy, barefoot and bare-legged. These skilled swimmers can also fly and, like predacious diving beetles and giant water bugs (more reasons not to wade barefoot), are able to locate isolated vernal pools from the air.

Although salamanders must have come to this pool by now, I don't find any. Nor do I see any egg masses. A thin crescent moon has risen and, with the stars, it brightens the water enough to keep the salamanders under the black leaf pack on the pool bottom.

In the still night, I hear mammals moving in dry litter in the surrounding uplands. I recognize the stepping of a deer. There are scurryings and pawings I cannot identify, though one shuffling digger is probably a skunk. Along the margins of the pool, shrews, mice, moles, and voles are no doubt at work. All the sounds I hear are terrestrial. Evidently I am the only night wader out here.

I come upon a bed of spermatophores just off a tangle of dead branches, and, in sedgy shallows on the north end of the pool, the first wood frog egg masses of what will probably become a large communal island of them, judging from the magnitude of the chorus I heard in the afternoon. I then discover a pair of wood frogs in amplexus, immobile on the leaf flooring. Their embrace will last the night, with fairy shrimp gliding all about them. My rippling departure from the pool and my heavy, booted footsteps in dry leaves as I ascend the huckleberry ridge and descend to the border of the red maple swamp cause all the other night walkers to be silent for a time.

Wood Frogs

April 15, 11:27 A.M. The occasional clear, piercing cries of a broad-winged hawk and the clamor of red-winged blackbirds along the flooded brook margins are barely audible over the guttural calling of male wood frogs from their favored breeding niches in the Reedgrass Pool. People hearing these calls for the first time frequently mistake them for the quacking of ducks, unseen ducks in the middle of the woods. Wood frogs generally beat spring peepers to their breeding pools by one or several days and give the season its first frog chorus. They may number in the hundreds, yet when they sense danger, they are of a single mind and but one voice, cutting off their urgent calling at once. Somehow, in the midst of a mating frenzy, they keep an eye out. They dive to cover, and the urgency of the mating season is subjugated, for the moment, to the demands of self-preservation. But these revelers can wait only so long to get on with the business that drew them to the vernal pool. In time an anxious male calls out. His first few cautiously spaced utterances may go unanswered, or unchallenged, but soon a second will voice his own ardor, a third will join in, and the irresistible tumult will burst forth anew.

The wild and heart-gladdening chorus I heard as I walked toward the Reedgrass Pool dropped off before I was in sight of it, causing me to wonder if the frogs had sensed some other potential menace. As I come up over the crest of a long sandy knoll, a kame left by the glaciers, above the wetland basin, a broad-winged hawk lifts up, rising from an area of tussock sedge mounds and stunted red maple saplings. His wide wings, brown above and strikingly white, tipped with black, below, carry him off to the high, wooded ridge to the east. The appearance of this winged hunter, who counts frogs among his prey, was undoubtedly what silenced the chorus. I do not see a ripple nor hear a single call as I wade into the Reedgrass Pool. The warmth and rain that brought the wood frogs here have nearly completed their work on the ice. One thin float remains, on the north side of a dense screen of alder and winterberry. It is dull and gray, pitted by rain, eroded by wind. The new season eats away at this last remnant of winter past, transforming its frigid pewter into water as clear as glass.

I wade to where the hawk took flight and discover, low on a mound of tussock sedge, at the water's edge, a freshly killed frog lying bleeding. The skin has been peeled away from his back and legs. He looks disturbingly like a person who has been flayed. Wood frog tadpoles are highly palatable, attracting many predators. As those who survive approach metamorphosis, their skins become increasingly toxic, adding a measure of protection to their heightened wariness and greater speed at escaping. The hawk was evidently dressing, or undressing, his catch to avoid the noxious effects of the frog's skin when I came along to interrupt his lunch. Evidently because of their toxic skins, the last wriggling tadpoles of wood frogs and American toads in drying ponds often go uneaten. They die not by predation but by desiccation, their massed bodies providing something of a breeding pool for flies.

The skinned frog had made it through his long overwintering until spring summoned him from within the dark, protective earth to this place of sun and bright water. Intent on mating, he failed to detect a swift-moving shadow in the sky, and his song today was the last of his life. Here is one of those meetings in time and place among living things and seasons that are difficult to fully comprehend. A great raptor, with a wingspan of three feet, has traveled far, perhaps four thousand or five thousand miles, on updrafts and wind currents high above the earth, to wintering grounds in South America and back again, to drop from the sky and seize a two-and-a-half-inch frog who spent the winter only a few inches in the earth, probably no more than a hundred yards from the spring pool in which he was captured. It is no great exaggeration to say that, by virtue of the broad-winged hawk and the wood frog, this vernal pool, set among kames and boulder ridges in the northeastern United States, has a link with the high mountains of northern Peru.

With a hawk sweeping down from the sky and me wading the pool like an enormously oversize heron, the frogs understandably keep out of sight. I withdraw to one of the Reedgrass Pool's deepest areas, by the only large rock in this sandy basin, a glacial erratic somehow separated from the boulder-crowded ridge. Spotted turtles may bask on its lichen-covered shoulders a week or two from now. I lean against it and look out on the pool, well hidden by a screen of winterberry, a wetland shrub so intricately branched it provides cover even in its leafless state. This is one of my favorite watching places, and I try to keep as still as possible, as long as possible, when I am here. This is not easy during plague times of black flies, mosquitoes, or deer flies — sometimes all of them at once.

From this lookout I have seen spotted turtles basking on mats of sedge or grass, pursuing insect larvae and tadpoles, racing about in wild courtship chases. Several times over my thirteen years of coming here I have seen the froglike heads of young Blanding's turtles, among the most elusive of the elusive, with their bright yellow chins just above the water. Swamp sparrows are always busy along the water lines, warblers and kinglets continually flit among branches just above my head. I have heard unseen bitterns call at my shoulder when the reed canary grass has grown to fill in all of the space above the water, providing bird and man alike a virtual invisibility that allows an uncommon closeness. On one occasion I watched a bittern suddenly emerge at a channel-edge opening, seize a green frog, lift his head and neck for a gulping swallow, then vanish in a screen of green and straw gold. It was as if the reed canary grass had transformed itself into a silent, stalking heron and then back into whispering grass. From this same watery thicket I have observed mating water snakes intertwine and developing spotted salamander larvae twitch in their eggs, deep within the turgid jelly of their egg masses. I have seen predacious diving beetles and caddis fly larvae bore into that same protective gelatinous coating to eat eggs and larvae. On later-season visits, when the water is only a little over ankle deep, I have looked on as tiny tandem damselflies have dipped into the lingering shallows, depositing their eggs, while metamorphosing wood frogs, still with tails, took their first hops on soggy mattings of grass.

Had I been here a little earlier today, I'd have witnessed the broad-winged hawk dropping from the sky and catching a wood frog. I am curious as to how this worked. I assume the hawk must have behaved like an osprey diving for fish and, with a precise strike of his talons, taken the frog from the surface of the pool or just beneath it. These frogs of forest floors are entirely aquatic when they are in vernal pools. They do not haul themselves up on logs or sedge mats the way the later-arriving green frogs and bullfrogs often do but keep low in the water. They have no interest in feeding now; their sole aim is to breed. At 46 degrees, the water is still numbingly cold, but these frogs are quick-moving and at peak activity, causing me to marvel all the more at the hawk's hunting agility. It is perhaps easier to envision such an abundance of frogs in a steamy swamp, but wood frogs are boreal animals, inhabiting much of Canada and a good part of Alaska. Their range extends north of the Arctic Circle. They are at home, and exceedingly lively, in icewater.

In time the frogs come back to the surface. *Nn-nyerck* repeated, then *r-r-r-, yurrk, yur-ruck,* one or two bold or impatient males call, advertising themselves to females. Soon the calls are repeated by others, joining and overlapping, until a multitude of frogs is calling at the same time, in a relentless chorus. How many frogs does it take to make such a skull-impacting sound? And roughly half of those in the pool are silent females. First the air comes boisterously alive with sound, then the water with movement. Ripples everywhere, rushes at the surface; these voices have bodies after all, long-legged bodies surging through the water.

Each season a great band of wood frogs mates in reed canary grass shallows at the edge of the deep cut just off the boulder. Another numerous contingent takes to a deeper hollow about forty yards from this site, in a broader spread of water with hummocks of inflated sedge, surrounded by reed canary grass and bordered along its shoreward margin by tussock sedge and a boglike shelf of sphagnum moss and cranberry. When their mating rituals have been concluded, there will be islands of eggs, on the order of five feet in diameter, worked into weavings of grass and sedge just beneath the surface at each breeding niche. Those who entrust their future generations to the temporary habitat of a vernal pool evidently know where it will dry up last. Within a few days of breaking out of the egg masses, the tadpoles disperse in all directions, into all depths.

Frogs swim almost at my feet, just beyond the winterberry; chasings, grapplings, escapings, and couplings resume, accompanied by the unrelenting guttural implorations of eager males. The chorus, if this noise can properly be called that, is wildly gladdening even as it hurts my ears. Within a critical mass of sound, I can pick out at times the brief, higher-pitched release call of a male who has been latched on to by another male. In such a crowd, with so many insistent embraces going on, mistakes can be made. I see that several females, who are larger than the males and noticeably swollen with eggs, are in the grip of two or three desirous suitors, none of whom is inclined to let go. Ardor is such among these frogs that females ensnared by several males sometimes drown. Aided by rough pads that develop on their thumbs during the breeding season, males take unyielding holds. They may clasp a female for hours or even several days. The ephemeral nature of the season and the pools in which wood frogs reproduce dictates the ferocious tenacity of the male's embrace.

I once saw a solitary pair in amplexus in a small, isolated pool late in the breeding season. I saw no egg masses. The manner in which the male gripped his intended mate suggested to me that he felt he had found the only female of his kind in the world, and he would never let her go. Another time I found a young bullfrog caught helplessly in the clasp of a male wood frog. Intervention seemed appropriate here, and it was easy to capture the tandem frogs, though the bullfrog made every effort to evade me. I tried to gently separate the two but the wood frog was as good as a living time lock. Gentleness getting me nowhere, I attempted a forceful pulling apart, again to no avail. I then worked carefully, but still forcefully, on the forearms and intertwined digits of the wood frog, seized so tightly around the bullfrog that it must have restricted his breathing. I worried that I might break one of his arms, but I finally managed to pry the wood frog's front feet apart (they were much like human hands) and open his forelegs enough to let the bullfrog slip from his grasp.

It troubles me to interrupt these surging lives on the awakening edge of spring, charged with and decidedly committed to sustaining their species. But I am not a wood frog. My feet are numb, my legs approach immobility, and my body is taking on a shiver, despite the April sun. Though I know it's not possible, I try to make my departure go unnoticed. My first slight turning, however, cuts off all sound but the ripplings of diving frogs. That sound, too, dies off quickly. The surface of the Reedgrass Pool grows still. An inadvertent magician, I have made three hundred frogs disappear. Since I have already disturbed them, I decide to check one of the traditional breeding niches, where they lay a great communal island of egg masses. This communal nesting is thought to foster warmer temperatures and more rapid development of eggs in the center. Or it may help prevent desiccation of the innermost eggs during drought years, when the pools may dry up before tadpoles hatch, in case a refill comes in time to rescue the stranded eggs. The massing may also serve to insulate central clusters from the deep freeze that may follow breeding in some springs. The density of communal egg masses may also restrict losses to predators who are able, in varying degrees, to dig into the protective jellied coating. In any case, it appears that a very high percentage of eggs escape desiccation, freezing, and predation, and develop into tadpoles who make their way out of the coating. It is at the tadpole stage that predation takes a heavy toll. This reduction in numbers is necessary to lessen an impossible competition for the vernal pool's rich, but by no means inexhaustible, food resources.

I see no eggs in place, but find that I am present at the initial moment. In sunken swirls of canary reed grass just beneath the surface, I sight a pair of wood frogs in amplexus. Heads down, they face each other, she holding on to grassy ropings with her front feet, he holding on to her. The female is in the act of depositing and attaching an egg mass, her long legs parted and extended around her sphere of eggs. At extrusion, the mass appears as a rounded, tightly packed black ball of eggs, like a wad of buckshot. The jelly coating will expand greatly over the next day or two, to its more commonly seen configuration. Each female lays from several hundred to two thousand eggs, in one or several globular clusters; the males, still in amplexus, release their fertilizing sperm over the eggs as they are deposited. The male's hind legs are folded forward, his webbed feet set against the globe of eggs. I cannot make it out clearly, but it looks as though he is helping her to extrude her egg clutch. The gesture of his clenched forefeet and set hind feet convey the impression that he is literally wringing the eggs out of his mate. I have to wonder how this mass of fecundity could have fit within her body. After deposition is completed, the female sinks to the bottom, her formerly swollen body sunken in, flaccid. She indeed looks as though she has been wrung out. The male swims away, indicating that his mate has laid all of her eggs. He may remain in the pool and perhaps attempt another mating, but the female, emptied of eggs, will leave the pool as soon as she has recovered from her exhaustion. Not wishing to hold up life processes that are from their very inception a race against time, I wade out of the Reedgrass Pool.

The Forested Pool

April 30, 1:17 P.M. Clear, melodic calls of a northern water thrush ring out from the stillness of a hemlock-shaded vernal pool. As young green frogs detect my approach, they hop, screaming and splashing, into the water from the wooded borders. I stand for a time at the southern end of this 120-yard-long pool, where an outlet brook dashes down small rocky spills and flows through a little pool ringed with mossy stones and profuse with marsh blue violets on its way to join a river a mile downstream. This is a richly vegetated vernal pool, with several extensive stands of winterberry holly and dozens of tree-mound islands, dominated by red maple and eastern hemlock, with occasional yellow birch, a solitary red spruce, and a shrub understory composed primarily of winterberry and highbush blueberry. After the water warms some, and before it dries away, herbaceous water plants arise in sunlit areas beneath openings in the tree canopy.

By virtue of its high crown of trees, this wetland could be classified as a swamp, or forested wetland. At the same time, owing to its topographic features and seasonality, and the fact that wood frogs and spotted salamanders breed here, it is a vernal pool habitat. Although it is linked with a river, this high woodland pool with its seasonal outlet is inaccessible to fish. Wood frogs; Jefferson, blue-spotted, and marbled salamanders; and fairy shrimp do not breed in waters fish can enter. It appears that they are unable to withstand the predation fish would bring to bear on their eggs and young. I have, however, often found the egg masses of spotted salamanders in waters patrolled by fish, generally where cloggings of vegetation might act, to some degree, as fish screens. I once counted eighteen egg masses lying on the perimeter of an open-bottomed pool, just out from dense sedge growth where young chain pickerel, six to ten inches long, hid, in their characteristic lancelike fashion, poised to torpedo after any passing prey. I have also discovered egg masses in side-water shelvings just off the main flow of swift streams populous with brook trout, black-nosed dace, fallfish, and white suckers. It appears that spotted salamander egg masses have some resistance to fish predation and that the larval young are unpalatable to fish or capable of avoiding them.

For their part, fish press the margins, even to the point of death, in seeking prey. As I searched a vernal pool in a hill region one night, I caught sight of a quickly turning form, brownish, with light spots and flecks, that spun out of my lantern beam and into sunken leaf drift. I gently stirred the leaves with the handle of my net, unveiling a sparkling, richly speckled native brook trout about seven inches long. The pool had two inlets, one a seep feeding in through level ground from a sedge and sphagnum source only twenty yards away, the other a spring-fed rill that tumbled over stones and slipped under boulders and tree roots. Both sources run dry each year well before the drying of the vernal pool they flood. No fish could come by way of these feeds. At full spring flood the pool has an outlet, a slip of water through a shallow, leaf-clogged channel that descends to the gravelly run of an intermittent stream. The trout had reached the luxurious vernal pool by way of this minimal and perilous flood-time fish ladder. In order to complete the final leg of his journey, I am certain he worked his way sideways through wet leaves, as I have seen adults and fry do in vegetation and even among small stones, in low water. He would have a splendid season in the vernal pool's cold, well-oxygenated, spring-fed water, with its abundance of insect and am-phibian larvae. But it would be a comparatively brief season, and in all likelihood a terminal one. Once the water dropped below the level of the lowest lip of the pool, the trout would be trapped. As groundwater-fed sources diminished, the eight- to twenty-inch depths of the pool would shrink away, becoming warm and oxygen-depleted. He might survive this phase, but he could not survive the summer's drying out. Having found a number of brook trout stranded in cut-off streambeds and streamside pools, I thought it doubtful that this one would retreat be-fore it was too late.

I am certain no fish could ever make the ascent from the river to the Forested Pool. But, like most intermittent streams that have not been in-tersected by roads, channelized, culverted, and stripped of their ripari-an, or streamside, natural cover, the outlet is a travel corridor for many animals, from juvenile green frogs to full-grown moose. I walked this stream course one February day when it was silent, stilled in ice, and drifted with two feet of snow. Along its narrow slalom run through leaf-less trees were sets of running tracks and long slides, unmistakable signs of a river otter's having used it as the final link of his passage to the river from a large meadow pond a half mile away. These networks of little streambeds need not hold running water to serve as corridors for wildlife.

The Forested Pool is holding at full depth today, a-swim with little velvety black wood frog tadpoles. Spotted salamander larvae, soon to hatch, are clearly visible in their egg masses. There is something in the nature of vernal pools, with their brimful springtime waters and teeming life, that belies the often harsh reality of their temporality. Like the amphibians who could not exist without them, vernal pools have two lives, one aquatic, one terrestrial. Vernal pool habitats are as varied as they are intricate and complex. Within their defining commonality, every vernal pool I have come to know has its own hydrologic and habitat signature, its own timing, its unique bestiary and botany. This seems to me to be the case with all wetlands.

I wade into the pool from a mossy, hemlock-shaded bank, threading my way through emergent shrubs, scattering wood frog tadpoles in all directions as I cross winterberry shallows to an island mound crowned by a tall, twin-trunked red maple. Its upper third is leafless from dieback brought on by seasons of prolonged flooding. Hemlock saplings and highbush blueberry skirt the taller maple trunks. All of these woody plants are rooted together, forming a stilted mound on what was once the base of a toppled hemlock. The trunk of this great tree, which went down decades ago, lies in the pool, providing footings for an archipelago of smaller shrub and sapling mounds. Deep accretions of sphagnum moss cover the bases of these brushy islands, as well as the sodden length of the hemlock log that reaches above water. A water thrush works her teetering way through the gnarled twistings of aged blueberry branches, bobbing with every step, repeatedly uttering her crisp, metallic call note, *whit . . . whit . . . whit*. A pair nests in or close by this forested wetland every year.

I have come here to look for other nesters, tiny ones who make no sound and keep out of sight in the plush overhangs of sphagnum moss, a little above the water line. Four-toed salamanders come here to breed. As their name indicates, they have four toes on both front and hind feet, while most salamanders have four in front and five behind. By this point in the season females with egg clutches should be here. The water thrush bobs and weaves her way out of sight and stops calling. I begin my search, carefully lifting a handful of saturated sphagnum moss from the thick outreaches and overhangs it has built out from root mounds and the waterlogged tree trunk, replacing the moss as I work my way along the water line. The third handful I lift reveals the red-brown back of a salamander curled up with her eggs. After a moment of stunned surprise, she slips away into the soaked and pliable inner depths of the

Nest-guarding four-toed salamanders (*Hemidactylium scutatum*)

sphagnum. Her eggs are adhered singly, in a loose gathering, to the pale moss in her nesting cavity. These diminutive salamanders, females averaging about three inches, the males a little smaller, mate in late summer and fall. In spring, females migrate to wetland nesting grounds and deposit their eggs from three to eight inches or so above the water line. Unlike the mole salamanders, who leave their breeding pools with the first night rain after they deposit their egg masses, female four-toed salamanders stay with their egg clutches, attending them until they hatch, in five to eight weeks. The larval young, upon hatching, wriggle down through the soggy matrix of their nest, which is commonly sphagnum moss, but may be other mosses, mattings of grass roots, or rotted wood, and drop into the water, where they live as aquatic gill-breathers until their metamorphosis about six weeks later.

I continue along the fallen hemlock. Lifting sphagnum from knuckled roots of blueberry mound, I uncover a large aggregation of eggs and a pair of guardian females. One has twisted over onto her back. Her snow-white underside, finely peppered with black dots, show sharply in the dark, shadowy moss pocket. This habit of rolling over to flash a white venter possibly startles would-be predators away from the eggs. Female four-toed salamanders frequently nest communally, with one or several staying to guard the entire complement of eggs. A single female's clutch usually contains less than three dozen eggs; a nest holding more then forty eggs is likely to be a communal one. The guardian females I have uncovered hold in place a moment, one upright, the other on her back. The distinct constriction at the base of the tail of this species shows clearly on both. When they are seized by a predator, the tails break off more readily than those of other species. The twitching, detached tail occupies the predator as the tailless salamander escapes. In time, a smaller, stubbier tail regenerates. The right-side-up female soon wriggles swiftly through the moss and drops into the water, to disappear in a dark hollow under her nesting mound. I quickly replace the moss covering over the inverted one, who has not left her post. It is hard to picture such tiny, soft-skinned animals, lacking fangs or claws, in the role of guardians. Yet they are evidently able to drive away a variety of predators, from ground beetles to shrews. Egg clutches that receive maternal protection appear to be considerably more successful than those left unattended.

Four-toed salamanders do not require vernal pool habitats in order to breed and so are considered facultative rather than obligate vernal pool species. I have found them nesting in a number of wetlands where spotted salamanders and wood frogs breed. But I have also found females guarding egg clutches in the sphagnaceous marsh and shrub-swamp backwaters of a large, open pond and in a sphagnum-laden seep with only an inch or two of standing water, sites that would not support breeding by obligate vernal pool species.

3:02 P.M. After finding seven nest sites, I conclude my survey of the Forested Pool. Piercing cries from high in the sky interrupt my departure. Looking up, I see a pair of broad-winged hawks wheeling in an open space in the canopy of budding red maples and dark hemlocks. Suddenly they sweep together and begin a spectacular spiraling free fall, tumbling over and under each other. They appear to clasp talons briefly, with one hawk right side up and the other on his or her back. I have never seen a bird upside down in the air before. They separate and, without a wingbeat, ascend high again on an updraft, then repeat their aerial acrobatics before circling high once more and careening out of sight. Broad-winged hawks have swept just over my shoulder here, as I've stood hidden on tree mounds in the pool. With shrill, plaintive, descending hisslike cries they have protested my passing too close to their nesting tree on my way to the pool. These raptors who soar the high clear air and haunt the dark woods are not considered wetland birds, but they hunt the Forested Pool regularly in its season and nest close by. By way of its water and its wildlife, the Forested Pool is part of an ecosystem that encompasses the intermittent inlet and its source, the floodtime outflow brook and its seasonal confluences, the great floodplain with its ever-flowing river, and the uplands all around.

Ariadne

May 10, 4:44 P.M. Mayfly hatch: glistening wings throughout the wetlands, in the near and higher air, over and along the brook, at the edge of the alder swamp, and everywhere above and around the Reedgrass Pool as I step in at its alder and willow border and wade to my watching place by the boulder. The mayflies rise, then, wings still for a moment, they fall. Again a sudden ascent, followed by another drop, all in midair. Gossamer-winged, double-tailed, they look like tiny cellophane kites with no means of controlling their flight, yet they hold precisely spaced places in the brisk and capricious breezes. At times they drop to touch the water, and this proves perilous for many of them. Unless perfect in their touching down, they become ensnared in the water's embrace. Its skin seems a magnet to them, and frogs are waiting. Seventy-five yards from here, along the brook channel, where water is too deep and swift for frogs, trout rise to mayflies caught in the drift. They are risking their fleeting lives to deposit eggs — but "risking their lives" may not be the best way to put it, for in this final winged form they exist only to mate and lay eggs. They do not even have mouths, for they will not be eating. This ephemeral existence as winged creatures of thin air, a stage that lasts from hours to a day or two among the many mayfly species, culminates a life of from one to several years as completely aquatic larvae, gill-breathers whose form gives little clue to the aerial appearance they take at transformation. It seems curious to me that the mayflies dip to the water in this vernal pool. It doesn't seem that their eggs could hatch and their larvae complete a life cycle where water is destined to disappear in as little as two months. Evidently this breeding multitude disperses and dispenses its eggs somewhat like seeds on the wind, touching down wherever water beckons. Some of the gleaming pools, like the sky-dancers that are drawn to them, are ephemeral. Eggs or larvae will fail in these, but out of the incredible numbers of mayflies, enough will deposit eggs in permanent water.

Now that mosquito larvae have undergone their own metamorphoses and flown off, by the tens of thousands, to nearby damp and shady places, amphibians seem more abundant than insects in the pool. There are scores of green frogs and bullfrogs, who have migrated here to take advantage of the good hunting. I cannot begin to estimate the number of spring peepers who have come to breed in the wake of the wood frogs. The peepers will linger and breed into June. The musical calls of American toads indicate that the several pairs who sometimes breed here have moved into place in their customary grassy pool-edge shallows. The prolonged, sweetly penetrating rolling trills of the males carry well, summoning females from uplands all around. The shorter, lower-pitched trill of a gray tree frog advertises that his kind, too, has begun to move in. But it is the streaming schools of thousands of wood frog tadpoles continually sweeping by me and fanning out everywhere among the mats and new spears of the reed canary grass that lead me to think that Amphibia at this moment outnumbers Insecta, even with the ubiquitous caddis fly larvae factored in.

The latest encasements of the growing caddis fly larvae reflect the progress of the season. As fresh shafts of reed canary grass come forth in the water and thrust above it, the larvae cut bits of bright new green as well as the faded gold straw of past years' sunken growth for the construction of their cases. They are thus cloaked in a weave of green and gold, perfectly camouflaged in the submarine grassy tangles through which they ceaselessly forage. It seems as if their constant tumble-bumble movements would offset any camouflage effect their house-coats might offer. One larva, clambering over sunken stems, has caught the eye of a brilliant predator in the clear water. A spotted turtle stalks forth, one whose radiant head and shell patterns I recognize at once. Since thaw, in my wadings of the Shrub Swamp, this vernal pool, and the intermittent stream that passes through the alder swamp linking these wetlands, I have had an eye out for these markings. The turtle they adorn and identify is one of several whom I have allowed myself the conceit of naming: Ariadne. This first sighting of her this season marks the fifteenth year I have known her. Over that time the theme of my spring searches has become "looking for Ariadne." I usually find her ear-lier in the year, either during the last week of March or the first few days of April, as one of the first spotted turtles to emerge from the Shrub Swamp, or, during the first two weeks of April, as one of the first to mi-grate into the Reedgrass Pool. This remarkable vernal pool is where I first encountered her, and even then, fifteen years ago, her plastron was already too worn for me to attempt to determine her age. I conser-vatively entered her in my notebook as being "at least twenty years." It is likely that she has been coming to the Reedgrass Pool for three decades or more by now, after reaching traveling age at ten years or so. She may be coming here even after my swampwalking days are done. The impor-tant thing is for the pool to continue after our respective times are up.

Ariadne stalks the lurching caddis larva as though it were a tadpole capable of suddenly darting away. She thrusts her head forward, seizes her prey, and begins to work on its encasement, rapidly snapping at it with her keen-edged jaws, raking it with her sharp-pointed claws. The house of straw, fortified with an interior wall of spun silk, holds up under the assault, its tenacious texture and structure rather than its camouflage serving to protect the soft-bodied architect. It is hard for me to see how the struggle goes, but in the end there seems to be a gulping swallow, and I conclude that Ariadne has managed to extract the larva. She pays no attention to a nearby mass of spotted salamander eggs, whose developing larvae twitch in the interior, algae-greened light. Several years ago I observed her dig into an egg mass and evidently get a few eggs, but the difficulty was greater than that entailed in extracting the caddis larva. Over the years I have seen many spotted turtles in many pools with salamander egg masses, and only twice have I seen the turtles make an attempt at them. Ariadne will be more likely to focus her attention on the endless parades of wood frog tadpoles. They are so alert now, and so quick, that she would do well not to try to chase them down in open water. More likely she will stalk and ambush them in the heavy vegetation. Ariadne drifts out of sight in the mazes of reed canary grass that she knows and navigates so well.

To this day, the sighting of a spotted turtle, particularly the first of the season, carries an aura of my first encounter with one. I was eight years old, wandering alone, when I entered the turtle's world. I remember the evening green of that place, the smell of the plants and water, the sky light on the pool, the glimmering of a brook that emerged from a shadowy wood. All around me the world was alive. There were ceaseless callings and splashings of frogs, flittings of birds and dragonflies. I had recently moved from an urban environment and had never seen anything like the wetland world that lay before me, never felt anything like what I felt in its presence. I saw movements different from any made by frogs, birds, or insects. I waited and watched. A turtle swam into a clear space in the shallows. It was intensely black, glowing with yellow spots and orange head markings, a stunning living thing that made my heart race. Shoes and all, I waded in and caught the turtle.

My bonding with that wild animal in her wild place was immediate and deep. That wetland no longer exists, but I have followed the species to new places the rest of my life. Because of that turtle, year after year, day after day, I enter the wetlands and move among their other animals and their plants, getting to know them in a way I otherwise never would have. The first spotted turtle was the Rosetta Stone for a language I had never even known existed before, a language that cannot be spoken. The turtle became my translator of and guide into an ultimately unknowable world, the embodiment of an ineffable realm I seek to know, in the sense of being there without needing to fully understand it. I have come to realize in later life that the turtle was my liberator, as well, from an exclusive bondage to the human world, from a form of political imprisonment and a denial of spiritual and intellectual freedom that I was already coming to resist. The Native Americans say that each of us has a totem animal. Clearly the turtle, and specifically the spotted turtle, is for me that living spirit-bridge between the human and natural worlds. I do not look for human meanings out here; one who looks for human meanings in nature will never see nature.

Ariadne will stay in the Reedgrass Pool as long as its abundant food resources hold out and the water depth and escape cover are adequate. She will leave sometime between the end of May and late June and travel to her nesting grounds. After laying her eggs, she will come back here and again stay as long as the conditions suit her. Although vernal pools are more commonly thought of in terms of amphibians, aquatic insects, fairy shrimp, and other invertebrates, they are prominent turtle habitats in many ecosystems. The Reedgrass Pool is unusually important in this regard. At one time or another during its seasons of ponded water, spotted, subadult Blanding's, juvenile snapping, and adult painted and wood turtles come here. Spotted turtles, which make extensive use of vernal pool habitats throughout their range, are the most abundant species here and stay the longest. Although they are considered facultative, not obligate, vernal pool species, I believe that spotted turtles are able to inhabit some wetland complexes only because of the rich seasonal foraging provided by vernal pools within those complexes. Spotted turtles may hibernate in wetland niches that cannot provide enough food for their peak activity season in spring. Like Blanding's turtles, they are able to radiate outward from their overwintering places to vernal pools a mile or more from any permanent wetland, following intermittent streams or crossing upland terrain. They feed heavily until the pool becomes too shallow or their prey runs out.

As the heat of summer comes on, and the water in vernal pools and other wetland niches falls below the levels that spotted turtles require, most of them estivate, entering a state of greatly reduced activity that parallels hibernation. They commonly take to terrestrial hideouts for this phase of their cycle, burrowing under forest litter or tunneling into thatch in dry, sunlit fields. Or they may estivate in wetlands that have largely dried up for the season, in the same muddy, root-bound niches where they overwinter. I have found adults and juveniles shifting about in shrub swamps during summer rainy spells. Their deeply tannin-stained shells suggest that they have been dug into shrub, sedge, and fern mounds. Spotted turtles may estivate for months, even when favorable water levels are maintained in their wetlands. But there are exceptions to this pattern. I sometimes find them fully active in aquatic environments when one would expect them to be estivating. This is more likely to occur in wetlands with deep, mucky bottoms complemented by exten-sive floating mats of sphagnum moss and/or heavy emergent shrub cover. If the broader wetland includes niches that provide the proper water depth, escape cover, and prey, some members of a local popula-tion of spotted turtles will remain active in those niches while others estivate.

If summer rains are heavy enough to refill vernal pools, spotted tur-tles are likely to return to them for another round of feeding. Deeper vernal pools, such as buttonbush kettles, can support overwintering by spotted (and in some cases Blanding's) turtles. The turtles are thus able to greet the incoming salamanders and frogs at thaw. This is especially true from southern New England south, where spotted turtles have been seen swimming at night among clouds of spotted and Jefferson sala-manders. The loss of vernal pools can leave some landscapes uninhabit-able by the spotted turtle, a once-common species that has suffered great decline throughout its range due to degradation, alteration, frag-mentation, and loss of habitat. I feel certain that in some ecosystems spotted turtles are dependent upon vernal pools in order to persist. In such situations, it would seem correct to view them as obligate vernal pool animals.

Blanding's turtles are the equal of spotted turtles in their ability to locate vernal pools, and both species may make long and arduous migrations to reach them. These turtles, so well adapted to palustrine wetlands like sedge marshes, shrub swamps, buttonbush kettles, and boglike, acidic harsh fens with sphagnum mats, may travel through high, dry forests of beech and hemlock or oak-hickory woodlands, as well as dry, open fields, to get vernal pools in which wood frogs breed. Protecting a wetland to its water's edge, or even to its broadest wetland plant and soil boundaries, clearly does not begin to address the habitat needs of spotted and Blanding's turtles, or of many other wetland species. It is necessary to protect buffer zones, migration corridors, and contiguous habitats.

Ariadne has not been out of sight for long before I have a very different reptile to watch, one I have never seen in the Reedgrass Pool, or, for that matter, in any body of water. Moreover, I have never before observed a northern redbelly snake out in the open in broad daylight. The midafternoon appearance in water of this extremely secretive, nocturnal snake is highly unusual but evidently deliberate. He hunts along the water line, his tongue flicking continually as he winds through miniature-forest tangles of branches and drapings and stiff mats of reed canary grass. He moves with measured grace in the vegetation, makes sudden sideways dashes across spaces of open water, then resumes his slow, sinuous stealth when he reaches another maze of plants. In his quick and fluid crossings he moves over the water as though he were a sidewinder traversing desert sands.

The slender little redbelly, with his gracefully small head, is only about ten inches long. He is not capable of swallowing even the smallest of the green frogs or bullfrogs here. It seems more probable that he could be swallowed up by one of them. He will not find the favored food of his species, earthworms and slugs, in this pool. The snake slips out of sight before I am able to witness him attempting to catch anything, and I consider the possibility that he has come here to hunt tadpoles, as do the ribbon snakes who migrate here from marshy backwaters along Alder Brook.

My encounter with the redbelly snake is one of those incidents of discovery that makes me more keenly aware of how complex and multifaceted a habitat the Reedgrass Pool is, and of how easily it could all be undone. Trenching a length of several yards at the lowest lip of this seasonal pond would be enough to end its history as a wetland, a history that goes back to the landscape shapings of the last glaciers. Some earnest hours with a shovel or pickaxe, or a few minutes with a backhoe, would end an ecology that has been thousands of years in the making. Dig a narrow ditch, and water would no longer collect here. It would steadily slip away and disperse among the lowland alders, downgradient to the south. The seasons of salamanders, frogs, and turtles would end immediately. Bittern, sora, spotted sandpiper, and Virginia rail would circle low over the hollow, find no water, bank away and not return. Wetland plants would disappear more slowly. With no annual period of standing water to keep them at bay, upland grasses and shrubs would move in. Tussock sedge, inflated sedge, blue flag, and winterberry would die out; even the tenacious reed canary grass would be supplanted. In time, upland trees from surrounding ridges would seed in, and the Reedgrass Pool would become a woodland hollow. Ditching and draining are not the only means by which such a wetland could be destroyed. Dump trucks and fill could achieve the same end in little enough time.

On varying scales and by varying means, this has been the fate of innumerable wetland habitats, from vernal pools a few yards in diameter to vast acreages of wet meadow, marsh, and swamp, their ecologies hardly known, if known at all. The natural landscape is being held hostage, being sold out, to human politics, economics, and fancy, exacerbated by the crushing pressure of overpopulation. Generally speaking, vernal pools are the smallest, most seasonal, most isolated of wetland habitats. Yet they are among the most ecologically complex of natural environments, inhabited by remarkably specialized species whose life histories are intimately interconnected. Vernal pools are a profound study in the convergence of the living and the nonliving, of plants and animals, earth, water, and climate coevolving and adapting to achieve the balance of their present moment. The migrations and metamorphoses of vernal pool amphibians and the seasonal journeys of spotted and Blanding's turtles are only a few aspects of a long, complex history that, up until some three centuries ago (the span of six or so generations of Blanding's turtles) had been playing out in an essentially unbroken landscape. The future of the vernal pools that are left, whatever it might have been otherwise, for the time being lies with the whims of human actions. It does not appear to be a very bright future.

The Reedgrass Pool is one of the largest vernal pools, and one of the most diverse in animal species, that I have come to know. In my time I keep a record of this place, as best I can. I am continually overwhelmed by its extent and biodiversity, as well as its time, its cycle of seasons. I could spend the entire flood season of many successive years in this pool alone and still have much to see.

6:36 P.M. After wading the pool, I return to the boulder lookout for some final surveillance. Almost at once I see a male spotted turtle knocking his way about in sunken branches and tussock sedge in the blue-flag shallows, shoreward of the deeper channel. His active circlings, dives, and surfacings go on for some time and have the heedless vigor of a male intent upon a female. He makes enough commotion for two turtles. Intermittently, as evening comes on, spring peepers take up their singing. A toad trills. I lose track of the turtle, then sight him again, as he surfaces clearly. As much as I'd like to see if he is familiar or new to me, I feel that he is on a courtship mission, so I do not attempt to make a capture. Often I must decide between catching a turtle to document a known individual or discover a new one and staying back to observe its behavior.

The male disappears once more, and when he suddenly reappears, he has a female in his grasp. She surfaces, bringing him with her, struggles, frees herself, and dives off toward the deeper channel. I advance to the outer edge of the winterberry thicket. The pair swims right to the toes of my boots, in a swirling of spots in darkening water that does not allow me to identify either one. They are soon off again and out of sight, though I can trace their animated race for a time by means of brisk stirrings in the canary reed grass. The spirited courtship of their species may take this pair from one end of the pool to the other and back.

They are gone but a moment when another pair scrambles by, knocking against my boots as they pass. I am truly seeing spots now, swirling and spinning, and suddenly organizing into shapes separated enough to show me that this is a triangle, not a pair, with two ardent males pursuing a female. In resolving the carapace patterns, I realize that the female is Ariadne. Another meeting, and another insight into the life history of this turtle I have known so long. I now have observed a courtship site and time specific to her, as well as two of her nesting sites and their hatchlings, two migration routes she travels on her way to this vernal pool (along which I have also seen her attended by courting males), her activities here, her annual overwintering area, and a specific hibernaculum within it. This picture, which has taken me fifteen years to assemble, seems surprisingly complete to me at times, but I know it is fragmentary. Two years ago I did not see her all season. A person following these long-lived animals over the years may come to believe that they will always be there, but I wondered, during the searches I did make that year, if she were still around and if I'd ever see her again. If I were able to radio-track her, I could fill in many blanks concerning her daily and seasonal movements and activities, but I am content for now to wade and walk the seasons of her wild places, with so much else to see, ever looking for Ariadne.

A wind has come up, alive and rustling in the reed canary grass. It soughs in the pines on the knoll above the Reedgrass Pool. The evening wind is their common voice, but the pines and the grasses have distinct tongues. I look up at the pines' black silhouettes and see that these trees hold hands with the wind. With wavelike bowings and risings, they seem to pass the wind from one to another. An earlier voice comes up anew, a voice of a thousand voices that intensifies as daylight diminishes, until I can no longer hear the wind. Spring peepers fill the edge of night with a shimmering wall of sound, a massive, pulsing union of shrill pipings. Somehow individual calls stand out in the deafening chorus, staccato bursts of sound, sharp, sweet, clear, penetrating, with a plaintive upward turn at the end. These are the advertising calls of males intent on mating, and one must wonder how the silent females single out any one voice and respond to its advertisement. Mingled among these are distinct trills, high-pitched, sweet, and clear, slightly longer, and also slurring upward at the end. As agreeably musical as these trillings may sound to the human ear, they are aggressive warning calls that erupt when another male enters a singer's territory of four to sixteen square inches — diminutive, but space enough for a three-quarter-inch to inch-and-a-half frog and his mate.

As gladdening and morning-filling as the mingled songs of birds at a May dawn can be, and as pervasive and penetrating as the night-encompassing cadence of insects in autumn can be, these world-filling, mind-altering choruses of spring peepers have no equal in the north-eastern landscape. There is talk now of the silence of the frogs, of their striking diebacks, and declines and the disappearance of species globally. Debate is centered on whether these changes are attributable to human alterations of the environment or are a reflection of natural population fluxes. As is commonly the case with such die-offs, the fundamental concern is that there may be a factor involved that will affect people. Perhaps the frogs, like the canary in the coal mine, are signaling some environmental hazard, be it global warming, acid rain, depletion of the ozone layer, hormone-altering or hormone-mimicking chemicals, some form of pollution that destroys the frogs' immune systems and leaves them fatally vulnerable to a skin fungus, something as yet undetected. In the absence of any clear picture emerging while the debate goes on and research continues, a readily perceptible cause of the silencing of frogs goes essentially unaddressed: the tremendous habitat loss that has come at the hands of the human species. It is a silencing that has taken other voices than those of frogs, as well as voiceless presences, all inevitably vanishing with the disappearance of the places in which they must live.

My own acquaintance with the silence of the frogs began more than four decades ago with the extinction of the wetland where I first heard the spine-shivering, soul-moving night chorus of the spring peepers. When I first went out to hear these frogs, I walked railroad tracks on a misted night so dark I had to feel for my footing. As I drew near the marshy pond in a red maple swamp from which the calling came, I turned from the tracks and felt my way along a gravelly clearing, enthralled by a crescendo that became heightened with every step I took in its direction. Feeling my way into bordering shrubs with my hands, and tracing my way to the swamp by footsteps in its increasingly soggy hollow, I was drawn to a center of almost unbearable intensity. It seemed at once madness and exultation. I could not join or understand, I could only listen. I became completely overtaken, mentally and physically, by the chorus of the frogs, as though I had become an instrument of their unrelenting communal voice.

These tiny frogs seemed to me to be the evocation of spring and life eternal. But within a few years they and their woods and swamp were gone, lost in the conversion of the landscape to human ends. The last time I heard them, I was standing in starlight on the third story of the steel skeleton of the first building of an industrial complex that would silence the frogs forever. Far too many silencings have occurred in the face of the proliferation of the human species. We hear ourselves only. To paraphrase Shakespeare, we have failed to hear the tongues in trees, read the books in the running brooks, heed the sermons in stones, and find the good in every thing.

Ascending the brushy, grassy slope of the knoll above the Reedgrass

Pool, I see the rising near-full moon among black-purple clouds. The turtles may not sleep tonight, as males pursue the moon-brightened spots of females' black shells in the night water. The spring peepers will not sleep. A long winter of sleep and snowy silence has ended. It is time to be awake and sing. The unabated shrill chorus is all but disorienting, yet at the same time reassuring, sweet, and musical. Resounding from the acoustical amphitheater of the wetland hollow, it seems it could carry to the stars. So many voices.

Metamorphosis

July 1, 12:38 P.M. Temperature in the mid-nineties, another in a siege of hot days with burning sun and drying winds. With less than an inch of rain since late May, it will be a season of total loss for the young of most amphibians that breed in vernal pools. As I approach the Reedgrass Pool for the first time since mid-June, I can smell the death. The scent of carrion grows stronger as I walk the waterless basin to the winterberry thicket where I stood in two and a half feet of icy water amid the tumult of breeding wood frogs only a few months ago.

I hear the incessant, buzzing whine of fly wings as I approach the last desperate holdout of hundreds of tadpoles and scores of spotted salamander larvae. Some two hundred or so metallic blue-green and yellow-green blowflies land and fly, land and fly, over a blackened common skin, the last remains of larval amphibians who died when this final pocket of water gave out. The skin extends along a channel section, as precise a delineation of the deepest point here as any human instrument could give. On the peaty floor of the pool, several carrion beetles work the scene of death. I see a solitary dragonfly. And then I see a lone amphibian survivor. With struggling hops, a nearly transformed wood frog emerges from shadows onto a mat of dried grass. His skin is shiny with a moisture he somehow keeps, but he sticks to the dry grass. His front and hind limbs are fully developed, but he still has three-fourths of his tail. I do not see how he can survive the continuing desiccation, but he may get by in damp shade until he can leave the pool basin and live as a frog in the woods. His glistening, dark-brown coloration would be well camouflaged on wet grass in a watery pool, but against the pale straw color of the dried strands, he stands out sharply.

Tiny flowers have appeared on the winterberry. In more favorable summers I have stood here in a foot and a half of water, its black surface like a star-crowded sky with floats of winterberry flowers, the dark depths teeming with tadpoles. Perhaps some others were ahead of this froglet's timetable, though I am doubtful. He would seem to represent the vanguard, possibly the sole representative, of his generation, based on the stage of the swimming tadpoles I last looked in on, most of whom did not yet show hind limb buds. They had a long way to go developmentally, and the water was evaporating quickly. The rank growth of reed canary grass, so valuable as cover to all of the abundant life of the Reedgrass Pool's water season as well as for its luxurious input into the pool's rich food chain, becomes a liability in times of drought. Most vernal pools have little or no vegetation and dry out primarily by evaporation. Those that do support heavy growth lose a tremendous amount of water to vegetation as well. Plants draw water up through their roots and transpire vapor out through their leaves. At the peak of plant growth and leafing out, one can almost see the water level drop in depressions that are densely grown in with aquatic grasses and sedges or swaths of buttonbush or other emergent shrubs.

A little farther along the channel, as I brush my way through shoulder-high and over-my-head reed canary grass, I come to another, deeper pocket, entirely layered with a film of skin that appears blackened, coal-colored on the umber substrate. This coating is the skins of hundreds of wood frog tadpoles, united in death. I wonder if the toxicity of the skin plays a role in its persistence. There is only the faint odor of carrion here. These were the first to die.

I press on to the northwest corner of the basin, the site of its deepest pooling, where another contingent of wood frogs and spotted salamanders breeds. A broad plateau that rises one to one and a half feet divides the Reedgrass Pool's deepest hollows. I do not smell death or hear the buzz of blowfly wings as I enter this breeding niche. But I find no water. I search among sedge mounds where the colony of wood frogs that breeds here lays its great communal island of egg masses each spring. One year I measured it at nine by two and a half feet. I find no water, no tadpoles. It does not seem possible that they all could have achieved metamorphosis. Were they all taken by predators? Such a difference from the other breeding sector, and such a departure from what I have observed in drying-up vernal pools, does not seem likely. My perplexity increases as I widen my search, until I come to the answer. A swarming mass of tadpoles, a living globe a little over a foot in diameter, writhes in a final muddy pocket at the base of one of the sedge mounds. The ball of tadpoles crowds back in under the dead-straw skirt of the mound. The burning sun, so hot on the back of my neck, must be lethal to these thin-skinned aquatic ones. They have no water that I can see, only a communal slime coating continually redistributed by their ceaseless swimming around one another. This regathering of widely dispersed tadpoles would seem to offer the same survival advantages as the communal egg masses, allowing those in the moist core to hold out a little longer against the drought. They are probably down to their final hours. It is difficult to pick out individuals in the constant movement of the many, but I can see various stages of development. Most have no limbs yet, many have two hind legs, some have all four legs. Showers and thunderstorms are forecast for late afternoon the day after tomorrow, but the rain could be too little, too late, insufficient to bring standing water to the tadpoles' final holdout.

Walking from the hollow, I step up onto a peaty ledge crowned with cranberries. As I scan its carpet of vines, I find evidence of another life drama, one that has played out to its end. Upside down, eye-catchingly bone-white, the carapace of a little snapping turtle lies on trailings of cranberry. I find no predator's tooth scrapes on the two-and-five-eighths-inch shell of a turtle cut down in the midst of his fourth growing season. But some animal bit through his shell at the left shoulder and cleaned him out. There are no notches on his carapace, so he is not one of the three- to five-year-olds that I have trapped and marked along migration routes to the Reedgrass Pool. This turtle lingered too long, evidently, and was overtaken in a waterhold that had shrunk too small to conceal and protect him. He may have been caught as he emigrated, although he would have left the pool during daylight and most of his predators are nocturnal. His cleaned-out carapace attests to the wisdom of not remaining too long in a vernal pool, a wisdom ingrained in and perpetuated by those who discern the danger in the dwindling water level and move on to safer cover, even though the foraging may be yet so rich, so enticing. A young snapping turtle has left behind his emblematic shield on the playing field of his existence; like a shield dropped on a battlefield, the carapace will endure.

3:17 P.M. The Sandpit Pool is the result of human work rather than that of glaciers. The excavation of this abandoned pit went deep enough to come into contact with the high water tables associated with spring flood season. This pool is therefore fed by groundwater, as well as by snowmelt, rain, and runoff. Vernal-pool breeding amphibians are quick to take advantage of pools that form in depressions and pits of human origin, such as those left after sand and gravel extraction or rock quarrying. Vernal pools also occur in natural sandy sites, in kettles and depressions of glacial origin that are deep enough to come into contact with groundwater or have underlying soil layers that are impervious enough to impede drainage. This pool is not part of my annual wetlands rounds, and I have not looked in here for two seasons. I steal up to a sand pile just behind a ring of alders that has become established around the high-water perimeter. From this hidden lookout on elevated ground I once watched a spotted turtle foraging in aquatic grasses, and on another visit I caught a juvenile snapping turtle here. I doubt that turtles come here in great numbers or stay long, for at its deepest, the pool holds no more than twenty inches of water, and much of it is less than a foot deep. Open, shallow pools like this put turtles at risk from predators, but because wood frogs, spotted salamanders, spring peepers, and American toads breed here, foraging turtles on the move from pool to pool will stop in to hunt during their active spring season.

There is still some water here, although the pool has shrunk considerably. This broad, shallow basin is like a giant evaporating dish, and it also drains as the water table subsides during dry spells. I leave my shading screen and step into the blinding, burning sun of the open pool, sinking a little more than ankle deep. Only about an inch of this is water. The rest is muck that has begun to accumulate along the pool's heavily vegetated rim. I find wriggling masses of tadpoles huddled in shallows shaded by sweet gale. Heat is evidently more of a problem than desiccation at this point. In full sun the temperature of the shallow water is 98 degrees. In the adjacent shade of the sweet gale, though still quite warm for animals that started out in icewater, it is a considerably more merciful 84 degrees. Although they have a wide band of shaded water in which they could spread out, these tadpoles have massed together like those in the waterless Reedgrass Pool. The great majority are wood frog tadpoles, but I see smaller ones among them, probably spring peepers. Some of both species spin off from the central amphibian mass and circle it in the grass-clogged shallows. In the center of the pool, where the water is five inches deep, the temperature is 95 degrees, almost as hot as in the sunlit shallows. Nonetheless, some tadpoles cruise here, among submerged, sparsely scattered tufts of pipewort and fringing stands of slender spikerush.

I am surprised to see a larval salamander resting on the bottom, out from under cover on such a blazing day. He speeds off, propelled by eel-like gyrations, through water and the thin mucky sediment layer on the firm sand of the pool bottom. I see where he stops and manage to scoop him up for a look. He has farther to go to metamorphosis than do the wood frog tadpoles. He has tiny, threadlike forelegs, tinier hind legs, and a brushy corona of gill fringes around the base of his head. His finlike tail is tattered and chewed-looking, quite possibly the result of encounters with his own kind. Unlike the vegetarian tadpoles, larval salamanders are carnivorous, voracious predators not disinclined to cannibalism. This watery bowl of abundant and diverse life has plenty of other hunters: predacious diving beetles and their larvae (called water tigers), backswimmers, and many varieties of dragonfly larvae, some of them bigger than tadpoles.

Feeling the need for shade myself, I wade back to the southwestern corner of the pool, where alders cast a shadow in which I can stand up straight. The water in the shadow is a roiling sea of life, with clusters of tadpoles wriggling wildly among themselves. Like their doomed brethren in the Reedgrass Pool, they are at varying stages of development. They appear to be robust in inverse proportion to their developmental status, with the legless tadpoles the most vigorous, and the four-legged ones closest to metamorphosis the most fragile, being bounced and jostled about on a living tide they all but drown in. A few of these tiny near-frogs separate out, and with a combined hopping and wriggling, move over sodden mattings of grass. The long tails that were not long ago their means of swimming after food and escaping danger now seem a hindrance, burdensome banners about as long as their bodies, which they are obliged to carry about for a time yet. Their swift but somewhat ungainly excursions onto grass are trial runs for their imminent abandonment of the floating world and initiation into life on terra firma.

I am always struck by how much smaller recently metamorphosed frogs and toads are than the tadpoles from which they have just transformed. Frogs and toads pass through great changes as they absorb their gills and undergo shifts in circulation, a reshaping of their mouths, changes in teeth, and, finally, absorption of their tails. There is a concomitant makeover of their digestive systems, as the long, tightly coiled intestines of swollen-bodied herbivorous tadpoles become the shorter food canal of carnivorous frogs and toads. Metamorphosis would seem more the province of insects than of vertebrates; nothing in the life histories of reptiles, birds, or mammals equates with the complexity of this amphibian transformation. The profound anatomical and physiological changes, including changes in body chemistry, that take place as they transform from aquatic, gilled, water-breathing, tailed, legless herbivores into terrestrial, lunged, air-breathing, four-legged carnivores appear to drain them of strength and body mass, leaving them less adapted for survival than they had been as full-grown tadpoles.

The physiological rigors of the process itself prove fatal to many tadpoles. In essence, tadpoles who succeed in living to the threshold of metamorphosis (but a fraction of those that emerge from the prolific egg masses) find themselves compelled to start over again as different animals in a different world. They acquire an entirely new form for a second life within a single lifetime. In the case of wood frog tadpoles, those who have mastered the water become, as their very world disappears, tiny, extremely vulnerable froglets who must master a totally different environment, one that must stretch out before them like a continent. In this inescapable destiny, these frogs seem to face an evolutionary double jeopardy.

July 4, 2:30 P.M. I return to the Reedgrass Pool to see if there are any survivors. Heavy rain came up at three in the morning yesterday, followed by intermittent showers through the day and a spate of crackling thunderstorms and torrential downpours as day gave way to night. The watery legacy of an incoming cold front's clash with established hot, humid air masses amounted to a bountiful inch and a half of rain. I step from the cranberry shelf into five inches of clear water that has collected around the sedges in the deep pocket. In an earthen basin, I wade in ponded water that was rain in the sky not many hours ago, and, a day before that, vapor in clouds high above the earth and far to the west. Had these hydrologic processes taken place twenty-four hours earlier, I would be wading among hundreds of rescued tadpoles continuing their metamorphic journeys to becoming wood frogs. But the rain has come too late. No amount of rain will help now. Even if the month or the year ends with what meteorologists report as an above-normal total, the loss for the Reedgrass Pool's wood frog and salamander population remains irreversible. Timing is more critical than totality. With living things, the right amounts of water, warmth, and food must come at the right stage of development and growth in order for their seasons, or their lives, not to be lost. If the timing is awry, seasonal averages of precipitation or temperature are of no comfort to the native plants and animals, which must ever work with and against the extremes by which the abiotic regime maintains its long-term balance. I find sunken and floating bodies, some within hours, it seems, of inheriting the earth, of never again being dependent on the pool for existence, except for those few days of explosive breeding that continue their species.

I suddenly remember one last pocket, a trench beneath a stand of silky willow in the northwest quadrant of the Reedgrass Pool. I have never seen wood frogs commit egg masses in this shaded site, but dispersing tadpoles might have gathered here as the pool dried up. I pull back willow branches and peer into half a foot of dark, shadowy water. All I see at first are dead tadpoles, whitened, many belly up, at the surface and in a huddled aggregation on the bottom, where they must have spent their final writhing hours in a ball similar to the one I witnessed three days ago. But a couple of quick dimples at the surface catch my attention, and as my eyes become accustomed to the shadows, I make out a swimming wood frog tadpole. Several more glide through a shaft of sunlight. These tadpoles were taken to their final possible minutes, perhaps kept alive by being at the center of the great mass of the dead and dying, spared by rainstorms that today are drifting far out over the ocean.

After watching for some time, I can make out only two dozen or so, two dozen out of thousands. The odds against any one of these tadpoles going on to complete metamorphosis and survival to breeding age, a year from next spring, are extremely prohibitive. No wonder a male holds on to a female so tightly in a breeding pool, though he may be surrounded by hundreds of others. Their evolutionary history has deeply imprinted upon this species a knowledge of the environmental uncertainty it faces. Wood frogs commonly have a life span of only three years. A succession of dry springs could extirpate a local population. Over time, immigration could restore the species to the habitat, but in the fractured modern landscape, many migration routes have been cut off. Spotted salamanders and their kin, with life spans that can surpass twenty years, are not so narrowly at the mercy of any one spring or series of springs. But they, too, face environmental uncertainty and require margins of time and space that are not granted by the diminished and fragmented human-altered landscape.

5:17 P.M. Things have gone much better for the teeming tadpoles in the Sandpit Pool. Their water has been refreshed and broadened, cooled to 71 degrees, and probably oxygenated. Dissolved oxygen, which becomes severely depleted in heated water filled with gill-breathing organisms, may not be so critical to the wood frog tadpoles now, however. Most of them seem to have gone over to air-breathing. No-legged, two-legged, and four-legged, they make continual turnings, belly up at the surface, white bellies tinged with a bronzed, pink iridescence, constant pale and brilliant flashes with tiny mouths opening, creating countless black holes in the sky-light-silvered surface film. Some tailed frogs with well-developed fore and hind limbs, on the verge of metamorphosis, have separated out, seemingly caught between two different worlds. Out of the water, not yet ready for dry land, they alternately rest and scramble on soggy rafts and islands of grass. The medium they see through and breathe in is no longer water but air. They do not congregate like the less developed ones, but move apart, their inclination already shifting from schooling to the solitariness that will mark the rest of their lives. Little near-frogs, some within hours now of leaving their natal pool, climb up on low grass stems or raised clumps, like green frogs or bullfrogs taking a perch on a log or lily pad in a pond. No longer wrigglers, they balance themselves and sit with heads and shoulders up, almost as erect as full-fledged frogs. There are dark lines in front of their eyes, and the black masks so characteristic of adults are beginning to show on their faces. Gold glintings run down the ridges on each side of their brown and gray-brown backs, with fawn and pinkish tints coming into their sides; black-flecked bands become prominent on their hind legs.

All the tiny frogs appear to be looking away from the vernal pool, as if contemplating the land that is at once distant and near at hand. They commonly rest with their tails in the water, head and shoulders out, as if balancing between two worlds, between two lives. They will not pass this way again. The meaning of their class name, Amphibia, taken from the Greek *amphi* ("both") and *bios* ("life"), becomes all the more clear. They have a life in water and a life on land; and the two lives, one as a tadpole, the other as a frog, toad, or salamander, are absolutely distinct.

Spring peeper tadpoles dart about in the same grassy shallows. Not seeing them surface, I presume they are still breathing through gills. They do not show limb buds yet and will need this pool longer than the wood frogs. Should the pool fail them, there will still be abundant spring peepers transforming in permanent wetlands not far from here, dispersing in great numbers through the red maple swamps, alder thickets, and vast surrounding upland forest. Unlike wood frogs, which breed only in vernal pools, spring peepers also breed in the vegetatation-choked shallows of marshes, fens, shrub swamps, and swamps. Each female, though no larger than an inch and a half, lays from seven hundred to a thousand eggs, which are distributed singly among submersed plants.

I watch as the burnished, pale-bellied wood frog tadpoles swim upside down for a time, following a quick hit of food or air at the surface. I keep looking at one or two in the crowded schooling that do not seem to right themselves, showing their white bellies all the time. Finally it occurs to me that in fact they are white tadpoles, swimming right side up. I wade toward the spot where one of these tadpoles disappears in a gang of dark siblings, muck, and mattings of sunken grass. Scooping with both hands, I come up with muddied water that is frantically alive with tadpoles. As I let this living soup slip through my fingers, I see that I have been lucky enough to capture the white one. I rinse all else away and cup him in clear water in one hand. I have never seen anything like this white tadpole, burnished with a golden tint. I move into the sunlight and turn him under my hand lens for a good look. His tiny iris is fiery red in the sun, burning carnelian with a garnet glint; the tadpole is a true albino. Both his hind legs are well developed. I wonder if he will live long enough to become a white wood frog.

I let my unusual captive go, and in a few minutes the tadpoles resume their activity at my feet, rising and turning at the surface, scraping plants for algae and, here and there, as four-legged metamorphs with tails, wriggling onto grass mats and hopping over them. I see one newly transformed wood frog who is missing his left hind leg. It looks as though only one hind leg developed. This may not be an insurmountable handicap during the short time remaining in his pool life, but on land, a missing leg will prove an impossible impediment for a species that lives or dies by leaping. Nearby I see a two-legged tadpole whose powerful swimming tail was not enough to save him. On his back, he twitches in grass near the surface. His movements are not his own. Dead, he is being shoved about by two predacious diving beetles about half his size, discounting his tail, who have killed him and are at work on his body. I make more scoops through the populous waters and find a foot missing here, half a leg there, many tadpoles with only a single fully developed hind leg, some on the left, some on the right. Perhaps this is not uncommon, and I have not looked closely enough in past seasons, but I do not think I could have been so unobservant as not to notice this many metamorphosing tadpoles with only one hind leg. The development of front legs is a variable business; but hind legs, which come first, normally develop in unison.

There seem to be too many missing hind limbs to be the work of amputating predators. Just as there is rising concern over the silence of the frogs, there is increased consternation over the number of deformed individuals being found. Leopard frogs, in particular, have shown abnormalities such as extra legs, sometimes growing from body parts such as the head, and extra or missing eyes. Deformities this extreme do occur naturally in this species at times, as a result of infestation by parasitic trematodes, but the numbers of occurrences and extremes of deformity appear to have accelerated to unprecedented levels. Abnormal limb development at metamorphosis has also been found in other species, including green frogs and bullfrogs.

I leave off my tadpole-catching and circle the broad, dried-down margins of the Sandpit Pool. It is a garden of small plants, fox sedge, pointed broom sedge, and green bulrush well scattered with lance-leaved violet, some bearing flowers quite late in their season. Some swamp candles display their final yellow-flowered glow, and, on wetter

Recently metamorphosed
American toad (*Bufo a. americanus*)

sand, spreads of dwarf Saint Johnswort show flickers of yellow flowers, which may continue until frost. The nutrient-poor nature of the mineral soil is reflected in the dwarfed stature of the woolly-fruit sedge, winterberry (hardly waist high), sweet gale, meadowsweet, and royal fern that ring the high-water mark. The sandy basin is evidently rather acidic as well as poor in nutrients, judging from its broad bordering swaths of large cranberry and colonies of diminutive, reddened round-leaved sundews. In this boglike zone I come upon some of the first of the pool's amphibians to have transformed, unbelievably tiny toads, only five-sixteenths of an inch in body length, that have left the water but kept to the pool basin. The size of coarse grains of sand, they hop briskly, setting about the business of being toads. Among the glossy, purpled cranberry leaves I find an outward-bound wood frog, stub-tailed, making leaps that are long for his size.

There are many fates in this arena, many destinies at this crossroads of changing forms, changing lives. Despite the reprieve of the rain, the pool is approaching its own annual transformation from a place of water to a place of land. All but the rooted plants will leave. This final water will dissipate as vapor in thin air. So obedient to gravity as water, in this new form it becomes airborne. There will be other transformations for this elemental liquid mineral as it goes from being cloud to rain and returns to earth. Nothing is lost in the transmigration. Perhaps someday this season's abandoning water will come back to this same pool.

There have been transformations in my own life — I see the skins of several shed lives — but nothing so tangible in form, so monumental in function. I would appear to be much the same wader in this pool, season after season. But all around me, every year, all of these wheels and cycles, metamorphoses that seem miraculous, incomprehensible (how did such things come to be?), become commonplace miracles in the end, at least among the creatures of these vernal pools. It is as though they would say to me, all of the living things and the vanishing water itself would say to me, "What, this is what you are, for your duration on earth? There will be no new form and life within your form and life, no new limbs or set of wings to take you to another world?"

Dragonfly metamorphosis

Marbled Salamanders

September 5, 1:17 P.M. Marbled salamanders do not live as far north as my home wetland areas, so to find them I travel 150 miles south to rock-studded hills crowned with oak-hickory forest. This upland landscape, at elevations between 850 and 1,150 feet, is laced with the precipitous descents and stepped meanderings of two permanent streams and many associated intermittent streams, and rich in seeps, springs, and vernal pools. I discovered a woodland vernal pool here in early July that was still populated with wood frog tadpoles, spotted salamander larvae, green frogs, bullfrogs, and spotted turtles, at a time when many other vernal pools had already dried up. Trills of gray treefrogs mingled with the calling of a northern water thrush, and the scent of swamp azalea was heavy on the air. As I waded this classic vernal pool, with its black water, central bed of fowl manna grass, stands of emergent winterberry, and emerald-mossed islands of ancient highbush blueberry, black huckleberry, swamp azalea, and sheep laurel, overtopped by a high red maple canopy, I felt nearly certain that marbled salamanders would migrate here for their late summer and autumn breeding. I hadn't seen these salamanders since I was a boy in Connecticut, turning over logs to look for woodland snakes and salamanders. These encounters were outside of their breeding time and therefore removed from the vernal pool aspect of their lives. Moving north in later life, in an effort to escape the heavy buildup and enormous habitat loss occurring in southern New England (a buildup and loss that are on the verge of overtaking me once again), I left these salamanders behind.

Now, in September, there is no water in the pool. Its sloping basin is lined with a dry upper layer of leaves over a damp black lower leaf layer, pressed flat by the weight of the water that once stood here, plastered down like a great herbarium sheet. It is a thin flooring, as seasonal recycling evidently keeps pace with the heavy annual input of fallen leaves from the surrounding forest. A circle of red maple and occasional yellow birches around the pool's perimeter gives way to acres of forest dominated by red, white, and scarlet oak and pignut hickory. The woodland depression that cradles the vernal pool seems so abandoned without its water. In its present empty state, I cannot bring into clear focus a vision of what the pool was like little more than sixty days ago. At the same time, there is an air of patient waiting in this hollow, an evocative sense of tempered expectation, that I find nowhere else in the surrounding forest. In one corner compressed and dried fountain moss skirts craggy, serpentine buttonbush stems. The moss stops at a uniform height on every unevenly growing stem, indicating precisely the pool's seasonal high-water mark and testifying that this dry basin is in fact a vernal pool. The moss, which undulates in long, trailing billows in permanent streams, is something of a resurrection plant here, waiting to plume out to a sheltering fullness that will harbor a great array of aquatic invertebrates and predatory salamander larvae when the water comes back. Curiously, the fountain moss grows only on the shreddy-barked buttonbush; none is affixed to winterberry or other emergent shrubs here.

Not sure where to begin looking, I stand among tall cinnamon ferns, scanning the high-water border of the pool, its gradually sloping sides, and its central depression. Three nights of heavy rain nearly a week ago should have inspired marbled salamanders to make their migrations to breeding pools. In an adaptive reversal of the migrations that the spotted, Jefferson, and blue-spotted salamanders make to vernal pools flooded by end-of-winter rains, these salamanders travel to the same habitats when they are dry, or nearly so, to mate and lay their eggs.

At this point in the season, the anticipatory males, at least, should have begun to enter vernal pools. It is possible that mating is already over and that females are guarding egg clutches, much in the manner of the four-toed salamanders. My search, which could begin just about anywhere, must begin somewhere. I scan the leaf-drifted rim of the pool. My eyes are attracted to a generous molding of leaf pack, draped over and collected beneath a jumble of fallen twigs near a small slab of fallen bark, a mixed-media thatching that has settled into a pocket among the buttressing roots of a red maple. Targeting this niche, trying to be guided as a salamander might be, I drop to my knees in dry leaves on the upper rim of the slope, above the high-water line, where there will be no hiding salamander that I might crush. I brace myself on one hand, extend the other to the limits of my reach. My first lifting of the ten-by-six-inch piece of bark, along with an inch-thick layer of leaves, uncovers a cluster of glistening eggs. They look like tiny ambered pearls. Marbled salamander eggs are deposited singly in a loose aggregate rather than in a jellied egg mass. My first impression is that the mother salamander has laid her eggs and departed, as sometimes happens; but even as that disappointing thought arises, I see a startling curl of marbled black-and-white back under a dark shelf of leaves. She is here. I lift another layer cake of leaves and reveal her, curled sinuously along the contours of half the little hollow that holds the eggs she guards. She is strikingly marked with irregular bands of silvery white, sharply contrasted against bordering bands of jet black.

I can't say who is more stunned, the salamander or I. The image of her, arresting enough in its own right, is enhanced by the facts that this is the first nest-guarding female I have found and that I discovered her with my first lifting of leaves and bark in a distant pool where I suspected, but did not know, that the species could be found. I can hardly stop looking at her, but I realize I must replace her cover at once if I am not to interfere with her maternal vigilance and possibly cause her to abandon her egg clutch. It happens like this sometimes, a blend of hypothesis and intuition, when one sets out to meet the favoring convergence of time and place and immediately finds the elusive object of intent. It happens, but so rarely. It is hard to express the gratitude I feel for a profound privilege granted. Whether a finding is immediate or years in coming, when it does come I drink it in as deeply as I can, allow myself an inner rejoicing that fills accumulated voids and sustains me until the next such moment. All but astonished once again by the very thing I have been looking for, as I admire this salamander I have come upon by such a curious route, I think of a researcher friend's favorite quote, from Louis Pasteur, which has become a theme for me: "In the field of observation, chance favors only the prepared mind."

I rearrange the salamander's covering and sit back on my heels, absorbing the details of the site, trying to file a clear search-image and not let the excitement of the moment blur the particulars. I need to make specific notes of the occasion. But I also have an uncontrollable urge to get on with the search for more salamanders and record events later. Following this urge is never a wise policy. Already I want to uncover the salamander and her eggs again, to refocus on the minute and greater details of the reality. But I don't want to disturb her any further. My goal is not to measure marbled salamanders or count their eggs but to ascertain that the species is present and get an idea of how many might breed here, when they might breed, and what types of niches they choose for their nests.

Entering the basin proper, I explore on hands and knees. Facing upslope now, I search a band around the perimeter, from about a foot to four feet below the high-water mark. Marbled salamanders do not lay their eggs in the deepest pits in the pool because autumn rains often bring about a partial refilling that could cover the eggs and instigate premature hatching. If the pool then dried up, the larvae, which must live here through the winter, would die. Eggs set higher along the rim of the pool would not be triggered to hatch until the pond was filled by more lasting waters. Some of the shrub and tree island-mounds have leaf-covered slopes with fallen branches. I search these as well. Other mounds drop precipitously to the pool floor, their elevated roots forming stilts that keep them above water. The waterless state of the pool reveals hollows and tunnels that go deep into the mounds, underwater hiding places for turtles and frogs when this is an aquatic world. Now they are passageways for small mammals: moles, red-backed voles, shrews, and the like.

And for another marbled salamander. As I look into a dark crevice I detect his black and white patterning and am able to extract a chunky, stub-tailed salamander. The sharp, pure white markings, versus the grayed white of the female, and the protruding vent identify this one as a male. Only about four inches long, marbled salamanders are considerably shorter than their spring-breeding relatives and appear proportionally stockier. Their mottled markings, even more striking in males, mimic the lacy shadows of fallen leaves, many of which have holes and scroll-like channels eaten out of them. But these mole salamanders rarely see the light of day. Even when they venture out at night, it is during rain, when there is no moonlight or shadow shapes. Here are animals of darkness adorned, it seems, for life in broken light and shadow.

One can wonder enough at their markings, but what of the turning in the pattern of the natural history of this species that has brought it to its unique timing with the seasons of water in vernal pools? In coming to dry pools (and, on occasion, waterless pockets in intermittent streams) in autumn, rather than flooded pools and pockets in spring, marbled salamanders counter the breeding behavior of nearly all other amphibians. It is damp beneath the guardian female's bark cover and leaf mulch, but her dark hollow is dry by salamander standards. One reason females stay with their egg clutches may be to help keep them moist until the water comes back. If hard cold comes on before the pond refills enough to cover her eggs, she will be forced to leave them and move on to her terrestrial hibernaculum. Although, as with four-toed salamanders, survival appears to be higher in eggs that are brooded by a female, marbled salamander eggs that have been abandoned can survive winter in a dry pool beneath a covering of leaves and snow, with successful larvae hatching in a springtime refill.

Mating too takes place in a very different environment from that in which the spring-breeding salamanders swim and congress. There are no weightless, acrobatic turnings in clear water for marbled salamanders; males and females meet on foot, on solid ground, to shuffle and

Courtship of marbled salamanders (*Ambystoma opacum*)

dance under the cover of leaves and branch tangles. In the absence of a water ballet, they posture and parade, with animated nudgings and shovings, as males attempt to attract and excite a female enough for her to be moved to select a sperm packet from the spermatophores they have deposited.

5:22 P.M. With the discovery of six nest-guarding females and the lingering male, my intimation of two months before has proven correct. More commonly, years must pass before intuition lines up with reality. The last two females I found were extremely difficult to locate. They were in a shallower extension of the pool depression, where three blown-down red maples lay. The trees had fallen recently enough that their dead crowns were still heavily branched, and the entangled branches had ensnared deep drifts of leaves that the pool's shredders and consumers had not yet reduced much. There were places I could not reach, but, crawling again, I snaked my way among the branches and uncovered the salamanders in separate sites, each under nearly six inches of leaf drift. One had found a natural pocket among a filigree of tree roots. The other appeared to have carved out a hollow with twistings of her body. Under bark, under leaves, all await the return of water. A tropical storm that may just now be starting to form over the Caribbean Sea might bring a deluge in several days' time that will recharge this pool basin, touching off the hatching of marbled salamander eggs and sending their mothers back into the forest. The mole salamanders, wood frogs, spotted turtles, and other life forms of these isolated catchments are often the children of hurricanes.

October 18, 10:28 A.M. Approaching complete recharge, the pool is filled to just below the bark-slab and leaf-pack roofing of the first marbled salamander nest I found in early September. The blazing scarlet and orange of the red maple leaves is darkening to maroon. More than half of the leaves have already fallen and are blanketing the pool. Those that have sunk still keep some of their glow on the bottom of the pool. Maroon-red and russet, the scarlet and red oaks give the surrounding hills the somber radiance of their final autumn color, toned with purplings of white oak. The oaks will make their contribution to the pool's leaf pack with the next wind-driven rain. Two recharges are taking place in this basin, the rain's refilling of the pool and the trees' replenishing of the leaf pack. This elemental mix will give rise to the vernal pool's complex and manifold life next spring. The choruses of the wood frogs and spring peepers that will come at thaw to shatter winter's quieting of these woods begin with water and leaves.

I look at the nest site for a time and at its surroundings, again trying to absorb and imprint an image. The scant specifics that led me to unveil a marbled salamander with my first lifting of leaves and bark are all the more obscure now, blurred by drifts of recently fallen leaves. Throughout my swampwalking, considering plants and animals I find, or fail to find, I continually ask myself, "Why here, and not there? If not here, why not?" The salamander larvae should still be in their eggs, as the water has not risen high enough to make the essential contact that will immediately trigger them to break out of their eggs and swim off into the recharged pool. That same watery touch will send their guardian mother back to the upland woods, where she will overwinter in the earth. Lifting the nest covering, I find that she is still here, curled close by her egg clutch. She has been at her post for forty-four days. I wonder if she ever goes off to hunt, or if prey come into her brooding site, or if she simply fasts. Twitching movements in the eggs catch my eye. The larvae within are well developed and very active. Perhaps they can sense how close the liberating water has come. At a season of so many endings, here is a beginning. While their mother sleeps away the winter, they will be active and growing, even when their pool is frozen over and drifted with snow.

Winter Pool

February 7, 3:57 P.M. Searching for vernal pools, I walk snowy wooded hills about a mile north of the Marbled Salamander Pool. Late autumn and winter are good times to look. Before freezing, the pools' sky reflections shine out in the leafless landscape; after freezing, their silvery glints contrast sharply with fallen leaves or dustings of snow. In deep snow or dense coniferous forests, they may be all but undiscoverable. There will be no frog calls to guide me today. Murmurings of intermittent streams may lead me to a pool, but, as so many pools have neither inlet nor outlet, it is the gleam of water or the sheen of ice that I rely on most. And it is a dull gray sheen set in sharp white snow that reveals a woodland pool on this heavily clouded afternoon. This treeless basin, about thirty yards in diameter, lying in a small leveling near the crest of a 950-foot ascent, would be discernible even if it were under two feet of snow. Fully flooded, it has an outlet, a narrow spill of water that slips slowly out from under the ice and flows nearly level for twenty feet before dropping away downhill in an icy-leaved descent. The films of algae throughout this outflow are the only green in the February landscape and the only living things I see in the water, which is between 33 and 34 degrees.

Circling the pool in quest of an inlet, I come to a crescent of meltwater about three feet wide on the opposite side from the outlet. Here the water is warmer, 38 degrees, suggesting that groundwater seeps in along this rim. Webbings of the same algae are suspended over and attached to the leafy flooring. I gingerly step onto the ice, planning to break a hole somewhere to open a window into the water life of the pond. Larval salamanders are generally more active and more visible at night, as they rise high in the water column to feed on daphnia and other microorganisms, but I have watched them in late January, swimming about in sunlit shallows free of ice, slipping in and out of sight among sunken leaves. As I muse on larval marbled salamanders, the ice suddenly lets go beneath me, without a warning crack or groan. I drop to the uneven bottom of the pool, one leg jarring to a halt in a foot of water, the other in a foot and a half. As sudden and surprising as my abrupt descent is, I see at once, in shatterings of ice and sloshings of water, a mingled swirl of fairy shrimp and marbled salamander larvae. I have never before quite so literally dropped in on the animals I was hoping to see.

With this startling simultaneous sighting of two obligate species, I can immediately declare this a vernal pool. My explosively opened window quickly becomes clouded by muddy roilings of fine, orange-tinged silt stirred up by my ungraceful plunge. As murky as the water becomes, I can still make out the jet black salamander larvae, the neon blue–white fairy shrimp with touches of rust and crimson and fluorescent white tail tips. At this point in the year, the largest of the fiercely predatory salamander larvae are, at about an inch long, no bigger than the fairy shrimp, a critical coevolutionary timing that enables these two species to coexist in a populous, tightly circumscribed environment. For a moment it seems I have broken through a magic looking glass and fallen into spring. But these are icewater animals at home in a midwinter world. In a little wetland basin set in a leafless upland expanse, I wade for a time among gatherings of two vivacious animals that are at the height of their respective stages of being while so much of the rest of the animate world has migrated far away or settled in to a lengthy sleep under ice and snow. Part of a great interwoven wetland and upland system, these tiny wild lives are fully alive in a little bowl of water under ice in the very heart of winter; only a vernal pool can keep them.

Soft rush (*Juncus effusus*) and sedges

2 THE MARSH

To find new things, take the path you took yesterday.
— John Burroughs

The Crossing

May 5, 10:23 A.M. A black bear's footprint, perfectly impressed in mud almost as black as a bear, records his recent passage through the marshy bottomland. The bear is quite likely aware of me and is making certain once again to keep himself unseen. I know the bears here only by occasional footprints in mud, sand, or clay, by ripped-apart logs, and by long shreddings of bark on trees. They know me far better by scent and sound and, near-sighted as they are, by many cautious, hidden watchings from near at hand. There is no way for me to let them know I mean no harm, these great living shadows about me.

Following a flooded muskrat trail, I enter the broad, wet, lowland landscape of Great Marsh. Throughout much of its forty-acre extent, this depression has the look of a grassy prairie. The only trees are isolated stands of black willow and lines of red maples along the permanent streams that meander through the marsh. Thickets of woody shrubs grow in scattered islands, pockets of shrub swamp set in an expanse of grass and sedge marsh. Marshes are emergent wetlands characterized by soft-stemmed, herbaceous vegetation, nonwoody plants such as cattail, bulrushes, bur reed, rushes, pickerelweed, and aquatic grasses and sedges. The tall trees that grow in swamps and the low, brushy growth of shrub swamps are absent from or play a minor role in their plant composition. Marshes, also called palustrine emergent wetlands, represent a continuum from being permanently flooded to having no surface water. Those that have no flood period or are flooded briefly and shallowly only during years of heaviest rainfall are known as wet meadows. Their soils, which typically feature a water level close to the surface throughout most of the year, support lush growths of wetland grasses and sedges and a bounty of flowering plants like spotted jewelweed, boneset, and joe-pye weed. Shallow marshes, which hold two feet of water or less, commonly contain great swaths of sedges, rushes, and grasses. Deeper marshes, with two to six feet of permanent standing water, tend to be dominated by extensive monocultures of cattail. This marsh, where I am making my first crossing of the season, embraces all of these palustrine natures.

I wade the muskrat trail through a cranberry-sedge meadow. Although not an architectural engineer of the beaver's caliber, the muskrat nonetheless makes a mark on marshy landscapes, maintaining watery runs through profuse vegetation, constructing straw-hut villages, digging out channels, and excavating bank burrows. The dominant plant growth of marshes is frequently so luxurious (an indication of the nutrient richness and productivity of marsh habitats) that it is as difficult to walk and wade through as forested and scrub-shrub wetlands. Many of the herbaceous plants produce dense tangles of stems, leaves, and blades that persist long after hard frosts have killed them back to their perennial roots and rhizomes. The dense, ensnaring, ropelike vegetation, combined with water and mud, creates an environment resistant to travel by all but the best-adapted animals. Fortunately for me, and for other more terrestrial beings who must pass through here, muskrats maintain a road system. Some of their routes appear to follow the meanderings of the water, others are as straight as man-made ditches. In fact, muskrats often appropriate abandoned ditches dug to convert marsh and wet meadow to hayfield, which may have followed historic animal trails in the first place.

Here in the open cranberry-sedge meadow I am an unusually tall traveler. Outsized, heavily booted, I feel somewhat like a moose, although that long-legged animal could actually pass through here with ease, and with considerably more grace than I can manage. In most wetlands I am engulfed by tall vegetation, but here I stand above most of the plants about me. The great sweeps of cranberry-laced woolly-fruit sedge, and colonies of cushionlike tussock sedge, pressed down by the weight of winter's ice and snow, will be about waist-high to me when their new blades are fully risen. The brushy islands of sweet gale and leatherleaf rise only a little above my waist. Even so, it is arduous going to traverse the meadow, which looks so soft and inviting from a distance. I keep to the animal trails, however circuitous they may be. White-tailed deer also follow the muskrats' trails but avoid their deeper swimming channels and dangerous quagmires. When I enter an unknown wetland, I often take deer trails as my initial signposts as to where to tread, where not to tread.

It is hard to say who does more to maintain this section of the trail, the muskrats or the deer. Turfy ridges are chewed up by the sharp-toed passings of many deer, yet watery runway stretches are strewn with shredded muskrat greens and have plastered-down muskrat feeding stations along their lengths. The deer provide passageways for many travelers in shallower sites, as do muskrats in flooded marshes and beavers in deeper wetlands and riparian corridors. When I have placed minnow traps in wetland deer paths for amphibian surveys at salamander breeding time, I have turned up as many as eighty spotted salamanders in a single night, as well as surprising numbers of red-spotted newts, spring peepers, wood frogs, young green frogs and bullfrogs, little chain pickerel, giant water bugs, water scorpions, and predacious diving beetles. Many animals too large to enter a minnow trap travel these same pathways. Although deer trails are seldom more than ankle deep in water, and then only during the wetter times of year, they provide niches for long-term residents as well as pathways for transients. I see that spotted salamanders have entrusted egg masses to deeper pockets under cranberry overhangs at the edge of this trail, as they have done in springs past. In more open sphagnum and sedge wetlands, spotted turtles may nest along the edges of deer trails, on ridges exposed to sun and just above the reach of floodwaters. Star-nosed moles and water shrews incorporate these sluiceways into their regular rounds, ribbon and garter snakes hunt them, looking for the young green frogs, bullfrogs, and pickerel frogs who live in and along the trails as long as any water remains. Small chain pickerel also hunt here, far from the dangerous, bigger-fish waters of the permanent stream. Flat-leaf bladderwort, a submersed plant that finds a home in the linear wetlands formed by animal trails as well as in the water's circuitous channels through this wet meadow, has begun to extend from its winter buds. By summer solstice, its white-green whorled branches will choke these narrow corridors. Almost animallike, these massed plants huddle on wet mud as the trails dry down, able to avoid desiccation while awaiting the return of the water. Deep green buds then form at the tips of their growing-season stems to keep them alive through the winter. This carnivorous plant has specialized bladders that entrap minute crustaceans and other small organisms, another sign of the rich world of invertebrate life that inhabits a niche created and maintained by walking deer and wallowing muskrats.

I turn north at a shrubby intersection, a four corners in a sweet gale stand, from which watery pathways radiate to the north, east, south, and west as precisely as compass points. I pass three large pitcher plants, the same clustered triad that has been in place here since I first came this way over a decade ago. They do not spread out, nor are they overrun by the surrounding vegetation. I know of no other pitcher plants for miles around, save one that has established itself as the crown of a sphagnum-covered stump in the boglike backwaters of a pond about half a mile away. I continually wonder how these and other plants find and hold their places in such vast sedge-dominated tracts, and think again of how there are wetlands within wetlands. I cannot make out the slender single leaves of the rose pogonia in the profusion of sedge swirls and cranberry vines, but its orchid flowers, which will accent the green world of the summer marsh with scatterings of pale rose lavender, must be coming forth. At summer's transition to autumn, when no trace of the orchids remains, pale tufts of few-nerved cotton grass will glow in the sun, bowing in the wind that blows over the bronzing sedge and ripening cranberries. It is probably wetter in this marshy corner and, judging from the boglike vegetation, more acidic than in the neighboring acres.

Chance events—the drifting of a windborne seed or its brushing from some animal's fur, feathers, skin, or scales to the favorable place at the propitious time—play an important role in plant distribution. Once a plant has gotten a foothold, in many instances it will play an active role in maintaining that turf by way of allelopathy, the production of growth-inhibiting chemicals that keep other species at bay. A species' growth habit may also influence the water regime of the immediate surroundings, as when plants divert and/or detain flows. Hydrologic factors (where, how long, and how deeply the water is distributed throughout the wetland complex and whether it is still or flowing), together with variations in water chemistry, microclimate, and microtopography, create slightly but significantly different environments. A fraction of an acre out of scores of apparently identical acres may provide the conditions that suit a particular species of plant.

Farther along, the north branch I am following becomes a foot deep, then deeper, as I wade on to the band of marsh that borders the Slough. Many marshes are associated with lacustrine wetlands; that is, they form along the shallower edges and backwaters of lakes. Others, such as the Slough, are linked to riverine wetlands, developing along the margins and in the floodplains of rivers and streams. The character of the vegetation changes as I wade along the borders of this sluggish creek, whose deeply sedimented channel holds three to four feet of water at spring flood. Mermaidweed, a submergent that stays green all winter, flourishes here. It is ringed by a broad swath of emergent marsh, thick with beds of blunt spikerush and bur reed, stands of soft and Canada rushes, soft-stem bulrush and three-way sedge, broad-leaf arrowhead and blue flag. In contrast with the bluejoint grass and beaked and tussock sedges, most of these plants are nonpersistent perennials that quickly disintegrate with the first touches of frost. Their lush new growth now rises to fill spaces left last fall. The crowns of several tussock sedge mounds are beaten down and littered with long green sprouts, chewed at the base. These hummocks are feeding stations for muskrats. Ducks feed here as well, attracted by the great spreads of blunt spikerush that choke the shallow edge waters and muddy banks and by pondweed and other vegetation in the marsh border and deeper central waters of the

Wool-grass
(*Scirpus cyperinus*)

Slough. Crayfish come from the bordering brook to feed on plant detritus, and where crayfish go mink are sure to follow. They leave piles of reddened crayfish castings at their own feeding stations and take muskrats when they can. Blanding's turtles, another of the many animals who favor crayfish as food, circle this marshy inlet as they make their rounds along Alder Brook and throughout the broader wetland. A pair of eastern kingbirds nests in the Slough's straggling line of living and dead red maples. All day long they launch stunning air raids from hunting perches on dead branches, in pursuit of dragonflies and other insects flying over the wet meadows.

I walk the line between the impossible muckbed of the bur reed at the edge of the Slough and the brushy outreach of leatherleaf that lines the sedge meadow border, to an upstream narrows. Here I cross the slow-drifting water and enter a small shrub swamp with mounds of royal fern and tussock sedge, crowded with wetland shrubs and stunted red maple saplings, interspersed with pockets of mud and water. Shrub swamps, with their deeper and longer-standing flood periods, develop a more pronounced microrelief than wet meadows. The cranberry-sedge meadow I have just left and the beaked-sedge marsh on the other side of this small shrub swamp are for the most part low, level wetlands. Their even floors and the generally even height of their grassy vegetation present a prairielike aspect in all seasons. These saturated-soil marshes are treeless, shrubless realms; the pit-and-mound terrain created in swamps by windthrown trees and mound-building shrubs does not tend to develop in marshes.

Near the outer edge of the shrub swamp, beyond which another wet meadow opens, I come upon a form worked onto a wide-topped mound and so artfully integrated into its setting that it seems part of it. But it is a unique and separate structure, saddled onto a turfy hummock from which royal fern unfurls, and built up into alder and sweet gale stems. Two feet by three feet and nearly a foot and a half deep, this construction has stems at its base but is fashioned primarily of grass and sedge blades, downy moss, and plant duff. It has a hole in the middle that looks like the entrance to some mammal den or burrow. But water, not earth, lies below the mounded platform. Reaching into its dark hollow, I pull out the skull of a small rodent. The skull, too clean to be from a kill of this season, could be more than a year old. Nothing about the mound suggests current activity. Fingering deeper inside, I find more skulls, a dozen in all, scattered through the plant weavings. Examining the skulls, I can see that they are those of little muskrats, and I realize that this is a marsh hawk's nest. I see these raptors hunting over the marsh and its environs for a week or two each spring on their migrations north and again in the fall, as they make their way back south; but I have not known them to stay the summer and nest here.

As marshes were drained over the course of settlement, marsh hawks, or harriers, were able to establish breeding grounds in the vicinity of large hayfields. Additional loss of wetlands, coupled with the conversion of hayfields to forest and development, has made it impossible for marsh hawks to nest in areas where they used to be abundant. Since about 1980, nesting pairs have all but vanished from New England south of the White Mountains. Some nesting occurs on offshore islands. The overall habitat in which this marsh is set, with its wetland mosaic and nearby hayfields, may be just extensive enough to support a breeding pair. The skulls make me think that one summer a population explosion in the marsh's muskrat colony enticed a pair of harriers to settle in and raise a brood. Even under ordinary circumstances, muskrats are prolific, capable of raising several litters of six or more each year. But in years of explosive reproduction (which occur on the order of once a decade), during which they can eat out an entire cattail marsh, the numbers of vulnerable young and unfit adults far exceed even the heavy predation normally brought to bear by such major muskrat-eaters as mink.

Leaving the shrub-swamp niche in which the marsh hawks nested, I find easier going in a muskrat channel cutting through a great wet meadow that is almost entirely filled in with beaked sedge. One other plant is able to find a place in the midst of this severely exclusive sedge: in midsummer, swamp milkweed will open deep purplish pink flower heads here and there, just above the highest reach of the beaked sedge. I bear to the left at a fork in the muskrat trail, wading between two small shrub-swamp thickets of sweet gale and swamp rose, to the deepening water of a bluejoint reedgrass marsh. Ecotones, where one habitat borders another, as where field meets forest or wetlands meet uplands, support a greater, often far greater, diversity and abundance of species than either habitat alone. The extensive, winding margins where this great wetland complex meets the surrounding uplands form an expansive and varied ecotone; but within the marsh itself, an interspersion of wetland elements forms edge habitat upon edge habitat, ecotones along the meetings of sedge meadow and grass meadow, marshy swaths of bur reed and bulrush with aquatic beds of floating-leaved water lily and pondweed, interfacings of cattail stands with open water, emergent marsh with shrub-swamp thickets and red maple swamp. Water shapes the patterns of these plant assemblages; the plants in turn influence the water. Together, hydrology and vegetation affect the distributions and behaviors of the animals that move among them.

A black duck explodes out of the mazes of bluejoint at my knees. A burst of powerful wingbeats, with a sound like small thunder, carries her out of sight in an instant. All spring these large, soot-black birds and I startle half the life out of each other in far-flung wetland recesses. Much of the time they keep to such heavy cover and are so quiet in the water that I rarely see them before they erupt into air-shattering, water-shedding ascents that could seriously challenge the heart health of anyone not accustomed to having noticeably large living things suddenly burst wildly, loudly, out of nowhere in remote wetland corners. For good measure, a black duck almost always throws in a frantic, nerve-shattering outburst of hoarse quacks. This female did not launch herself until I all but stepped on her. A bird that does not make a move until I am within such desperately close quarters is almost always sitting on her nest.

Having already frightened the duck away, I decide to look in on her nest. Though it lies less than two wading strides from me, it takes a while for me to find it. Characteristically well concealed, it is a grassy shape among sedge and bluejoint swirls, canopied by a natural arch of winter-toppled bluejoint grass. Ten pale gray-green eggs lie in a grassy bowl lined with down. Ducks do not carry in nesting material but fashion a nest by pulling grasses, leaves, moss, and such in from the immediate surroundings. A lining of down, which the mother pulls from her breast, is added as incubation proceeds, and she covers the eggs with down whenever she leaves the nest. Nest-building and incubation are the province of the female alone. Once egg-laying begins, drakes depart. During the monthlong incubation period and afterward, there are many opportunities for skillful predators, such as fox, mink, and raccoons, to take the eggs or ducklings, if not the brooding hen herself.

This black duck's main ally in successfully raising a number of young is the cover provided by the complex nature of her breeding habitat. Great Marsh is extensive, unfragmented, and unpolluted. It features a bewildering array of intermingled wetland types, an interspersion of marsh, shrub swamp, and forested swamp, along with areas of open surface, and aquatic-bed habitat that will soon bring forth a profusion of floating-leaved and submergent plants. Breeding habitats of such unbroken extent and high complexity have declined dramatically. The ducks of the prairie pothole region, for example, are not as favored as the black ducks of this bluejoint marsh, with its contiguous marshes surrounded by broad natural buffers. The pothole region, some 300,000 square miles of glacier-scoured prairie terrain in south-central Canada and the north-central United States, originally comprised many thousands of marshes, sloughs, and ephemeral ponds. But 70 percent of the wetlands of the Canadian portion has been lost, and many thousands more of these wetland basins in the United States have been drained for agriculture. The hens of the prairie pothole region (home to half of the waterfowl native to North America) must nest in isolated niches ringed by open land that has been converted to cropland and suburban sprawl. The contiguity and interspersion that formerly characterized these vast tracts of wetlands have been eradicated; habitat complexity has been overtaken by environmental simplicity. The nightly rounds of raccoons and foxes have been greatly facilitated. In contrast, a mink or any other predator would be greatly challenged to locate the duck nest I have stumbled upon.

Feeling that the black duck hen is watching me, I wade away from the nest. I complete my crossing of the inundated meadow and turn along the sparse line of red maples, keeping to a natural levee that borders this run of the brook. An animated tiny bird catches my eye as he darts acrobatically among dead branches above my head. A sudden brief blaze of crimson from his head identifies him as a ruby-crowned kinglet. I see that the object of his energetic excitement is a female kinglet, who appears content to let her suitor do all the dancing. While earlier-returning birds have already committed eggs to nests, these migrants are engaging in courtship en route to nesting grounds farther north. Even seen against the sun, his brilliant crown flashes incandescent. When he hides it, he becomes at once a small, nondescript bird, barely noticeable but for the white eye rings circling his intent black eyes. He tumbles and hops, wheels and spins, in an impressive high-wire act all around the female, who crouches on a branch, her head hunched into her shoulders. She trembles her wings, holding their tips close against her body. The male flies across a little pool to dance among tree branches. His melodious, incessant singing carries loudly, clearly; it seems as outsized as his rubied crest in the marsh landscape.

These birds of boreal evergreen forests, mixed woods, spruce bogs, and their ecotones are seasonal frequenters of the wetlands I wander. I often see them in the alder thickets around the Reedgrass Pool in springtime. In autumn they apply their acrobatics to catching insects in willows and alders along the intermittent stream that feeds into Alder Brook, the permanent stream whose floodwaters nourish Great Marsh. He flames his crown once more, a little king indeed, and becomes, for a brilliant moment, an electrifying element in the panoramic marsh landscape of early May. Such little emblems can be so vivid that they enliven acres of space and growth: the crimson slash on the head of a four-and-a-quarter-inch bird, the scarlet shoulder patch of a red-winged blackbird not so much larger, the sharp white flag of an alarmed white-tailed deer.

There are other aerial acrobats about, filling the great sky space above the marsh. A flock of tree swallows weaves thin air with life. One pair has left off sailing and gliding on high to attend a nest in an abandoned woodpecker hole in a dead red maple. No jewel could gleam more brightly, turning in the sun, than the brilliant backs of these freewheeling birds. Neither web-footed swimmers nor stilt-legged waders, these are birds of the wing. Yet they are very much birds of wet meadow, marsh, and open water. They are not of the water itself, though they touch it at times with precise, high-speed skimmings of their tiny bills. Rather than inhabiting the dense wetland vegetation that is home to so many of their avian kin, they live in the space above it, high and low, the great airy openness that is the skyward portion of the wetlands. They, too, are nesting now. It is at their arrival-pauses and entrances to nesting holes that I am best able to see the metallic sheen of their blue-green backs.

I walk and wade sodden turf, pools, and channels along the maple line to a glimmering riffle, a sand and gravel shallows, where I cross Alder Brook. I push through a hedge of alder and red maple enlivened by the yellow flashings, incessant tail waggings, trills, and twitterings of palm warblers and wade on into the deepening water and mud at the edge of a cattail marsh. *Kidd'-ick, kidd'-ick; ki'dik-kid'ik-kid'ik* — the metallic rasping of a Virginia rail's call comes from close by, behind a woven wall of cattail and coarse sedge. There is no seeing into their bewildering growth and crisscrossings of light and dark. Nor is there any way to flush this wader from his cover for a quick look. He will only run, invisibly, deeper into the marsh growth, where no eyes, let alone feet, can follow. I know these rails are here, know them by their calls, and count my few sightings of them in all my years in the wetlands as great favors. Of the many secret lives of the marsh, the Virginia rail's is one of the most secretive. These birds seldom call in broad daylight, preferring to sound out at dawn and dusk. Turtle nesting season brings me to wetland margins at daybreak and twilight and at times after dark from late May through June. Most of my hearings of these elusive birds come at these times.

Sora come here, too, at least some years. Even more elusive than Virginia rails, they also tend to call at dusk and dawn. The one year their calls became a background for my wetland rounds, I heard them at night, spaced series of *keek . . . kee-yawk'*, in darkness and by moonlight, around midnight, and again at dawn. In all my time in marshy tangles, I have seen a sora only once, when a black-faced male stepped from rank growth of reed canary grass into a small opening in the shallows of the Reedgrass Pool. I had been motionless for some time. It is during stakeouts, or protracted periods of motionlessness as I catch up on my notes, that I have had most of my close encounters with the most wary and secretive creatures. On one occasion, as I wrote in my notebook while sitting on a fallen tree in a covering of dead branches, a coyote came within fifteen paces of me, investigated a mammal burrow I had recently looked into myself, and went back the way he came, never knowing I was there. I will never come closer to achieving the invisibility I desire. Another time, as I leaned among alders and kept watch on a stretch of open water on a winter brook, a mink all but trotted over my boots as he pursued his rounds along its snowbound banks. There was essentially no cover among the alders in January, nothing more than stems and shadows; my absolute stillness was again the key to not being detected. Snowshoe hares, wood turtles, snakes, frogs—many animals know the value of keeping still.

Unlike the coyote and the mink, the sora eventually noticed me. Looking up, he appeared transfixed for a time, as if trying to decipher my face. He may have found it as quizzical as I found his, with its red eyes and yellow beak. His solution to the puzzle was to casually step back into the screenings of reedgrass, confident that he would never be seen again.

Beyond its sedgy, rail-concealing margins, the cattail segment of Great Marsh is permanently flooded. Water levels drop in summer, and in drought years mud flats are exposed in shallower sections. But there is always water here. This emergent wetland is intermediate between a shallow marsh, with water depths between six inches and two feet, and a deep marsh, which may have water six feet deep and feature extensive areas of open water. As in many cattail marshes, the black, mucky substrate is up to my thighs in most places, every bit unwadeable. At times I gain access to muckier regions by wearing plastic overshoelike devices that strap over wading boots or old sneakers. They are rimmed by flexible baffles that spread outward as a foot is set down and compress as it is lifted; the foot does not sink so deeply and is far more easily withdrawn from the suctioning grip of the muck. These "mudders" were designed to imitate the feet of wading herons, whose long toes spread wide upon being set down and contract when raised.

There are, however, places in this marsh, as in many wetlands, where the water depth, insubstantial substrate, or both preclude human wading by any means, and the vegetation excludes any floating device. The quality of their mud and water, as well as their populations of biting and bloodsucking invertebrates, their sudden snakes and antagonizing plant growth, tends not to draw crowds to marshes and swamps. In an era of globally expanding human presence, during which an endless array of equipment has allowed us to enter just about any corner of any habitat, from sheer mountain cliff to coral reef, the self-protecting nature of these wetlands has kept them among the final holdouts from human intrusion. But even these wilder margins can be shaved and interiors made accessible so that great acreages of wetlands as resistant as the Everglades can be converted to suburban sprawl and fields of sugar cane. An increasing number of habitats have been diminished and degraded by overvisitation. Driven into smaller and smaller corners of less and less cover, and encircled by expanding human activity, species decline. Ecosystems become ecologically, aesthetically, and spiritually impoverished. I wonder how much comfort Thoreau would take from knowing that the site of his cabin, now Walden Pond Reservation, is limited to a mere 2,000 visitors per day. He who wrote that he had three chairs in his cabin, one for solitude, two for friendship, and three for society, would now require an extra 1,997 chairs for society some days and would have to go far afield to find solitude.

Determined swampwalker that I may be, I am kept out of much of this cattail marsh. As in many wetlands, the muck here is more than an impediment, it is an impassable barrier. I cannot make my way through most of the cattail stands, nor wade the muskrat channels. The pools of floating-leaved and submersed plants and the spaces of open water are well beyond my reach. They are the realm of muskrat, Blanding's turtle, black duck, and dragonfly. It is an agreeable standoff. I am cautious about becoming an overbearing presence in any of the wetlands rounds I keep, and this marsh assures that I do not become one here. I content myself with circling the wadeable margins, getting glimpses into the interior through reedy curtains of cattail.

This marsh has formed, as marshes often do, along a stream section flowing through a poorly drained depression in the landscape. Dam-building by beavers commonly has a hand, or paw, in the establishment of marsh habitat. Favored by topography, hydrology, and the work of the beaver, cattail has become established in this marsh to the extent of forming a monoculture. Once a stand of these aggressive colonizers becomes entrenched, it begins to spread outward via creeping rhizomes, weaving beds so thick they supplant all other vegetation. A one-acre stand may consist of no more than a few plants, enormous clones that have arisen from a single seed. The capacity to spread by vegetative reproduction via networks of prolifically sprouting underground and underwater stems is an important characteristic of many wetland plants. It is a fortuitous event for the seed of a wetland plant to even sprout in a marsh or swamp environment. Once established, however, seedlings of rhizomatous species can expand into sizable colonies, often displacing all other vegetation.

The exuberant songs and piercing alarm calls of red-winged blackbirds ring in my ears as I wade a muskrat channel among cattails. Wherever there are cattails, there are red-wings; wherever there are cattails in sufficient standing water, there are muskrats. Many of last year's persistent stalks and leaves still stand taller than I do. New green straps rise among them, the three-dimensional tapestry of this year's growth, which will grant me some of the sora's secrecy in later-season wadings. This marsh is unusual in being divided into two sectors, the main one composed of the more common broad-leaved cattail, the other a bed of narrow-leaved cattail. The latter is more common in coastal freshwater and brackish marshes. Where the two species occur together, they may hybridize. Indifferent as to whether their cattails are broad-leaved or narrow-leaved, a colony of red-winged blackbirds breeds throughout the marsh, weaving well-concealed nests among stalks and leaves a foot or so above the water, often beneath a canopy of old blades bent over and interwoven by the winds and snows of the past winter.

I take a watery avenue that leads to a muskrat village, a pondlike clearing in a bed of broad-leaved cattails more thickly grown than most forests. The open water, a clearing that in all likelihood was created by bottom-scooping muskrats and is maintained by them, is the setting for half a dozen houses and a number of satellite feeding stations, platforms, and rafts. It looks like a deserted village, but I know that some residents are at home, prudently in hiding. Their lodgings are built primarily of dead cattail stalks of seasons past, with thatchings of beaked sedge and other coarse vegetation and a finish plaster of finer plant material and mud. A few sticks may be incorporated on occasion, but in contrast with the wooden lodges of beavers, muskrat houses are constructed with herbaceous plants. The muskrats — inadvertent water gardeners — build on little islands they make from heaps of mud and decaying plants dredged up from the adjacent bottom. Cattails are to muskrats what aspens are to beavers, a staple of their diet and a primary source of raw materials for their building projects. Still-water muskrats, as opposed to those who live in bank burrows along streams and rivers, eat the starchy rhizomes of the cattails, cut down their stalks and blades to construct houses, and excavate their root mats and encasing mud to dig channels and raise islands. All of these activities help check the insistent spread of these aggressive plants, which might otherwise completely fill in an emergent wetland and render it unnavigable and uninhabitable by many wetland animals. The open pools and channels maintained by these large aquatic rodents also enable pondweeds, water lilies, watershield, bladderworts, water-milfoil, and other aquatic-bed plants to grow in this marsh.

An incoming muskrat, unaware of me, surfaces at the mouth of a lesser channel in her cattail village. She carries a mouthful of greens, succulent shoots of springtime sedges she has harvested elsewhere in the marsh. She may have young who are ready to be weaned but are not ready for cattail stems. She freezes at the surface as her tiny black eyes, rounded well out from the sodden fur of her head, take in my unintentionally menacing figure, half hidden in dry stalks. Ordinarily she would dive and double back the way she came in an instant, swimming underwater for two or three minutes before surfacing as much as two hundred feet away, well out of my sight. But she is evidently on a mission and does not want to either turn back or relinquish her precious cargo, which has probably been obtained at some effort. I wish, as I often do, that I had some animal tongue to convey that I am harmless. I have no

Muskrat (*Ondatra zibethica*)

taste for muskrat nor desire for this one's coat or salad. But muskrats have many predators and enough of a history with humans and their guns and traps that this one can take no assurance from my stillness and unspoken good will. Terror and courage mix in her wild heart. She goes down directly in front of me and begins a swim across open water that strong instinct must tell her to avoid. I feel certain now that she has little ones to feed. Even worse, she has to struggle mightily to submerge, owing to the buoyancy of the sprouts she carries. Propelled by partially webbed hind feet that are broadened by a fringe of stiff hairs, assisted and steered by a powerful rudderlike tail, muskrats are excellent swimmers, capable of swimming forward and backward with ease. But this burdened one has trouble making progress. As she strikes out for the safety of her house in the village, the unfortunate discomfort of her slow-motion swim in a clear pool treats me to an uncommonly prolonged view of a muskrat trailing dinner greens.

5:40 P.M. Leaving the cattail marsh, I brush through a hedge of sweet gale. Throughout my crossing of this marshland, I have traveled to the calls of red-winged blackbirds. It is impossible to wade a cattail marsh in May without agitating red-wings. Frequently they have sounded drawn-out, high-pitched whistles and low, nervous cluckings, their expressions of alarm, as I have come too close to their nests. Their ear-piercing, descending alarm calls (or are they warnings?) are so beautifully shrill and haunting that I am often tempted to linger near the nests, unkind as that would be, just to hear them call again. Lingering isn't necessary, in any case. They nest in such numbers throughout this marsh and its shrubby borders that almost anywhere I go, I sooner or later pass by a nest and stir up their penetrating cries. The males wing and perch all but in my face at times, flicking their jet black tails in continuous protestation.

In sidling through the sweet gale, which grows just above shoulder height here, I turn at a favoring angle and descry a nest, a cup of woven sedges. The coarse strands of the outer structure are bound around a number of sweet gale stems; its inner lining is made of very fine grasses. The nest is both hidden and shaded in the emergent shrub hedge, a little less than a foot above the water, which is six to eight inches deep here. Cradled within it are four blue eggs ornately inscribed with dark brown and purple squiggles, an Arabic script that looks legible enough to be read. The eggs are nearing their time to hatch, which in red-winged blackbirds coincides with the metamorphosis and aerial emergence of mayflies, dragonflies, and damselflies. Each of the two or three broods these birds raise each year is timed to a wave of metamorphosis by aquatic insects. I am reminded once again of precisions in timing, to which I wish I could become better attuned.

6:11 P.M. Along the interface of a sweet gale meadow and a sedge meadow I come upon a second blackbird nest, worked among tall sedge shafts, a few sweet gale branches, and a slender alder stem. The four eggs in this nest are also adorned with calligraphic umber-maroon scrawls, but the blue background has reddish to pinkish washes here and there. The fledglings that pip from these eggs will all be of one red-wing mind, sing the same songs, become birds of a black feather, indistinguishable from one another, save males from females. Or so it could seem. As eggs, each is a signed original. And later, among the migrating flocks that turn in the air as if with a common mind, and may seem all-in-one, there will always be, as there is with all living things, the individual within the species.

Alarm calls give way to untroubled evensong as I wade a muskrat trail that leads to the base of a white pine knoll, my point of departure from this great marshy basin. When I come back in a week or two, it will be aglitter with the wings of mayflies, dragonflies, and damselflies, and the red-winged blackbirds will be feeding their young.

Snapping Turtle, Dragonfly, Black Bear

July 4, 2:38 P.M. From its border of soft-stem bulrush and bearded sedge to its central cattail island, Bulrush Marsh is a green sheen. Every square inch of the surface of this five-acre emergent wetland has been closed over by a collective of floating plants, primarily watermeal, a minuscule plant that floats at or near the surface of quiet waters. Barely the size of the head of a pin, less than a sixteenth of an inch long, watermeal is the smallest of flowering plants. But in colonies it is capable of blanketing acres of marsh and swamp, particularly in wetlands rich in nitrogen. Watermeal makes the lesser duckweed, which has established its own floating colonies here and there, seem outsized at three-eighths of an inch. Adrift among the watermeal and duckweed are two aquatic thallose liverworts: purple-fringed riccia, which floats on the surface, much like a duckweed, a slender riccia, which hangs suspended in tangled masses just beneath the surface mat. Easily escaping notice as individual species, these tiny water plants collectively form something of a freshwater Sargasso Sea in wetlands that favor them. Together with copious admixtures of plant detritus, they form a floating world, a marsh-covering mat about a quarter of an inch thick known as the neuston. Mingled among the plants of the neuston, and suspended at various depths in the water column beneath it, are dark green globes that range in size from about a sixteenth of an inch to a little under half an inch in diameter. Picturesquely named green jelly balls, they are conglomerations of protozoans and algae that come together and form a common organism.

Screened by bulrushes, I stand midthigh deep in the wadeable moat surrounding the great, inaccessible quaking-bog-like cattail island that occupies the center of this marsh, watching for some sign of a Blanding's turtle. The neuston is a keen attractant for these turtles, much as vernal pools are early in the season. They forage on the abundant prey that live in it, including snails, freshwater clams, aquatic insects and larvae, tadpoles, and minnows. The mat also provides the heavy cover Blanding's turtles favor; they hang suspended in or just beneath it, striking out with their long necks to capture prey and at times basking within its heat-collecting vegetation, their carapaces just breaking the surface. Every time I shift my watching place, I set off an eruption of screaming, splashing green frogs. The bullfrogs, nearly as numerous, with a few thrashing exceptions sit in stoic silence, even when I cause waves in the dense floating mat they have settled into.

Green is the color of this midsummer marsh. Frogs in every shade and variation of its ruling color sit in the greenery of emergent, floating, and floating-leaved plants. For good measure, many frogs are coated with watermeal, which tends to adhere to their heads and backs. I once saw a basking painted turtle who was so thoroughly coated that he was as green as a red-eared slider—a related species of southeastern wetlands. One standout in this verdant mélange is a large bullfrog, whose broad head is a startling turquoise. Now I see a living emerald, a shining, recently metamorphosed gray tree frog, flattened against a broad-leaved cattail blade, just about glued in place by means of his suction-cupped toes. As his name implies, he will be as gray as granite or beech bark for most of his later life in upland woods, although if he spends enough time among leaves and ferns he will change color, taking on a green cast to match his background. At this time of transformation, however, he bears the most brilliant green I have seen in the marsh.

My attention is drawn away by jostlings in the bulrushes and separations among floating pondweed leaves, the first movements other than scrambling frogs that I have detected in the overwhelming stillness of the marsh. The plants telegraph that a turtle is on the prowl. Perhaps a Blanding's turtle is foraging in the submersed, water-filling suspensions of bladderwort and milfoil and the underwater stems and leaves of pondweed. I mark the movements and begin a slow advance. Another stirring in the vegetation reinforces my impression that a turtle moves, but the movements are more suggestive of a snapping turtle than a Blanding's.

Despite my intimate familiarity with the wetlands, I do not always feel easy about reaching into their teeming waters or mucky substrates. Sight is no help if one's eyes are above the watermeal-covered surface, and if I attempt to open a window in the neuston, anything lurking beneath will flee. All reckoning of what lies beneath must come from touch and feel. My reluctance to make a quick grab comes not from visions of snapping-turtle jaws or water-snake teeth but the fiery, painful bites of backswimmers, predacious diving beetles, and giant water bugs. Having been most painfully twice bitten over the course of my swampwalking, I am four times shy, even though those two bites now average out to only one every twenty years. Beyond thoughts of insect afflictions, an element of unknowing holds back my hand and arm at times, particularly in waters as hidden and heated as these. In my boyhood I would slide through such places on my belly, wearing only shorts, standing up now and again to casually pluck off the leeches I had acquired, but that is a time and a swampwalker past.

Floating leaves become still once more. The one pursued is aware of the one pursuing. What awareness have we of each other beyond rough perceptions of movement, estimates of size? My mind carries a limit-setting, parameter-establishing field guide of the life forms of this time and habitat. Only so many species of such-and-such sizes and behaviors can be here. Why, then, do I occasionally feel uncertain when reaching into water and mud? And what visions, however clear or vague, do my movements conjure up in my quarry? Perhaps the turtle's image-bank links this timeless afternoon with a memory from the time of the dinosaurs.

I am pretty certain who my turtle is now, and I have a reckoning of where he is, roughly how big, and which end is head, which end tail. Fingers spread wide, my left hand slips through the veil of watermeal and pondweed, my arm extends into the water. As I work my hand through the heavy soup of submerged vegetation, my fingertips sense their surroundings somewhat as the feelers of a brown bullhead do, though with far less sensitivity and information-gathering capacity. My experienced hand proves unerring in this instance. In all this watery insubstantiality, my searching fingertips touch down on something resoundingly solid. I immediately recognize the domed shield of a turtle. My fingertips spread out over a wide, shallow carapace that can house only a snapping turtle.

This is not my favorite way to find snapping turtles, even though I know that under water, in dense cover, with an entire marsh in which to escape, this turtle will not turn and attack. Only if I were to lift him above the surface or carry him onto land would he attempt his powerful, lightning-strike self-defense. I slide my fingers back along his carapace to its jagged rear margin and close my hand around the thick, spiked base of his tail. I can sense the turtle's entire muscular body tensing. The biggest snapping turtles I have encountered weighed in the vicinity of fifty pounds. This one is not so big, but he feels considerably larger than his movements in the water plants had indicated. Not comfortable with my hands-on measurings of the girth of his tail, the turtle yanks it suddenly to one side, drawing my knuckles across the sharp, sawtoothed marginals at the rear of his shell. I am sure that if an otter or, in shallows or on land, a raccoon or coyote were to clamp jaws onto his tail, the snapper would use this same defensive thrust to draw the predator's nose across this cutting edge. I accept the turtle's emphatic protest and let go. The greened surface of the marsh surges with his forceful leave-taking, then quiets back down to its prevailing stillness. A slight trickle of blood comes from the knuckle of my ring finger, testament to my contact with the serrated armor of the snapping turtle.

4:23 P.M. As I take my last look across the sheening marsh, a sturdy dragonfly lands on the top of my wading stick. A ten-spot, he is dusky and blue-gray, his checkered wings and the softly radiant blue-powder dusting of his abdomen are attention-getting, in lieu of the brilliance of color and iridescence that emblazon his abundant kin in the marsh. Perched just above my hand, level with my chin, he appears willing to bear the closest inspection. Intensely territorial, the males of this species often wheel at high speed close by me, with dizzying changes of direction, aggressively driving other dragonflies from their air space. At rest, black-and-white wings spread wide, this one seems as tranquil as the afternoon. He seems to be staking a claim on my wading stick. If I were to plant it here, he would undoubtedly add it to the perches from which he surveys, hunts, and defends his marshy territory. But this beaver-chewed length of red maple with some bands of reddened bark left on it, polished by rubbings of my own sweat mingled with seasonal ablutions of bug repellent and sunscreen, is one of my favorite wading sticks. Expecting my winged companion to take off at once, I pull up the staff and relocate it for that difficult foot-extracting first step out of the mud I have settled into while admiring him. But he holds his place. With each successive shift in my wading, he stays put, without the slightest vibration of his glistening wings even as I lurch from the last of the muck up to more solid ground. He is coming along for the ride. The *caballito del Diablo*, "little horse of the Devil," as the Spanish call him, accompanies me as I turn from the marsh along a drier edge of meadowsweet flanked by red maple and gray birch. I take no special care, use my walking stick as I would if it carried no passenger, but still he stays on, even as I step out onto an open field. Then, perhaps having rested enough or feeling too far from home, he flashes off.

I am not alone for long. Once I am on the firm earth of the field, I take a few steps to look down the line of trees between it and the marsh. A shifting shape, startlingly large and singularly black, takes over the landscape. At last I encounter a black bear. It takes a moment of curiously blended amazement and complete expectation for the reality to sink in — the tracks I have seen over the years do have owners. The bear

Black bear
(*Ursus americanus*)

moves on all fours, with a graceful, unhurried, utterly silent loping across the open space. He is blacker than midnight, blacker than ink, a sleek black like nothing I have ever seen. He seems to drift through and above the pale stalks of the little bluestem grass. Swirling winds that have come up with the afternoon's passing evidently carry a trace of my scent to the bear. He stops, then rises to full height on his hind legs and looks in my direction. He appears to stand as tall as I do above the thigh-high bluestem. A bear this size can only be a male. I see his small, glinting eyes. He does not seem to see me where I stand, motionless, just beyond the edge of the brush. I would like to watch from a more hidden place, as I don't want to frighten him off, but if I so much as duck now, the bear will be gone. His fawn muzzle contrasts sharply with the total blackness of the rest of his great body. His full-height surveillance apparently revealing no threat, he drops to all fours and continues his silent loping through a screen of grass and sweetfern. I lose sight of him in the swampy tree line and wait for any sound of him splashing into the marsh. But if he does enter the water, he does so as silently as he crossed the dry field.

A minute passes, two; then the top of his head and his rounded ears come into view as he heads directly toward me. Only at this moment, and only for an instant, do I feel any uneasiness. Characterized far more by restraint than ferocity, black bears rarely attack people; only 25 killings of humans by black bears were recorded across North America between 1900 and 1990. Data from the National Center for Health Statistics show that for each death caused by a black bear over that period, there have been 67 caused by dogs, 374 by lightning, and more than 90,000 by way of homicide. Closer to where I stand with the bear, only two human fatalities caused by black bears have been documented in New Hampshire, both more than two centuries ago. I do not feel any fear. In any case, there is no place for me to go. I cannot outrun, out-climb, or outswim a black bear, and my car is far away. A shout or hand-clap would send him fleeing. But I have waited a long time to see him and do not want him to go.

The bear may well know I am in the vicinity, but evidently his poor eyesight has kept him from seeing me, or he would probably have bolted. The black bears here most likely know my scent and sounds, have a knowledge of my comings and goings over time. If my patterns do not change, they will not become unduly alarmed. Again the bear rises to full height, his tan muzzle pointing directly at me, from about forty paces away. In one of those moments that seems frozen in time, or completely outside of time, I regard this remarkable animal, so large in the landscape, so much belonging to it. Standing on hind legs, with rounded ears up and cocked, powerful shoulders sloping, massive fore-arms held out in front of him, great forepaws drooping at the wrist, the bear is beyond impressive. He raises his muzzle. His twitching nose, much better at deciphering his surroundings than are his small but in-tent eyes, works the air. After testing the wind for a time, he drops down to all fours again and ambles back the way he came, turning to cross the field exactly where he did before, as though retracing his steps. On he moves, with occasional brief pauses but without rising up again, and disappears in dark shadows of the woods across the field. As he vanishes, I am struck again by the color of his coat. He is blacker than any shad-ow, and shadow-silent. He doesn't so much as rustle the stiff-twigged brush, the dry midsummer leaf and branch litter of the tree line. In the great black bear I have seen a living emblem of the remaining wildness of these wetlands.

At six o'clock I leave the marsh. My hand on my walking stick can still feel the spiked strength of the snapping turtle's tail; my knuckle bears its healing cut. I look at the beaver-chewed bevel at the head of my staff, where a dragonfly rode. The black, black image of the bear is sharp in my mind. I think of the snapping turtle, the dragonfly, the black bear, and the space we share, the time on earth we share, with our different eyes open, under the same sun.

Nest-to-Water Journey

September 23, autumn equinox, midday. As the time of turtle-hatching continues, I walk more than I wade, making my annual circlings and crisscrossings of sparse, sandy nesting areas adjacent to the marsh, looking for hatchling turtles on their way to water. As summer turns to autumn, the year's last sultry days alternate with vibrantly clear, cool spells and the first touches of frost. Loud crickets, glowing gold crooks of gray goldenrod and shiny-fruited dewberries along dry field edges; swamp dewberries ripe, cranberries ripening, and field milkwort flowering in damp moss and lichen hollows; nodding ladies'-tresses blooming: all the key emblems of turtle-hatching season are at their height. With the turning to afternoon, drifts of cumulus clouds, small and cottony, ride sweeps of cooling wind from the northwest. The sky is a vault of September blue, radiant with sun. Scanning the ground, I cannot see into shadows at first. The abrupt, intense contrast between lights and darks blinds me in broad daylight.

Half an hour into my ground search, I encounter a tiny traveler, little over an inch in carapace length, bound for the marsh eventually. The crimson hieroglyphs that border his clay-colored shell are dulled by the dry, persistent coating of sandy loam that he has dug out of within the past day or two. His head is dusty from his travels over sparse terrain. The hatchling painted turtle halts in midstep as I kneel for a closer look. His eyes are bright with September light, lemon gold, brighter than goldenrod, with a jet black slash and round pupil sparked with sun. This turtle, so new, has the look of an ancient wanderer, one who has walked the earth for a thousand years. How alive with light, how moist his new eyes appear, the bright eyes of a turtle who has never been in water. What vision does he carry, of the wetland he is bound for, the watery environment he will enter and, once having entered, rarely leave for the rest of his life? What kind of image does instinct hold, what blend of knowing and learning, of expectation, recognition, and surprise? Everything this hatchling sees or smells, senses in any way at all, must be new to him, and yet in some way must be known. From what point deep in

Hatchling painted turtles (*Chrysemys p. picta*) in hibernation

time, from what sensings by what life forms, did the original cues of his emerging earth-knowledge come?

The painted turtle whose path I have crossed is an autumn nest-emergent, an unusual case for his kind. The hatchlings of virtually all other turtle species in the glaciated Northeast dig out of their nests between mid-August and mid-October to journey to the wetlands where they will overwinter. The vast majority of painted turtles, on the other hand, although they too complete their development in the egg by late summer and pip from their eggshells, do not dig out of the nest until the following spring. Their first hibernation occurs on land, at depths of one to three inches, in the nesting chambers dug by their mothers. Remarkable physiological adaptations enable them to survive below-freezing temperatures in the nest. The mechanisms by which these hatchlings survive temperatures as low as 13 degrees are not clearly understood, but they appear to involve supercooling, in which an organism becomes colder than the freezing point of its tissues but does not freeze unless it comes into contact with ice crystals, and freeze tolerance, in which cells remain undamaged by intracellular as well as extracellular freezing. Hatchling painted turtles may employ both of these survival strategies at different times over their long hibernation. Both eggs and little turtles are vulnerable to being dug up and eaten by skunks, raccoons, and other predators of turtle nests, up until the ground freezes. When the ground thaws in spring, skunks begin their digging searches again, looking for hatchlings who have survived the winter in the nest but have not yet warmed up enough to dig out and begin their springtime journey to water. This traveler at autumn equinox may have left siblings behind in the nest, where they will stay until a month or more past next year's vernal equinox.

I straighten up and stand back. The hatchling resumes his walk along a glittering path of sun upon sand, an unassuming turtle little bigger than my thumbnail. He is probably bound for the marsh, though he may not get there today, nor travel to it as directly as I once would have thought. He may be a day or two into his life's first migration, and he may not complete his travels for several more days. As a result of interceptions like this, along with lengthier observations of the nest-to-water journeys of hatchling painted, snapping, spotted, and wood turtles over the years and the revealing fieldwork of a friend who tracked hatchling Blanding's turtles, I have abandoned my earlier conception that most freshwater turtles head straight to the water the way hatchling sea turtles do. In a field study I conducted with another friend, we applied dustings of fluorescent powder to the shells and legs of hatchling wood turtles. At night, using ultraviolet light, we could track the turtles by following specks of powder they left behind. Over time, we lost most of the trails in open ground, where there was nothing for the powder to catch on, or in untrackably dense cover, or in heavy dews and thunderstorms, which washed the powder away. Turtles we did manage to follow tunneled into dense grass, disappeared in rock jumbles, and dug into leaf litter. One spent the night in a deer's footprint in the damp hollow of a waterless vernal pool. Another ended up as a brightly colored fragment, a tail and a bit of carapace, still showing fluorescent powder, lying, along with seed coatings and husks of sweetfern nutlets, on a flat-topped boulder that served as a chipmunk's feeding station.

We were able to follow a dozen trails in their entirety, from nest to water. The trails told varied stories. One hatchling did go directly from the exit hole of his nest to the permanent brook in which he would over-winter. His migration may have taken an hour or less, as the stream was only thirty yards from his nest. His directness was far and away the exception. Other hatchlings from his nest made wide turns, arcing away from the water, traveling circuitously through hayfield, dense grass-and-forb old-field, and brushy tangles, before eventually wending back toward the brook. Most of the nest-to-water journeys took several days.

One of the hatchlings proved to be a veritable Odysseus, turning his back on sloping terrain that descended to a permanent stream below his nest site (counter to all the other hatchlings from this nest area, who headed downhill), traveling back and forth across the face of the steep bank of his nest in an abandoned sandpit for several days, finally ascending that bank, crossing a hayfield, and heading downhill again. The final stage of his journey took him through deep-matted grass and goldenrod, dense blackberry hedge, and a line of trees, to a final sloping descent through a riparian, green-shadowed forest of sensitive fern beneath an unbroken alder canopy. This brought him at last to the root-bound banks of a brook — a different brook from the one to which all other hatchlings I had ever observed from his nesting area had oriented. After a pause on the speckled gnarls of a brookside alder's root-hold, a little past noon on the twenty-sixth day of his great migration, he dropped into the clear waters of the stream. As I watched the hatchling wood turtle at the pivotal moment when he first entered the stream, a moment beyond which I could not follow, I felt that he had found his home at last. But of course he had been home all the while.

This journey, taken over such great time and distance, had been made by a wood turtle, very much a species of streams, rivers, and riparian wetlands, yet one that is equally at home in upland habitats during its terrestrial summer season. I have seen hatchling wood turtles keep to small forms (shallow, nestlike depressions that they fashion to their own size and shape under cover in grassy vegetation, forest litter, or earth) for several days; and I have watched them begin to feed long before they entered water. Unlike all northeastern turtles except the eastern box turtle,

Cryptic basking of hatchling wood turtle (*Clemmys insculpta*)

wood turtles can eat out of water. They find hiding places and basking sites that are quite concealed though reached by little spotlights of sun and drink water left by heavy dew and rain. I could see that hatchling wood turtles, so well adapted to life on land, might not have to make a rush for water. They need only reach it in time for hibernation in the water before a hard freeze. But what of the hatchlings of a highly aquatic species like the painted turtle? These graceful swimmers of open water seldom come ashore. When they do, as females must to lay their eggs and as males and females, young and old, do in making their annual overland rounds to the marshes, swamps, and ponds within their activity ranges, they travel in nervous haste. Unlike wood turtles, they cannot eat out of the water.

Not far from here, on a heated midday late in April several years ago, I came upon five painted turtles in the process of unearthing themselves from the nest in which they had spent the winter. Three were out of the nest, craning their striped, earth-encrusted necks, blinking sand away from their eyelids, taking in their first light of day. A fourth peered from the shadowed oval of their common exit hole. A fifth was waiting within, but not for long. Here, if anywhere, I thought, I would witness a dash from nest to water. Acres of open marsh lay nearby, its closest sedge and sphagnum border less than thirty yards away. The level terrain between the nest and the presumably beckoning waters was only sparsely vegetated, a near-desert of sandy turf, warm and brilliant in the sun of an April noon hour. Only a narrow line of brush and saplings screened the broad vista of the marsh. Even without this screen the hatchlings were too low to the ground to see the water. But every known or suspected cue by which hatchling freshwater turtles might find their way to water would seem to be clearly, irresistibly leading the way to the marsh. Tree canopy rose up opposite the wetlands, a dark shape against the horizon, an image that is thought to send hatchlings traveling the other way. The vast, open sky above the marsh was brilliantly before them, radiant with the light that is believed to attract them. I myself could catch the scent of the marsh and feel the humidity that radiated from its warming wetland acres. I had to assume that the orienteering hatchlings had a far keener sense for the presence of water than I did. My only advantage was my height: I could see the marsh. But with all the other signals, I had to think the hatchlings could as good as see it themselves.

The nascent turtles made their moves. One made a very short initial journey, scurrying about twelve feet from the nest in a direction away from the marsh, and dug out of sight in shaded duff beneath a stand of sweet fern. Two others headed due south, paralleling the edge of the marsh thirty yards to the east. One of these traveled about twelve yards and burrowed into closely crowded clumps of little bluestem grass. The other went on a sustained two-hour march, continuing due south. His entire journey paralleled the marsh, but he never turned toward it. I saw him pause but once as I sneaked from one watching place to another, trying to keep hidden while not losing sight of any of the little ones. Two hours into his resolutely straight-line march, he suddenly veered sharply to the west, away from the water, and headed for an isolated tussock of little bluestem grass. I watched as he dug quickly out of sight in its base.

As these three hatchlings traveled over the sunlit field on journeys of minutes or hours, their two siblings turned their backs on the wetlands and set out directly for the deep-shaded margin of an upland wood. I trailed them among the shadows as they moved in under aspen, oak, and pine. They separated, but fortunately kept close enough to each other that I could keep track of them from a single hiding place. Each paused on dry leaf litter and held still. After five or six minutes, one shouldered under the leaves and began to dig into forest litter. I marked the site with a twig and did the same where his brother or sister also slipped under a covering of fallen leaves. After the marcher of the open field had concluded his day's travel, I returned to these wooded sites. I carefully removed the leaf layer and fingered into forest duff at the first one's hiding place, sifting through a wide area and digging nearly three inches deep before finding him, well buried and tightly withdrawn into his shell. I am not sure I have seen a hatchling wood turtle, a species as much at home on land as in water, dig so deeply out of sight in a hiding place along his nest-to-water journey. Where the second turtle had disappeared into the litter, I found a round hole in the earth just beneath the leaves. It was the entrance to a small mammal's tunnel, most likely one used by moles and voles. I dug in and soon came to the hub of radiating tunnels, leading off in all directions. The hatchling's one-and-an-eighth-inch shell easily could have passed along any of these subterranean routes. I dug and sifted throughout the surroundings but never found the turtle.

Not one of these painted turtles, so emblematic of marsh and pond, headed to the wetlands on his initial day out of the nest; each took instead to field and forest. How long would their journeys be, how circuitous their routes to water? It even occurred to me that, given their ability to overwinter within a shallow nest chamber in the earth, some of the occasional autumn-emergents might leave their nests, separate, and dig into another earthen site for the winter.

The five hatchlings confounded all my expectations. If the two who took to the woods had climbed trees I could have hardly been more surprised. Yet I have seen hatchling snapping turtles, about as submarine a freshwater turtle species as there is, make wide turns and extended detours through exceedingly difficult field and forest terrain when a simple downhill run would have brought them to backwater wetlands that would seem any little snapping turtle's dream. On other occasions I have watched them migrate directly to the water's edge. Several times I have watched hatchling spotted turtles scramble, disperse, and dig into terrestrial hiding places much as the little painted turtles did. One spotted turtle I followed tunneled under a small log and stayed there for twelve days before resuming his journey. Other times I have seen them dig into a minimalist wetland pocket of ten by twenty-five paces or so, with only a few inches of ephemeral water and no soft substrate, and successfully hibernate through a northern New England winter there. I am certain the site would have been fatal for an older turtle but have come to believe that hatchlings of all these species possess physiological survival mechanisms that do not persist beyond that critical first winter.

The unpredictability in all of this may well be a key consideration. There is great survival value, for the individual and hence for the species, in avoiding the predictable, in scrambling the patterns to which predators could become too precisely attuned. The first message to hatchlings just out of the nest may be to disperse and hide; the migration to water can take some time and cover some space. There may even be a component for gene dispersal among colonies, and perhaps populations, at the hatchling level, as suggested by a wide-ranging wood turtle who ended up in a brook primarily inhabited by a separate colony from that of his mother and siblings.

I have observed those two groups of wood turtles (who are no doubt part of a larger regional population) for eleven years and, except for two adult males, have never witnessed crossovers, even though their resident brooks are separated by an upland rise only four hundred feet wide. The roaming males (who evidently travel longer stream routes rather than the overland distance in their mingling) certainly provide for an exchange of genes between the two colonies. It is interesting to see the potential for such exchange at the hatchling level. This potential is a long-range one, as the hatchling would have to survive for twenty or so years before reaching sexual maturity. But given time, and intact habitat, such workings must be capable of beating what would seem insurmountable odds to much human reckoning, and in fact be an integral component of the nature of life.

I have come to think of the nest-to-water journey as a complex and critical component of an individual turtle's life, with profound implications for his or her species. My repeated encounters with turtles over the years leads me to believe that they never forget a place to which they have been, that they construct an ongoing map of all the wetlands and uplands they traverse. Hatchlings must begin their mapping with their first steps from the nest. When I see a hatchling at the dark mouth of the exit hole he or she has just opened, tiny foreleg poised for that first step onto the earth, I think of the Chinese proverb "A great journey begins with a single step." Any hatchling turtle's life journey may be a matter of minutes, a single round of the seasons, or a course of well over a half century.

There are migrations within migrations. Once the hatchling has reached water, it must find a survivable niche within the wetland for overwintering. Each hatchling must orient to the aquatic habitat that meets the requirements for his species. I have seen painted and spotted turtles nest side by side along the edge of this field. The hatchlings of the former make their way to the marsh; those of the latter travel in another direction to the Shrub Swamp, where their species hibernates. I have yet to observe crossovers. In my earlier years of swampwalking, when I came upon a hatchling like this afternoon's migrant, I would pick him up and carry him to the nearest, best-suited wetland habitat edge. Best suited, that is, by my reckoning. I no longer do this. I know something about turtles, but I am not a turtle. It is not up to me to determine which is the "right way," which the "wrong way," for a hatchling to be traveling. If a hatchling fails in his orienteering and perishes on his nest-to-water journey, it may benefit his species, his death preventing the possible passing on of a genetic flaw in the population, well before the individual reaches reproductive age. How many survival tests has a turtle passed, how many selective pressures surmounted, before he or she becomes a breeding member of the population, which in spotted, wood, and Blanding's turtles generally takes from fifteen to more than twenty years? It seems that the first, and perhaps some of the most significant, trials are faced on the nest-to-water journey.

As natural habitats dwindle, wildlife management plans are drawn up for a growing list of endangered and threatened species. Efforts to preserve declining or isolated populations of turtles, such as disjunct colonies of Blanding's turtles or a disappearing subspecies like the Plymouth redbelly turtle, include screening nests against predators and collecting hatchlings for "headstarting." The hatchlings are typically kept warm and active and fed year-round, a regimen that promotes far more rapid growth than would occur under natural conditions, then released into whatever habitat, often compromised, remains. But circumventing or countermanding natural development processes, such as the nest-to-water journey, is not likely to be in the best interests of the individual or the species. Such human manipulations may well have the effect of disseminating genetic weaknesses that would have been suppressed by the dying of hatchlings unfit for their particular habitat.

There is a human tendency, arising from genuine concern and a taste for being proactive, to rush in and expend money and effort on heavily managed programs designed to save the last of the big cats in Africa, the remnants of an isolated box turtle colony in the northeastern United States. It is hard to criticize the concern. But it arises from misguided sentiments and leads to unwise policy. Somehow the solution is never allowed to be a pulling back to a respectful distance from the natural landscape, finding a proper human proportion within it. We are unwilling to step back from the marsh and allow its rightful margins to stand, to let its complexity and biodiversity, its very destiny, play out along ancient and ongoing pathways. Our overwhelming anthropocentrism does not allow the solution to take the correct form, of limiting our own numbers and presence to create a balance in the biosphere. Instead, people encroach everywhere, in ever-greater numbers with ever-greater demands. We line the wetland with houses, then ask what we can do to help the turtles. We are the problem, and under the terms of the day, we cannot be the solution.

It is beyond ironic that we can all but never say no to the housing project, shopping mall, hotel, highway, golf course, or expansion of agriculture, but that after the habitat has been fragmented, funds, agencies, and groups can be drummed up to cage the final nests, relocate buckets of eggs, fast-forward hatchling turtles in aquariums, and dump them into encircled habitat remnants. The most direct, simple, and viable solution, to simply leave the place alone, has no place in the debate. It is rarely a matter of whether or not a project is to go forward but *how* it is to go forward, with various token, ecologically meaningless compromises and mitigations, together with management plans for the lost landscape. We look to feel good when we should feel ashamed. "Wildlife management" is a sorry contradiction in terms. There already is a management plan. It has been unfolding since life's appearance on earth.

6:46 P.M. Mist and gathering darkness; I cherish this warm, moist, closing-in mood of September. As the light fades, there is an earth-glow from the nesting fields; the little bluestem, dull bronze and purple, seems to give off its own light. A surreal amber-orange light fills the darkening autumn air now, falls on my hands, on my notebook page. The light seems to come not from the sky but from the earth. Mist slips down the slopes, among the trees across the marsh. The middle landscape is silvered into invisibility. The marsh is an untroubled light-reflecting plain. The hatchling turtle whose travels I followed for a time is hidden away in the swirls at the base of a bluestem tuft. The final light of day dies out, soft silver, blurred bronze, in feathery stalks of grass that arch above his hiding place. The turtle is on his way, even as he sleeps. The marsh will be there at the end of his nest-to-water journey.

Turtlehead (*Chelone glabra*)

3 THE SWAMP

Wollemi. (Look around you.)

— Australian Aboriginal saying

Swamp at Noon

June 15. I enter the swamp at noon on the third consecutive day of the year's first turning to high heat and humidity, one of those breathless "Panama days," as I call them, that I can relish once I lizard into them. It is a little over 90 degrees in the shade, and the humidity is close to 90 percent. Through the red maple canopy I get occasional glimpses of almost hurtful sky light and blinding sun, reflecting from cumulus congestus clouds, majestically ascendant, glaring, crisply edged white domes and towers that may well mass into mountainous cumulonimbus formations, the thunderheads of late-afternoon storms.

A swamp is a wetland forest of tall trees, living or dead, standing in stillwater pools or in drifting floods of water or rising from seasonally saturated earth. In contrast to the open-to-the-sky worlds of aquatic beds, marshes, and wet meadows, and to the often dense but low-storied shrub swamps, a swamp is typically a vaulted, often enclosed place, with high columns of tree trunks and ceilings of leaves. By specific definition a swamp is a wetland in which trees (woody plants twenty feet tall or taller) make up at least 30 percent of the vegetative cover, with the tree canopy partly or completely closing out the sky. Soils in swamps range from saturated to semipermanently flooded and are usually rich in organic matter. In many swamps, wetland shrubs form a second canopy in the densely to lightly shaded understory. Beneath the shrub layer there are commonly third and fourth layers composed of herbaceous plants and ground cover, respectively.

As wet as the season has been, standing water has begun to fall away from the swamp I walk and wade. A young green frog, looking like an enameled pendant of gold-flecked malachite, with inlays and leafings of tourmaline, bronze, amber, and jet, is set in a mysterious mirror of shallow water. It, too, seems an ornament of some swamp artisan's design, amber and jet, greened with the light passing through the leaves of high maples, fronds of low ferns. I do not find the steamy, low-lit ambience of this edge-of-summer swamp stygian. I am in no netherworld but one of light and the living, however hushed, however shaded and subdued it may be.

Nor is this a world outside of time, though its history is ancient, its appearance Carboniferous. The frog, whose moist, ever-twitching nostrils are the only indication that he is not, in fact, the work of a gifted jeweler, has his roots in that great era of the amphibians, some 350 million years ago. But he is a modern amphibian, not a primitive form that has succeeded in holding on while life in the main has continued along its resolute evolutionary track. Some living relics do persist on earth, seemingly exempt from the passage of time. The coelacanth, a 350-million-year-old relative of lobate-finned fishes ancestral to amphibians, still lives in oceanic waters off the west coast of Africa. In the mid-1990s a primitive tree species, thought to be extinct for millions of years, was discovered in a vast nature park in Australia. The park is called Wollemi, an Aboriginal word meaning "look around you." The prehistoric trees were discovered by a ranger who was spending a day off looking around an unfamiliar corner of the park. In a narrow gorge he noticed conifers unlike any he had seen before. Climatic upheavals and enormous changes in living species, including the rise of flowering trees, had passed this species by. Though such living fossils, animal and plant, are found from time to time, life, with rare exceptions, has moved on, redesigning its seemingly endless forms and functions again

Green frog (*Rana clamitans melanota*)

and again. But for all the transformations, many common roots remain in the living. There are moments when the gulfs across time seem not so great. The sun-glinted, gold-leafed eye of the frog at my feet seems to have been looking out on the earth since the dawn of life.

The red-orange newt who prowls into view in clear shallows near the frog adds to the prehistoric feeling. He, too, could pass for the work of an enameler, carnelian touched with carmine, spotted with ruby and speckled with obsidian. But this three-inch, juvenile red-spotted newt is no leftover from the days of dragonflies with two-and-a-half-foot wingspans, though his past, as a species, goes back many times farther than mine. I wonder about our separate and collective futures as species. Untroubled by any wonderings I can detect, the newt, still in his red-eft stage, goes about the business of being a red eft. He interrupts his pendant posings with sudden darts, snapping up things I can barely see or not see at all — water fleas, minute aquatic insects, larvae. As I watch this animal go about life in the same physical world in which I live, though his world is in so many dimensions so utterly different from mine, I wish I could look through his keen gold-ringed eye and see what he sees in the water and how he sees it.

A tiny beetle becomes entrapped on the ineluctable surface film just above the red eft. His six-legged struggling does not go unnoticed. The eft, maneuvering awkwardly — backing up, tilting from side to side as he shifts his legs, arching up from the bottom over which he has been stalking — makes several lunging attempts at the surface, finally capturing and swallowing the beetle. The young newt was born of an egg deposited in underwater vegetation by a fully aquatic mother. It lived an aquatic, gill-breathing, larval-salamander life for several months, then underwent metamorphosis and left the water to be a terrestrial being. After several years of life on land, under logs and slabs of bark, on dampened pine duff and the mossy, ferny flooring of an upland forest, he now begins his return to the wetlands, on the verge of another transformation. A close inspection reveals the darkened green coming into his granular-skinned back. His tail shows traces of a finlike, vertical broadening. Over the course of the season, this forest walker of dark, moist days will move on to more permanent waters than the swamp can offer, and by autumn will have become a graceful swimmer, an aquatic animal for the rest of his life. He will turn bronzy green with a lemon-gold belly, retaining his peppering of black dots and the staggered line of black-encircled ruby red spots along his sides. As clumsy as he was in catching his prey at this stage of development, the red eft was far more in his element than the beetle, a creature of earth and air, who became completely helpless upon becoming caught by the tension of the swamp pool's surface film.

Frog and newt rest in the ambered clarity of sunlit water, where a shaft of the midday sun burning high overhead slants through the red maple canopy. Just beyond them the water is yellow-green, tinted by sunlight passing through the translucent fronds of royal fern. The darker green, spore-bearing, modified leaf tips of the fertile fronds are beginning to show. These enduring, mound-building ferns of swamps, marshes, and stream borders grow to a height of six feet. In wetlands with pronouced microrelief, they form arching lattices over my head as I make my way among the mucky hollows at their bases. On such occasions, these indeed regal plants appear to be Carboniferous tree ferns, and their resident swamps seem as old as coal. But royal ferns are more recent forms of nonflowering plants that arose at the time of the earliest amphibians. The great majority of ferns living today appeared quite some time after the ancient era they evoke, many of them within the past 100 million years. They have developed alongside of, and taken their ecological places among, the flowering plants, which within that time span have come to dominate the planet's vegetation and to exert a powerful influence on the terms of life on each. The ferns I move among, however much they may appear to be the growth of a dim and distant past, have arisen with the rushes, sedges, and grasses, the rose pogonia and swamp rose, leatherleaf, buttonbush, and red maple, and thus far have traveled stride for stride with them, along a common path in time.

Ancient ways are still at work among the living, with their elements of direction, randomness, and chance, their endless variation working over time. New turnings are invariably in process. The climate is always changing, however imperceptibly. Vegetation is slow to respond to climate change, but in the end it must. Animal life, in turn, is in a continual state of response to changes in vegetation. The living world is constantly working things out, generally with an incomprehensible gradualism over a very long span of time. We humans are not separate from the long history of life on earth, but in large measure we have estranged ourselves from it. And in a stunningly short period within our own brief history as a species, the past two or three centuries, our proliferating, space-and-resource-consuming global population has altered not only the terms of its own existence but the conditions of life for all other species on earth. We leave no sufficient space for the nonhuman world to pursue its own historic workings, follow its own unfathomable directions and destinies.

It is difficult to understand the diversification of life into the ten million or so species alive in the world today, much less the billions that have died out along life's journey through time. It is all the harder to divine the presumable single ancestor of some four billion years ago, and the means by which that incalculable diversification has taken place. No doubt biodiversity has been critical to life's persevering beyond several great waves of extinction, and the innumerable lesser extinctions that have gone along with the rise of new species. The abundance and diversity of species is now severely threatened by the planet-altering activities of a single species: *Homo sapiens*. As I look around myself, midshin-deep in a red maple swamp, I can only be grateful that in the face of the enormous loss of natural habitats, wetlands chief among them, these living things, which have made such a long communal journey, are still here, continuing, for now, that journey to its unforeseeable turning points and unimaginable end.

The questions of our origins remain ultimately unanswerable. We have a few clues as to where our own species came from, but we are at a loss when it comes to the broader matter of our beginnings. It would be hard to say that we know where we are, and it is virtually impossible to say that we know where we are going. Fossils provide glimpses into life's past and some insights into the origins of the first hominids. Ironically, we become awestruck by, and enshrine, the few fossilized remains of past life, yet we run roughshod over the miraculous life on earth today (including each other), as well as the marvelous systems that sustain that life. As revealing as the fossil record may be, it is acutely incomplete. The vast majority of living things that have come and gone on earth have left no trace of themselves. In most cases the fossilized remains are but a fractional record of the organisms that left them, bits of their hard parts, nothing of their soft parts, no real record of their behaviors. It may be a heady thought to consider that several hundred thousand fossil species have been found and named, until one realizes that this outwardly impressive number represents as little as 0.0001 percent of all of earth's species.

Although I know of the oceanic origins of life on earth, it is in swamps and marshes, freshwater wetlands, that I find my keenest sense of life's past, my sharpest intimations of life's journey in time, and my own moment within the ongoing. My kind has existed for only the most recent fraction of an instant in the duration of life's streaming through time. The features that describe me as a species, the aspects that I share with no other animal, my large brain and upright posture, evolved less than 6 million years ago, a sliver of time in the 400-billion-year history of life. But in the deep core of my cells lie pathways that lead to all the kingdoms of life on earth, the bacteria, protozoans, algae, fungi, plants, and animals. In my present form I am but one of the innumerable expressions of life. In my specific form I am new here, and I am the stranger. Yet I am ancient, and I belong. It occurs to me that in human terms (the word "strange" cannot really be applied to nature), I am the strangest thing in this swamp.

Dead-Tree Swamp

June 27, 3:17 P.M. At the abrupt transition where a brook flows from a wooded, canopied swamp into an open dead-tree swamp, I stand in the shade of a high wall of cool green leaves. Looking through a narrow opening in the verdant screen, I let my squinting eyes adjust to the intense summer light of the great open space. The day's glare is heightened by sunlight on acres of bleached skeletal trees, dull bone white and gray-white, a drowned forest standing and fallen in the black waters of a beaver swamp. As my eyes become accustomed to the shimmering light, so sharply contrasted with the dark recesses along the stream where I have been looking for salamanders all day, I see a great blue heron hunting. A young bird, he takes one strike, lifts his head up and back, his long sword of a bill to the sky, and makes several quick snaps as he extends his neck straight up and swallows. I suspect that the swamp may be blessed with one less frog, though it might have been a fish. Frozen in place now among the crisscrossing grayed branches of deadfalls, among shadows tinged with great-blue-heron blues and grays, the bird could have become immediately invisible to me had I not kept my eyes fast upon him after his gulping and swallowing. In slow motion I extricate my binoculars from the jumbled contents of my backpack and slowly raise them. Vigilant himself, even as he searches for wary prey, the heron would be off at once if his keen eyes were to detect one flicker of movement through my shielding screen of leaves. He keeps as still as the breathless afternoon for a time, then moves again, taking several slow strides, each accompanied by a rhythmic, gradual curvilinear extension and retraction of his serpentine neck. From time to time he redirects his head, his long, sharp bill poised, his avid eyes ablaze with focus and intent. His movements are effected with such heron stealth that even in motion he could pass unseen. The heron is in his element and at one with it, seeming to be the landscape come to life at some moments and to dissolve back into it at others. He reminds me of a wood turtle I stirred, with my wading stick, from a deep pool in a stream earlier in the season. The turtle was turtle at one moment, with a favoring angle and light, and simply part of the stream's broken water, shadows, and sandy, stone-strewn bottom the next. In their native settings, so many of these living things I try to watch are magicians, masters of disappearance.

The heron shoots his head to the water and retracts it, a bronzed, water-glistening fish wriggling sideways in his bill. The catch was skillful, but not exactly the lightning strike one would imagine necessary to snatch a fish from the water. It was a thrust tempered by measurement, timing, and lethal accuracy. A heron must be sudden, but not rush things; movement must be neither wasted nor revealed. It is very difficult for fledgling great blue herons to master the stalk or ambush as well as the strike. Many do not live out their first season. The one I watch appears to have become a consummate fisherman at a tender age.

There are three heron nests in this swamp; two are empty, but I can make out three young in the third. Majestically, a pair of adults circles in, appearing hugely blue-gray in the hazy sky just above the living crowns of the upland trees at the edge of the swamp. Drifting like kites, or like feathered puppets worked by invisible strings from above, they sweep among the dead trees in graceful glides, an impressive sort of parachuting that allows ascents and sweeps, as well as descents, without a wingbeat or perceptible shift of flight feathers. It seems remarkable that they stay aloft, given the stillness of the air and the measured slowness of their flight. Following their aerial surveillance, they drop to roost, one on the nest, the other on a large branch in a neighboring tree. The parents are decidedly larger than the solitary hunter I have been watching, who is in turn well beyond the nestling stage.

The arrival of the parent birds at the nest, a great platform of sticks about a yard in diameter, initiates strange antediluvian croakings, low and guttural, from the juveniles. The previously silent young keep up their pterodactyl clamor, oddly muted yet distinct in the humid silence of the swamp, throughout the entire five- or six-minute feeding session, as the attending parent shifts his bill from one open mouth to another. The feeding completed, this one moves off to the dead tree in which the other adult continues the statue-still roosting he or she (the sexes are indistinguishable) has maintained since landing. The heron who tended the feeding cleans off his bill with long strokes on his roosting-branch, alternating sides of bill and branch, like someone sharpening a scythe. I wait, expecting the second parent to move in and continue the feeding, but that one roosts on.

Keeping just back from the outer edge of the forest's screening border, I circle the swamp's eastern margin. Eastern kingbirds are acrobatically darting after dragonflies; a flock of tree swallows continually wings above the jagged crowns, sifts among leafless branches, and sweeps low over the water. At nightfall, when these diurnal sky patrollers are lodged within their nest cavities in the dead trees, big brown bats will emerge from their daytime roosts under slabs of sloughing bark to take up their nocturnal winging of the same air spaces.

With bursts of blue flight and loud, rattling calls, four belted kingfishers arrive and spread out high among the dead trees. These birds are usually solitary, and except for a mate during the breeding season, do not tolerate others of their kind in their territories. A female, emblazoned with a rust red belt, perches for a time on a dead branch about fifteen feet above the water, so close to my lookout that I can look her in the eye. She cranes her neck, twists and angles her head this way and that. Her high-dive fishing style allows her a broader surveillance than the close-at-hand vigilance required of stalking herons. In contrast to the herons, who are most of the time mute and motionless, neither stillness nor silence appears to matter much to kingfishers. It may be to their advantage to startle fish into revealing movement. This one constantly changes position on her ambush-branch, scanning the water, arcing and tilting her head, and from time to time rattling out her loud calls — wild, startling eruptions in the silence of the swamp. Her ragged crest, large, intent eyes, and sharp, heavy beak, more dagger than sword, complete the wild effect of her insistent cries. I have on several occasions seen kingfishers make successful fish-snaring dives, and each time it has seemed a marvel that these high-divers can pluck swift fish from the water, a skill more amazing than the heron's. But, I have also seen osprey catch fish with their feet. The kingfisher keeps up her fidgety scanning for some minutes. Nothing worth diving for catches her bright eye. She leaps from her perch and clamors off, an erratic blue streak disappearing in a forest of leafless trees.

Skyow! . . . skyow! — hoarse, penetrating cries from a green heron break the swamp silence that follows the kingfisher's departure. Something has flushed the heron from his wading or stalking along the deadfall branches at the water line in search of little fish or crayfish. When beavers built the dam that created this dead-tree swamp, they changed more than the habitat; they changed the very voices of the wooded landscape. Just behind me, space is leaf-filled, light is leaf-filtered. In all but the driest times, water whispers and murmurs over gravel bars, among stones, and through debris dams. At thaw and during spring spates, there is a constant rush of stone-splash. Upon entering the broadened, backed-up, still water of the dead-tree swamp, the brook loses its varied voices.

On the living-tree side of the dividing screen of leaves, along the upper run of the brook and throughout its riparian corridor, intricate warblings ornament the shadowy woodland quiet. Mellifluous northern orioles, lilting titmice, and fluting hermit thrushes weave tone poems throughout the summer day. As the afternoon deepens into twilight and darkness, thrushes and veeries keep up a haunting evensong, superimposed at times with a catbird's extended evening raga. But in the open, sun-bleached dead-tree swamp, bird voices are characterized by penetrating cries, throaty croakings, and startling rattles erupting at widely spaced intervals in the deep silence. The beavers' swamp has also given frog voices to the summer landscape. Isolated *plunks* and *twangs* of green frogs on occasion build into roiling choruses that suddenly

drop off again to silence. Individual bullfrogs break out
with resonating runs of *thuh' -
thuh-thuh-rhhumm'* that at
times incite communal choruses building to swamp-
filling crescendos.

A pair of wood ducks wings
in and settles out of sight. A
black duck hen glides among
branch tangles in the water
with a rather compact trail of
seven ducklings in tow. When
they sight something to eat,
they dart out from their common way, then quickly fall
back in line. With so many
dead trees in water open but

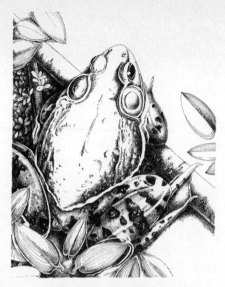

Bullfrog (*Rana catesbeiana*) and
floating-leaf pondweed (*Potamogetan natans*)

for scarce floats of pondweed and scattered rafts of duckweed, this
swamp might seem at first a sparse environment; but in fact it is a rich
and biologically diverse wetland. Although the trees have been dead for
some years now, they persevere as structure, architectonic columns,
platforms, bridges, and rafts. By virtue of all the lives within and among
these dead trees, even as they gradually go down into the water, they are
yet a living forest. They will persist for many years, high in the air, deep
in backed-up waters and silting-in muck of the impoundment, until the
cycle moves on and the swamp becomes pond. For now, even in death,
the trees continue to dominate and define the landscape.

The Red Maple Swamp

August 12, 2:17 P.M. I head toward the faint trickling sound of the Red
Maple Stream, a watercourse two to three strides across that edges one
half and cuts through the other half of the twelve-acre Red Maple
Swamp. From early April into May this stream is a brisk run of clear
water over coarse sand, one and a half to two and a half feet deep, which
floods into the swamp. During that season the brook is a migration

route for snapping and spotted turtles, bound upstream for active-season niches in Bear Pond and Great Marsh after overwintering in the backwaters of the permanent stream that this brook joins below the Red Maple Swamp. Today, at the height of summer, with the upper tree canopy and middle shrub layer leafed out, and the herbaceous lower cover at densest growth, the stream is much slower and narrower, barely ankle-deep and half hidden under the arches of royal fern and tussock sedge that reach out from both banks. But for a single spill over a water-logged red maple trunk, the brook winds through the swamp without a sound. The Red Maple Swamp, subject to repeated and prolonged flood-ing, primarily in spring, features the familiar pronounced microrelief of forested wetlands: plant mounds standing twelve to eighteen inches above the mucky pits that surround them. At flood times, water stands in these hollows, often level with the tops of the mounds. Muck lies a foot to a foot and a half deep on the solid floor of the topographical de-pression in which the swamp sits. I cross the brook. Its sandy, gravelly bed provides me a couple of solid steps, but these give over to sinking footfalls in the gripping, mucky sediments along the opposite bank.

Moving away from the brook, I enter the heart of the Red Maple Swamp, where sedge peat provides better footing. Red maple is the quintessential tree of forested wetlands in the glaciated Northeast. In many parts of this region, red maple swamps cover more of the land-scape than all other freshwater wetlands combined. This species can tol-erate a wide range of wetness and almost invariably comes to dominate wetlands in the floodplains of streams and rivers, headwaters of streams, groundwater seepages, and shores of ponds and lakes, as well as isolated upland depressions. It is also found in a broad range of upland habitats throughout the eastern United States. Red maple has likely been a pre-dominant feature of northeastern wetlands since the return of life after the glaciers, but its current overwhelming prominence has probably come as a result of disturbances such as logging and fire and of the dis-appearance of American elm. Once a major species of forested and floodplain wetlands, the stately, vase-shaped elm has been decimated by Dutch elm disease. Red maples are the only trees I see about me in this central sector of the swamp. The trees appear to be under duress. Dieback has left bare branches throughout their crowns, and their leaves are appreciably smaller than normal. The canopy, thirty feet overhead, is thin, a lacework of sunlight and shadow. Though well adapted to wetness, the red maples may be struggling with the hydrology here. This swamp is a groundwater depression, a wetland that is in contact with, or close to, the water table throughout the year. In addition, the Red Maple Swamp is flooded by overflow from the brook in winter and spring and by heavy rains associated with the tropical storms of late summer and autumn. The tree-crowned mounds, and the deep pockets of organic soil around them, indicate that this swamp sees prolonged flooding followed by extended periods of soil saturation during the growing season, when there is usually no surface water. The high degree of wetness here evidently tests the tolerance of the red maples. Although some standing water may remain throughout the year in forested wetlands, red maple swamps ordinarily cannot become established in sites that are fully flooded for more than a year. In swamps that lie under water for more than a third of the growing season, red maple and other species of forested wetlands, such as eastern hemlock, northern and Atlantic white cedar, black gum, green ash, and swamp white oak, as well as the wetland shrubs typically associated with them, are restricted to mounds elevated slightly above the seasonal high-water level.

The red maples here are struggling with one another at their crowns even as they struggle with the water regime at their feet. All of them are growing as sprout clumps that rise from stumps left standing after this wetland was logged off about forty years ago. Each clump consists of three to six trees, each of which is striving to outcompete the others and become a single great tree. I push aside the sedge and fern cover on a mound and reveal a sawed-off stump that has nearly been closed over by the spreading basal growth of three main stems. After the tree was cut, scores of shoots sprouted from its stump and root crowns. Browsing by deer and moose was probably one of the factors thinning the competition for a place in the sun, and stronger sprouts shaded out rivals. Some stems have died out only recently. The bark is still sound on them, and they are nearly as tall as the three survivors. But their leaves are gone, and for them the race for the sun is over. Each stump will likely end up with from one to three main trunks, and these will grow until loggers or storms fell the forest once again, and the process starts anew.

In the stillness of the August swamp, a rustle and scraping of bark, a small sound from a small bird, catches my ear. A brown creeper is making her rounds or, more precisely, her ascending spirals, up a dead trunk, working at bits of sloughing bark with her curved bill, searching for insects. In addition to the dense, multilayered growth favored by many species of birds, wooded swamps commonly provide abundant snags, dead trees, or parts of trees in various stages of decay. Even though red maple, yellow birch, American elm, eastern hemlock, and other trees of forested wetlands are well adapted to flooding and saturated soils, they are often under stress from these challenging conditions. After a succession of wetter years, crowns die back, main branches and trunks die off. High winds, ice, heavy snow, and occasionally lightning wound the trees. Since wetland soils are typically shallow and waterlogged, swamp trees are rarely able to sink deep taproots or anchoring roots into the earth, as upland trees do, and are therefore considerably more vulnerable to windthrow. Trunks are snapped off, large branches are broken, bark is stripped away by neighboring trees crashing down.

Unlike animals, trees cannot heal a wound by repairing or replacing injured tissues. Instead they wall them off, compartmentalizing them by means of chemical and physical barriers, and subsequently form healthy new growth around them. A succession of organisms, from bacteria and fungi to slugs, insects, and other small animals, moves in to utilize the nutrients and spaces opened up by a tree wound. These organisms in turn provide an important food source for many birds and other animals who live in surrounding uplands as well as in the swamp. Over time, killed-off sections of trunks and branches decay, and birds and mammals dig into the rotted wood to create nesting sites and dens that are protected by sound deadwood or a barrier of new growth in the living part of the tree. Hairy and downy woodpeckers, tree swallows, nuthatches, tufted titmice, and black-capped chickadees nest in smaller cavities and branch-stub holes. Larger decay compartments serve as nesting sites for ducks of forested wetlands, including the wood duck, hooded merganser, common goldeneye, and ring-necked duck. They also provide hidden daytime roosts for nocturnal species like the barred owl, great horned owl, and big brown bat. Rotted-out decay columns in the trunks of large trees, encased in sound, living wood, provide dens for animals as large as raccoons, opossums, and fishers. In the bottomland hardwood swamps of the southeastern United States, immense bald cypress trees, attaining heights well in excess of a hundred feet, can develop decay cavities spacious enough to accommodate black bears. At the opposite end of the scale, the brown creeper searching for insects in the snags of this red maple swamp needs only a loosened strip of bark under which to fashion her nest.

Given red maple's capacity for colonizing wetlands, it is not surprising that this regenerating, cutover forest is virtually a pure stand of the species. It may have been centuries, even millennia, ago, during a succession of years when flooding was shallower and briefer in this basin, that winged red maple seeds helicoptered in on the wind and germinated on tussock sedge mounds. Over time the maples set down stiltlike, mound-forming roots and became established enough to overtop the mingled vegetation of their footholds, then expanded to form a canopy over the entire wetland. Once established, a red maple swamp becomes deeply entrenched. This tree reproduces primarily by way of stump sprouts and root suckers, forming tenacious root mounds. The ability to vigorously sprout anew from the bases of drowned or windthrown main stems confers a decided advantage in a sodden domain where most trees cannot survive. Seasonal flooding and the overall wetness of the environment either prevent germination of other species or kill off any seedlings that do manage to sprout. Although other trees are rare in red maple swamps, there is often a dense shrub layer, composed of such species as winterberry, alder, highbush blueberry, silky dogwood, maleberry, northern arrowwood, and swamp azalea. The shrub canopy commonly covers more than 50 percent of these swamps, under a red maple canopy that often exceeds 85 percent of cover.

Beneath the shrub canopy there is usually enough light and space for rich herbaceous growth. This lower level is itself arranged in layers, from cinnamon and royal ferns, bluejoint grass and the taller sedges, to carpets of sphagnum and other mosses, over which wind trailings of glisteny-leaved goldthread and swamp dewberry. The birds of a forested wetland reflect the tiered nature of its plant structure. Their ecologies have coevolved to partition space and resources in ways that allow expanded numbers and diversity. Species such as red-eyed vireos and black-throated blue warblers keep principally to the high tree canopy; black-and-white warblers, veeries, and yellow and Canada warblers occupy the middle to lower layers; northern water thrushes and wood and hermit thrushes favor the pool edges and wet ground litter.

The shrub layer in this red maple swamp grows to a rather uniform height of nine to ten feet above its mounded footings and is composed almost exclusively of speckled alder and winterberry. Below it is a three-to-four-foot-tall herbaceous layer, a grassy, ferny expanse of bluejoint reedgrass, tussock sedge, and royal and sensitive fern. I brush among the mounds, investigating the smaller and less numerous plants that have taken their places among the lush foliage of these dominants: marsh fern, spotted jewelweed, turtlehead, halberd-leaved tearthumb, rough bedstraw, and blue flag in soggier hollows; tall meadow rue, bladder sedge, crested shield fern, bugleweed, and swamp jack-in-the-pulpit on drier hummocks. While the diversity of plant species in any one swamp is typically rather limited, red maple swamps feature a rich diversity of vegetation regionally. Although forested wetlands dominated by red maple have their namesake tree in common and an overall environment that at first glance might appear generic, each is unique in its forest structure, hydrology, and other site characteristics. This individuality is particularly manifest in the plants of the herbaceous layer. There are many variations on the red maple swamp theme, including red maple–skunk cabbage swamps, red maple–yellow birch–cinnamon fern swamps, and red maple–highbush blueberry–swamp azalea swamps. Each of these principal assemblages provides habitat for a range of wetland plants, from shrubs to mosses, liverworts, and lichens. In addition to this wealth of plant species, forested wetlands dominated by red maple and other hydrophytic trees provide critical habitats for a great array of animal life. Collectively, the forested wetlands in an ecosystem often equal rain forests in their biodiversity.

The value of the collective regional diversity of red maple swamps is rarely given due consideration as planners split straws and shave margins in attempts to assign wildlife-value functions to individual wetlands. In the connected natural landscape there is a constant biotic and abiotic dialogue among wetland habitats. They are integrated; there is no finite point at which one ends and another begins. We make "wise-use" decisions based not on ecological integrity but on the economics of

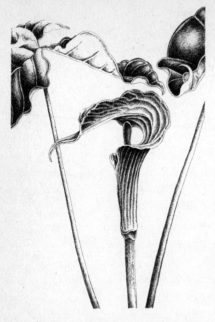

Jack-in-the-pulpit (*Arisaema triphyllum*)

human greed, designating a "prime" wetland here, an expendable one there, permitting ourselves to take a wetland away from the living landscape and frequently presuming to recreate it elsewhere. These actions are customarily taken with little or no in-depth, site-specific investigation or inventory and with no grasp of a particular wetland's place in the broader ecological scheme. The landowner-by-landowner, lot-by-lot conversion of land to human purpose fails to take into account the inescapable interdependence of habitat elements in the natural landscape.

I follow a well-worn animal trail to the outer edge of the swamp. A few gray birches have found a soggy niche in which to grow beneath the red maples, just in from an alder and black chokeberry edging that opens to a sedge swale. On the other side of this wet meadow is another shrubby ecotone of alder and chokeberry, then an upland rise densely crowded with white pines. I stand in shallow water, one foot in a red maple swamp, the other in a wet meadow of beaked sedge. A gray treefrog trills, a mosquito whines, a mourning dove calls from the white pine grove, familiar sounds spaced in the silence that has prevailed since I moved out of hearing range of the brook's solo spill. Now a yellowthroat breaks out with his emphatic *witch' ity, witch' ity, witch' ity, witch!* These lively masked birds sing throughout the day from spring well into summer, but even this vociferous one seems to feel that a moment's singing is sufficient for this sultry hour, and falls silent.

Engulfed in plants, I feel that I could set down roots myself if I stood long enough in one place among them, my feet embedded in muck. Photosynthesis seems palpable. I breathe in the scent of pure growth.

Into this green world drifts a green-jacket dragonfly — a female or

Yellowthroat
(*Geothlypis trichas*)

possibly a juvenile male. Adult males turn frosty blue, though they retain their green eyes and face. She flies low, cruising corridors in the beaked sedge a foot or so below their sunlit ceiling, turning among shadowed vaults under the arches of tussock sedge. Wheeling and darting at sudden intervals, she pursues midges or other insects I can barely make out. Somewhere between yellow-green and lime green, green as the swamp and the sedge swale, she seems to become a part of the plants on which she lands. Her flights are brief, spelled by protracted periods waiting in well-camouflaged ambush. When perched, she keeps her wings thrust forward, shielding herself from the sun. She takes again to open air, swift and sharp-turning, skimming bowed sedge blades. Another green-jacket hunts the alder overhangs above the sedges, and I see several more in the grassy mazes of the open wet meadow. These fierce predators will eat their own kind, but evidently there is enough prey here to keep them from turning on one another. The one who has kept close by me lands on my vest, a guardian dragonfly. She flashes into the air and takes a deer fly just off my left shoulder, wheels and lands on a sedge strand a few feet away. I see her jaws working, hear her chewing.

Turning back into the red maple swamp, I find a wide pathway pushing out through the sedge meadow. It is not the narrow, well-worn trace of a long-time deer trail but the recent route of what seems a larger animal, a bear or moose. There is no footprint I can read, but whoever passed here made a decided impression on the rampant growth. And he provided a convenient passageway for me. When I follow a beaten path like this, I needn't try to avoid trampling plants or making a trail myself. The path leads through an especially dense sector of the swamp. Grass, sedge, and fern are shoulder-high. Tall meadow rue lives up to its name, towering eight to nine feet above its foot-high mound. Relatively open swamp becomes trackless thicket. In the increasingly populous, heavily developed Northeast, red maple swamps are often the last hide-outs for the last holdouts, serving as refugia — sanctuaries for plants as well as animals — and migration corridors, where moose, bear, deer, bobcats, river otters, and others can find asylum from humans and dogs. These swamps are especially important as travel corridors, since they commonly occur along lengthy, interconnected watercourses. A moose or bear could easily evaporate before my eyes here, or before my eyes could detect it. For my own part, I never have the feeling that I will encounter another person when I walk and wade a swamp, be it scrub-shrub or forested wetland.

Thoreau stated that he would rather sit on a pumpkin and have it all to himself than be crowded on a velvet cushion. To have a bit of the landscape to oneself, to not be crowded in the landscape of the current epoch, one is almost obliged to withdraw to a swamp. Some supremely tenacious and resolute members of our own species, the Seminole Indians, took refuge in wetlands, the Everglades, to avoid being captured by the United States Army and forcibly relocated far from their homes. Seminole means "runaway," and these swamp refugees hid runaway slaves among themselves in one of the rare places where humans could escape from other humans.

I may or may not be following in a black bear's wake, but I am certain that this swamp is an important part of their wetlands-uplands seasonal circuit. As wetlands continue to be diminished, and the surrounding uplands are eliminated altogether, the remaining swamp habitats become increasingly critical for plants and animals that are not primarily

Tall meadow rue (*Thalictrum pubescens*)

wetland species. Plants and animals that are facultative wetlands occu-
pants (technically, being found there about a third to two thirds of the
time) but live generally in uplands become more and more dependent
upon swamps and marshes as fields and forests are converted to human
environments. Grossly inadequate as regulations are at protecting wetland habitats, there is virtually no regulatory protection for nonwetland
habitats. Species that can use wetlands have to do so increasingly to
survive.

The Louisiana black bear, a subspecies of the American black bear, is
one of the larger animals to have taken a last stand in forested wetlands,
the bottomland hardwood swamps of the southeastern United States.
These river swamps, which are inundated most or all of the year, are
forested by flood-tolerant species of gum and oak as well as bald cypress. Abutting the river swamps are forested wetlands that are flooded
about a third of the year. Overcup oak, water hickory, water locust, mag-
nolias, and bays grow there, as well as red maple, silver maple, and black
willow. In addition to the Louisiana black bear, two of the rarest mammals in the United States, the red wolf and the Florida panther, are dependent on the remaining bottomland hardwood swamps for their
survival. Not surprisingly, these ecosystems are part of the litany of wetland loss: the 30 million acres extant at the time of European settlement
have been reduced to 12 million acres. Logging has had a major impact,
but, as in most areas, agriculture has been the primary cause of wetland
loss in the Southeast, where swamps have been drained to accommodate
crops of cotton, corn, and soybeans.

I leave the animal trail, which leads into ever-denser growth, and
make my own way back to where I entered the swamp, listening for the
familiar musical burbling of the fallen-log spillway to help guide me to
the brook. When I come to it, I part an edging of alder and silky dogwood, step down from bankside hummocks, and follow the watery,
sand-bottomed pathway the running stream keeps open along the
western border of the swamp hollow. At my customary turning point,
I leave the brook and ascend the slope that leads to a white pine knoll,
where low wetlands grade into an upland rise. I stand for a time among
the last tall cinnamon ferns and look back on the abiding red maple
swamp. Though logged off about forty years ago, it nonetheless en-

dures. Forested wetlands like the Red Maple Swamp represent the greatest degree of plant development that occurs on freshwater sites in the glaciated Northeast. The wetness, deep accumulation of organic matter, low availability of nutrients and root-zone oxygen, and, in many cases, the acidity of the soils create a prohibitive environment for the establishment of upland forest. Although woody peat may build up to depths of ten feet or more, a process that can take thousands of years, swamps do not become dry land, because the water table rises with the accumulation of organic material. Therefore, unless they are filled or drained, forested wetlands will persist indefinitely. Unless they are filled or drained . . . There are no assurances in the modern, continually human-altered landscape. But as I leave the Red Maple Swamp, I try to carry the belief not only that this wetland will continue as a wetland but that it will keep its wild heart, perhaps even become wilder, however its face may change over time by way of wet years and dry years, beaver dams and hurricanes.

Seeps, Springs, and Swamps

December 13, 1:14 P.M. A remarkably mild day for mid-December, with an air temperature of 52 degrees. There are only scattered patches of snow in the upland forest. Down in the lowlands, swamps and marshes are frozen over, silent and snow-covered; the season's first siftings of snow melt off south-facing wooded slopes but linger on the ice that has locked in the still-water wetlands, probably until thaw. During early-winter breaks like this, streams come alive in rock-studded, wooded hills. While the deeper wetlands sleep, I follow brooks against their flows, trying to trace them to their sources. Tracking streams in winter takes me into wetlands I am less familiar with, usually wooded swamps set in upland hills.

Today I head up a brook I have known only as a lowland meander through a red maple swamp. Here it runs down a steep slope, a rocky descent whose banks are lined by traceries of forested wetland that give way, within a few yards, to upland forest of oaks, hickories, American beech, hemlock, white birch, and sugar maple. Among the tree-trunk forms and textures I see — and feel as I take handgrips up the slippery banks — is a large ash tree. It holds the edge of the bank, its buttress roots winding into the stream and under the streambed and emerging to coil along the opposite bank, much in the manner of a yellow birch or red maple. The way this tree has taken its stand in the brook makes me think it must be a black ash, a tree that commonly grows along brooks. But the tightly interwoven, diamondlike pattern of ridges and furrows in its bark indicates white ash, a tree I have known only from upland forests. There are no leaves and branches, and winter buds are well out of reach, so I may have to wait until next spring to positively identify it.

My long-term acquaintance with wetlands over the seasons, a familiarity that goes back to boyhood, to a time when I could not name a single tree and did not even know the spotted turtle by its correct common name, let alone its Latin name, has produced an imprimatura, a background screen, of the recognized, against which the new, or the familiar in an unprecedented setting, stands out sharply, catching my eyes from the most peripheral point. It may be a detail as minute as the texture of bark, the form of a tiny leaf, a winter bud. For years the names of things did not matter to me. The fact that I could not name any of the plants and animals around me took nothing away from what it meant to simply be there. It never occurred to me to look things up in field guides. But over time, the knowing of names made me more keenly aware of the distinct living things that had been given these names, with their unique forms and functions, their individual natures, their places within the whole. There is great value in learning a name, though it is but one aspect of learning the identity. As my life goes on, I work to expand this knowledge, but I will never know the names of all things, let alone be able to read the complete signatures of all things.

I move on up the brook to where its flow dwindles to a trickle. As the streamlet narrows to nothing, its narrow line of bordering forested wetland broadens dramatically into an extensive red maple swamp with a deeply mossed, uneven flooring. There are velvety mounds of an emerald cushion moss and ornate layerings of a bright green fernlike moss, both of which I am familiar with but whose names I have yet to learn. The hummocks here are not plant mounds but moss-covered stones and fallen logs. Glacial erratics crowned with polypod ferns stand about the swamp. Some are set on smaller stones, rollers or ball bearings of sorts, that helped the ice shift them about. Resting just where the glaciers left them, these stones seem ready to move on at any moment, as though biding their time until the return of the earth-moving ice. The emerald floor of the swamp forest gleams with silver, lead gray, and milk white shallow steppes of ice, accreting on stones and crystallizing in mucky hollows, where seeping water has been caught by the colder days and nights of December's deepening grip. But water keeps its fluid form as well, where it is still warm enough or is moving swiftly enough. I keep looking for a spring bubbling forth among mossy stones, the aboveground appearance of the subterranean water that has enabled a groundwater-slope swamp to become established here, on a steep hillside at an elevation of over a thousand feet, in the midst of acres of upland forest. Swamps are not restricted to lowlands. Wherever water is constantly present in or on the surface of the land, there will be a wetland; there are swamps, marshes, fens, and bogs on precipitous mountainsides and on high mountaintops.

I continue up the seeping slope to where the swamp flooring becomes a great shallow bowl, tipped up sharply at its far end. There is no more stream to follow. Beyond this point, the water's trail lies beneath the forest floor, moving over bedrock, through soil and crushed stone, a presence in earth that came from clouds and will return to clouds. Water has no beginning and no end. It is metamorphic and cyclical. The variations of this liquid mineral's interactions with earth in its freshwater form alone, to create freshwater wetlands, appear endless.

Undefined by any specific stream as it comes to the surface, water issues forth from a broad, sodden hollow of sphagnum moss and stone. It slips continually from the lower lip of the wetland bowl but, because it is constantly replenished by groundwater, it never runs dry. The growing season ended three months ago, but I find stalks of cinnamon fern and persistent fertile fronds of sensitive fern; I see spathes of skunk cabbage and remains of false hellebore, wisps of grass and sedge. Typical of hillside seepage swamps, the shrub layer here is minimal, just scattered spicebush. The tree canopy is unusually open, even for the leafless time of year, because many of the trees are stiff-branched ashes rather than fine-twigged red maples. Trees with many-divided compound leaves, like the ashes, do not develop crowns dense with twigs, as do trees with simple leaves, like red maple, yellow birch, and American elm. The tight, diamond-ridged furrowing of the bark again indicates white ash, but I cannot remember seeing this tree standing toe to toe with red maple in such wet footing. Black ash and green ash are trees of swamps, streambanks, and floodplains, but black ash rarely grows this large, and, in the Northeast, green ash is generally restricted to warmer valleys. A branch recently broken from the high canopy shows me the ash's winter buds. The leaf scars beneath the buds are deeply notched, a distinctive field mark that confirms these trees as white ash and reveals another aspect of their nature. Now that I can accept them as swamp trees, I see them throughout this hillside seepage swamp, codominant with red maple.

Above the reach of the groundwater seep, the forest floor changes. The damp silence of green mosses gives over to dry wind-whisperings of fallen leaves. Spent fronds of cinnamon ferns and waiting cowls of skunk cabbage fringe the highest soaking reach of the seep. Immediately above them, lowbush blueberry and black huckleberry begin their brushy crestings of the upland hill and its ledge outcrops. Along this wetland-upland ecotone, white ash yields to shagbark hickory, which in turn quickly gives way to the pignut hickory, red and white oaks, beech, white birch, and white pine of drier ground. I have come to an amphitheater, quiet and still in winter, a tableau vivant of tree, moss, and stone. In this December stage set for the long-playing drama of water's seeping emergence from earth, I feel witness to the larger script of the history of this planet, the stories of water and life upon it.

When I set out to follow a stream to its starting point, I never know what I will find. Last year, on the last day of January, tracking a lively slip that entered a vernal pool, I ascended a broad, shallow trough of ice and free-spilling water, cobbled with mossy stones and miniature mounds of grass and sedge. As is often the case when I trace a stream to its source, at times I had to follow the stream by sound as it bubbled out of sight beneath jumbles of rock or under the forest floor. When I couldn't see or hear it, wetland plants helped show the course of the underground brook. The most distinctive of these, brilliant blazings of winterberry, followed a ribbon of wet soil through upland forest. I lost and found the run several times, and on occasion thought I had come to its beginning. Finally, high in upland hills, I came to a spring that poured forth in an almost perfectly circular pool of open water, about five feet in diameter and a foot deep. Framed by moss-covered stones, skirted with filigrees of ice, surrounded by thin crusts of snow, it seemed a pool from another season, with its floating mats of algae, some brown to near-colorless, others tinged with green. The groundwater issuing forth, newly exposed to the January cold after its underground passage, was a winter-warm 44 degrees.

Three days later I took a route I had had in mind for years along the slender intermittent stream that feeds Spring Brook, the familiar seasonal brook that spotted turtles travel to reach the Reedgrass Pool. Tracking this rill up a cascade of rocks, boulders, and glacial erratics, I surprised a short-tailed weasel, pure white but for his black-tipped tail, in a cave of stones and startled a snowshoe hare from a thicket of beaked hazelnut in a boulder yard. The land around was all upland forest except for the narrow line of red maple, yellow birch, and black ash that bordered the stream. This thread of water, alternately splashing and trickling spills that ranged from inches to a little over a foot in width, moved over ledge and under stone. I lost and found it several times as I made my way up the wooded, boulder-laced hill. I was near the 950-foot summit when, through trees upslope, I saw a shining. I had to discount my first thoughts, that it might be a snowbank or an outcropping of white quartz. As I drew closer, I could see that it was a sheet of ice catching the last of the afternoon's sunlight.

The granite ledge was glazed with palisades of frozen water twelve feet high and thirty feet wide — horizontal, gray and white cloudlike ripplings of ice, crystal-clear coatings several inches thick that magnified the gray-green lichens they encased, and glassy columns filled with sun-sparkles that shone like stars. High up, near the crown of the ice, viewed from just the right angle, were two fields of red-magenta glintings, like neon, one composed of tiny points of light, the other a flecked sheet, an afternoon aurora radiating from ice. Leaden shoulders of opaque ice framed the glowing field of frozen water, and dark footings of ice descended to a seep of clear water at the base of the ledge, the beginning of the intermittent stream. The ice façade was entirely surrounded by dry gray rock, with sparse crusts of moss and brown, crisply curled lichen. At its summit, the ice lay as a thin clear shield on exposed ledge, surrounded by acres of leaf-drifted upland forest, more ledge

outcrop, and boulders. There was no higher or wider water. I was standing at the emanation from earth of one of the key sources of water sustaining my well-known wetlands below, the broad lowland mosaic of
Spring Brook and its surrounding alder swamps, bluejoint and sedge
meadows, Great Marsh, the Shrub Swamp, Alder Brook, and Red Maple
Swamp.

Northern arrowwood (*Viburnum recognitum*)

4 THE SHRUB SWAMP

And solitary places, where we taste
The pleasures of believing what we see
Is boundless, as we wish our souls to be.

— Percy Bysshe Shelley

Opening

March 28, 10:30 A.M. In late March I look for the first open water. As I snowshoe to the Shrub Swamp, the only place I see water free of ice is in the briskly running central channel of Alder Brook, where I record a water temperature of 36 degrees. I take any increment above 32 as a sign of spring. The brook's backwater sedge marsh is icebound, but some meltwater lies against its steep west-facing bank, welcome evidence of thaw. The beavers have made a new channel through this marsh. A clear strip of ice delineates the narrow course they have cleared through the dense woolly-fruit sedge. Winter's thick, persistent covering of ice obliges the beavers to submarine their early spring cuttings along this channel to the open water of the brook. A muddy dragway is worn through alder stands surrounding their new doorway to the water; it is mud season in the beavers' dooryard, as it is in mine. They keep this entrance clear, trimming back the ice as neatly as they have clipped its bordering shrubs and the upland birches and aspens on the slope behind them. Most of the remaining edging of the sedge marsh, a brushy belt of sweet gale, buttonbush, winterberry, alder, and meadowsweet, has gone unpruned. Close by me in this cover, a song sparrow sings. His clear, exultant, birth-of-spring notes remind me that I should not be impatient with the ice: there is not much of March left to enjoy.

Advancing to the Reedgrass Pool, I find that it, too, is still frozen over. Its milky ice has collected a two-inch layer of water from the early-morning precipitation, which vacillated between rain and wet snow.

Rings of open water have melted away from the bases of heat-collecting emergent sedge hummocks and shrub stems. Through the slender windows of this meltwater edged with clear ice I catch glimpses of caddis fly larvae, who have already been at work under the ice mantle, cutting, eating, and building their cases from last season's reed canary grass. Insect larvae are among the few animals that can be active in water so close to being ice. These narrow openings also allow me to take water temperatures at thaw, revealing slight but important differences in various niches.

As I approach Bear Pond, a pair of great blue herons sails over it. Surveying for open water, they find no place to touch down. Clear trumpetings reverberate in the muted morning. Straining my eyes, I see a solitary Canada goose striding on the ice along the border of the leatherleaf islands. One might think she is calling for the ice to open. Like the red-winged blackbirds, great blue herons, hooded mergansers, mallards, and other returning ducks, the goose will have to look to the brook for water. I am sure all of these end-of-winter returnees from places far away are spending most of their time along the river and its floodplain as they wait for the still-water wetlands to open up. As quickening life presses from all directions upon winter's retreating heels, the smallest space of open water becomes a magnet to migrants and a crucial medium for those who spent the winter under the ice.

I continue on to the Shrub Swamp, sinking in ice-crystal snow as I cross the nesting fields, where the snow cover has shrunk down enough to let the brushy crowns of sweetfern and persistent shafts of little bluestem show. Somewhere beneath this final winter blanketing (if this indeed is the last of the snow), encased in chambers in the hard-frozen earth, are hatchling painted turtles, survivors of the long winter, waiting the last weeks until the earth warms enough for them to leave their nests. No matter that I know their story rather well, it seems remarkable to me that I am snowshoeing over baby turtles. I pass through aspen and oak, gray birch and white pine. At a familiar sentinel pine with three trunks, crowning one of the last upland rises on the margins of the low-lying wetlands, I enter the Shrub Swamp.

I walk again on frozen water. One new to this maze of woody plants might not realize that ice lies beneath the snow and water beneath the ice. The wetland shrub thickets are laced with persistent beaked sedge and royal fern. Their straw and fawn colorings do much to warm the alder-and-snow landscape on a gray March day. Slushing through granular snow and shattering through air-pocketed layers of thinner ice, I shoulder my way among the alders. The depression that holds the Shrub Swamp was crushed into the land by the weight of the glaciers or scoured out by their relentless grindings. It seems to hold a glacier now, though one that is only a foot or two thick, not a mile or two. I move to a channel where alders yield to shrubs of a deeper flood zone: sweet gale, leatherleaf, swamp rose, winterberry, and black chokeberry. Occasional red maple saplings rise from mounds formed by intergrown blendings of shrubs, royal and cinnamon fern, and tussock sedge. Though its standing water falls away to a few inches-deep channels and pools at high summer, the Shrub Swamp is too wet for the maples to grow to tree size, so it cannot develop into a forested wetland. I am in a thicketed world that smells at times like winter, but there is a strong scent of thaw on the day's raw wind that comes only with March and melting ice. A new flush of color tinges the twigs of these shrubs all around me, and their small buds have begun to swell.

I walk an ice trail two or three feet above the mucky bottoms of channels and pools. Though their leaflets are gone, the persistent shafts of royal ferns stand waist-high to me now. Their sun-filtering, tropical-appearing new growth will spread green vaults over my head as I wade the water-and-mud depths here in summer, and the alders will leaf out to a twelve-foot-high canopy, closing out much of the sky by the end of May. I would like to be able to walk on water after the ice melts. Even now my fairly easy going ends abruptly as I progress to where the season-transforming touch of thaw is having its effect.

I am brought to my knees as my snowshoed right foot breaks through ice to black water along a sedgy channel margin. Drifting water has been at

Pussy willow (*Salix discolor*)

work beneath the ice here, undermining winter. Crawling, grasping alder stems, I get to my feet again. The snowshoes will not work from here on. I take them off, knock them free of wet, heavy snow, and stand them to dry in an alder clump. I study the hole I've opened. Next to the place I broke through, where channeled water thinned the ice, it is six and a quarter inches thick, crystalline white and crunchy for the top half inch, then hard for the rest of its depth. In the distance I hear the animal-like moans and groans and sporadic low roars of the far thicker ice on the pond. It is bound fast to every shore, and it will be some days, perhaps as much as two weeks, before it lets go. But here in the Shrub Swamp, ice is giving way, eroded from beneath by the slow movement of water curling in from the spring-flooded brook three hundred yards away. On sunny days the ice is weakened from above and within as well, by warming sunlight and by the heat collected from the ascendant March sun by stems and hummocks and then radiated into the ice.

As I continue on in neoprene waders, travel becomes increasingly difficult. At unpredictable intervals, one leg suddenly breaks through, and I am brought to my knees again. Even without the encumbrance of snowshoes I have a hard time regaining my feet as I am gripped by bottom muck and as edgings of snow and ice give way beneath every kneehold or foothold I try to take. The "walking-falling" aspect of my progress through wetlands is never more extreme than during these first times out to the winter sanctuary of the spotted turtles, when ice and snow add a dimension of uncertainty to the already unsure footing. I stagger across a final caving ice sheet in a broad swath of sweet gale. Beyond this point, ice-out has begun in the Shrub Swamp. Steadily drifting water glimmers throughout the Tangle, a deeper, more densely vegetated hollow within the Shrub Swamp that is the primary winter refuge of many of the spotted turtles I follow. Among these turtles' remarkable orienteering skills is the ability to determine that such niches will provide protection from freezing and predation over the winter and will open up to allow the earliest possible emergence from hibernation.

After snowshoeing a logging trail, a field, a wooded slope, and fast-frozen wetlands, I have entered the Shrub Swamp, a watery bowl of about five acres or so, set in hundreds of acres of snow- and ice-bound uplands and wetlands. It has opened up within the past twenty-four hours. As with the salamander rains, I do not want to miss the ice-out that brings forth the first spotted turtles here, so I snowshoe out and back over several days when I know the melting off is near. I step down into nearly waist-deep water. The water that drifts through the Shrub Swamp is not visible when I look directly ahead. But there is ample water here at thaw and other times of flood, as there is in the entire mosaic of wetlands extending along both sides of the permanent stream's lowland run. Water slides through this depression within a depression, passing among roots and rhizomes, sifting through weirs of shrub stems, coiling around enduring mounds and levees created by shrub, fern, and sedge. At times of high water, all components of the palustrine system to which the Shrub Swamp belongs, from sedge meadows to bluejoint marshes, other scrub-shrub wetlands, and red maple swamps, become fully charged, serving as the brook's flood storage. Given that a one-foot rise in water level over a single acre amounts to 300,000 gallons, there is an incalculable amount of water here. Along many streams and rivers, draining and filling and removal of beaver dams has greatly reduced the flood storage capacity of wetlands.

My peripheral vision takes in mounds and sheets of snow, the once-surprising backdrop that I have come to know as typical for this setting when the first spotted turtles emerge. This open bowl, which becomes a cold sink into which frosty air flows like water following autumn sunsets, becomes a solar-collecting heat trap as the sun retakes the higher sky in March. The spotted turtles climb up onto hummocks on the first sunny days following ice-out to absorb heat radiated from sun-warmed sedge and directly from the penetrating rays of the early spring sun. Living solar batteries, the turtles take the energy of the sun's heat with them for a time when they drop back into the numbing water. As they cool down, they can tuck in for the night or for the inevitable series of snell, cloud-covered days that come with spring. They can abide through the capricious season's late snowstorms. When the sun shines forth again, they crawl back up onto their basking mounds once more to collect the heat that brings them fully back to life.

The water temperature here is 42 degrees, just above the 41-degree margin referred to as biological zero. Below this temperature, most plant and animal life becomes dormant; above it, activity begins. Central runs of the brook and the river open earlier than the Shrub Swamp, and at far lower temperatures, sometimes fractionally above freezing, but these are essentially currents of deepwater habitats, unfrozen only because of their movement and devoid of life. Spotted turtles, even in the depths of their hibernating state, are intimately cued to the temperature that marks biological zero. Once the dividing line is crossed in the direction of warming, even by minimal increments, the spotted turtles (locally known by the fitting name "sun turtles" when I was a boy) begin to stir.

I wade a channel just wide enough to allow me to slide one leg in front of the other. With this first wading here since last November, I have again a feeling of returning, a sense of entering the season itself. Spits of rain whiten, then flatten, no longer drops falling but wheels slanting, spinning, spiraling. Shivering from the cold as rain turns to snow, I search the sky-reflecting surface, the clear and black depths of the water. A swamp sparrow trills from a brushy blur of sweet gale and leatherleaf. Thick, wet snow turns slowly in still air and silence, interrupted now and again by spells of distant song from red-winged blackbirds out along the brook.

12:21 P.M. I thread my way through well-known channels, my eyes intent on the water. If there were sun or any detectable warmth radiating through the cloud cover, I would be watching for spotted turtles basking in sweeps and swirls of fallen sedge and fern, but on a day like this I don't expect them to leave the water. But one never knows. Unlikely conditions have led me to witness unlikely events. Something catches the corner of my eye, an unmistakable domed form with subdued speckling, a spotted turtle shell out of the water. A male lies prostrate, immobile, on the cold mud of a tussock sedge mound, all four legs and his neck and head fully extended, eyes closed. This hummock was packed down by a muskrat who had recently used it as a feeding station. It is clear that the turtle is under great duress from hibernation and extraordinarily vulnerable to predation. Terribly weakened by the prolonged period of zero-to-insufficient oxygen and a subsequent buildup of lactic acid within their systems, some turtles emerge from overwintering partially paralyzed or otherwise incapacitated; they often fall victim to predators and lose feet, limbs, or their lives. This turtle's need to elevate his metabolism must have been so critical that he all but involuntarily crawled onto the hummock, to lie unalert and completely exposed, seeking as little as an extra degree or two of heat and a measure of life-restoring oxygen.

On the cusp of the season, the dividing line of his living or dying has come down to something as narrow as the dividing line of biological zero. I pick him up and recognize him at once. One of the older turtles I am familiar with, he could be struggling out of his fortieth hibernation or more. Earlier in his life he was chewed upon by some predator; extensive surface areas on both sides of his carapace have been gnawed away, so there are no spots on them. He is one of the Shrub Swamp colony that travels to the Reedgrass Pool for the vernal pool season, still a week to ten days away from its wood-frog awakening this year. Those frogs, along with the spotted salamanders, peep frogs, and American toads, are still hibernating in the frozen, snow-covered upland earth when the spotted turtles of the Tangle are first basking. An hour or two of sun or even less would probably restore this turtle, but sunshine will not be forthcoming today. He is completely torpid. As I touch his head and legs, he does not withdraw them. He is not capable of protecting himself within his shell. The cold within him is winter-deep.

If he doesn't drop back into the sheltering water at the end of the day, he could well freeze to death overnight or be eaten by a predator. It would be interesting to know if this turtle could survive this critical condition. If he is not here tomorrow, I could look for him in the Reedgrass Pool a week or two from now, when the spotted turtles will have made their annual pilgrimage there. If I never see him again, I could not be certain of his fate, but I could guess. In any event, in this instance it is impossible for me to refrain from interceding. I slip the spotted turtle into the zippered pocket of my swamp vest and wade on.

High Summer

August 12, 3:44 P.M. Eighty-eight degrees, close and still. In the border-region of the Shrub Swamp, the drill of the crickets is low and incessant, muted but shrill. A constant pulse of insect sound travels everywhere with me now, day and night, as I pass through upland woods, cross open fields, and enter the Shrub Swamp. Occasionally the long-drawn-out buzzing drone of a cicada sounds from the white-pine slope. The penetrating,

27 July–

I wade a corridor
of water and open sun-
light through the button-
bush swamp. These
emergent shrubs are
heavily in flower, and
well-attended by bumble-
bees, a watery equivalent
of Yeats' wooded "bee-
loud glade", brilliant.

Swamp notebook page with buttonbush (*Cephalanthus occidentalis*) prolonged, descending drone seems a perfect incantation for these afternoon hours that blend the intense heat, sultry humidity, and profound stillness of high summer. Now and then the wind stirs in the upper alder canopy, and in the sun-speckled shade below there is an occasional tremble of shrub leaf, sedge, or fern.

My entrance channel into the Shrub Swamp, which is snow-covered ice at the opening of the Tangle and a shimmering corridor of water in spring, is now a dark, waterless pathway of knee-deep muck. In order to make my way along it, I grab alder stems and stretch my legs to find footholds on their knotted roots or against firmer sedge and fern mounds. As I move closer to the Tangle, I have no choice but to wade through mud. The shrub and fern mounds are inconveniently spaced to serve as steppingstones and too wavery and crowded with stems at their crowns to grant me a toehold. The plants have barely enough room for their own footings.

There is no season of easy passage for larger animals in this wetland so favored by the spotted turtles. No great blue heron could touch down here. Evidently the turtles do not care to have much company. The pit and mound structure here, so perfectly suited to spotted turtles and swamp sparrows, is an architectonic expression of the wetland's plants, past and present. Beneath the abrupt unevenness of the microtopography, the firm underlying floor of the basin in which the Shrub Swamp

Spotted turtle (*Clemmys guttata*)

sits seems remarkably even. This substrate, exposed in places by cuts of swifter water, appears to be mineral.

"Where are they now?" I often wonder about the spotted turtles as I track them over the seasons. This question becomes prominent when I visit the Shrub Swamp in high summer. Many of those who left the Reedgrass Pool as it dried up probably withdrew to this wetland. Hatchlings and juveniles, who do not travel to that vernal pool or other outlying seasonal niches until they are six to ten years old, keep to this occult place through all the seasons; it is nursery as well as hibernaculum. Estivating turtles who have not retreated to the Shrub Swamp have tunneled under fallen logs or dug into the litter on the floors of the surrounding forested uplands or into the turf of grassy field margins. Without the benefits of radio-tracking, I am not likely to locate those who have taken to terrestrial sites. I do find spotted turtles in the Shrub Swamp at high summer, especially after thunderstorms. Heavy rains, even if they bring only an ephemeral flooding, occasion some shifting about as late as mid-November. But, from summer solstice on, the turtles move sporadically and with great furtiveness, quite in contrast with their appearance at the end of hibernation and their prominent, dazzling springtime presence in the Reedgrass Pool.

The turtles of the Tangle travel all over the Shrub Swamp and well beyond it to the wet meadows and marshes, the intermittent streams, the edge waters and beaver channels of the permanent brook, its upstream-bordering sedge marsh, the Reedgrass Pool, the backwater fen, marsh, and shrub swamp elements of the pond, as well as all the adjoining upland spaces. One female I first found ten years ago in an alder and cinnamon fern zone of the Shrub Swamp, fifty yards or so from the Tangle, has reappeared over the years in the upflow region that feeds into the Tangle, the Reedgrass Pool, the sphagnum/sedge fen and pickerelweed-laced marshy backwaters at the north end of the pond, and a beaver backwater on its western margin. The most widely separated of these points lie six hundred yards apart, but I certainly do not know all the sojourns of her life. Another female, whom I have seen only three times in a decade, I first saw nesting in a sphagnum hollow at the edge of the Shrub Swamp. I found her two years later as she emerged from hibernation in a stream bordered by bluejoint and red maple near the Slough, eight hundred yards or more from that nest site. Over the course of

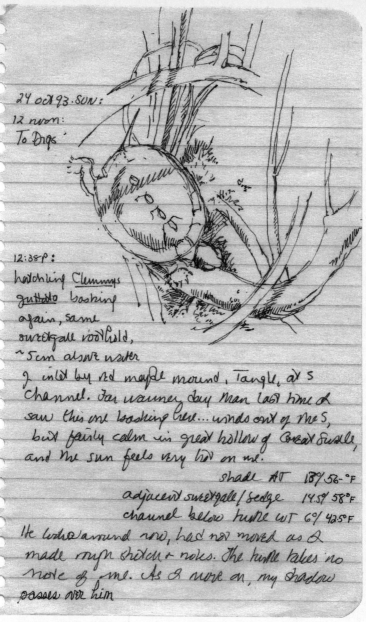

24 Oct 93 · SUN:

12 noon:

To Dgs:

12:38p:

hatchling Clemmys
guttata basking
again, same
sweetgale root field,
~5cm above water
g inlet by red maple mound. Tangle, at S
Channel. Far warmer day than last time ch
saw this one basking here... winds out of the S,
but fairly calm in great hollow of Coreax Suadle,
and the sun feels very hot on me.

shade AT   18°/56-°F
adjacent sweetgale/sedge   14.5°/58°F
channel below turtle wt 6°/42.5°F

He looks around now, had not moved as I
made rough sketch + notes. The turtle takes no
note of me. As I move on, my shadow
passes over him

Swamp notebook page with hatchling spotted turtle (*Clemmys guttata*)

these turtles' long lives they may cover miles. Such wide-ranging movements underscore the futility of discussing wetland buffer zones of fifty, a hundred, or even three hundred feet. What are these little measurings to the spotted turtles or the galaxy of other living things constantly moving among the wetlands?

Spotted turtles require a mosaic of wetlands with pure water and a range of surrounding uplands. Similarly, wood turtles are dependent upon a blend of clear-water rivers, streams, riparian habitat, and terrestrial habitat. These two species, which are so intimately bound to their home ground (they cannot run like deer, fly like birds, or scatter like the seeds of plants), require a continuum of wetlands and uplands of the highest natural habitat values. These turtles are indicator species: where they flourish, the ecosystem is able to sustain biodiversity. They are umbrella species as well: if the environments remain suitable for the persistence of these species, they will support high numbers and a rich diversity of other animals and plants.

The Tangle seems to have stayed essentially the same since my first visit here, save that over the past several years beaked sedge has proliferated, spearing up through mounds of tussock sedge, royal and cinnamon fern, and shrubs, infiltrating formerly open pockets and pools, and crowding the margins of the primary channels. This colonial sedge, which has already claimed acres of wet meadow in the surrounding wetland, is not an aggressive alien, like purple loosestrife, but a native that appears to have a similarly formidable capacity for supplanting other vegetation in habitats that favor it. Muskrats come here at spring flood, when the entire Shrub Swamp is navigable, to harvest the sharply triangular new spears of beaked sedge, eating the tender white bases and discarding the tops. The muskrats do not seem to make much of a dent in the expansion of the sedge, which is shoulder-high to me, and after first sprouting it becomes too tough even for muskrat teeth. In any event, with the falling away of the water, the muskrats have withdrawn to the cattail marsh and permanent brook.

The incursion of beaked sedge may have started with seedlings that germinated during an uncommonly dry year. As is the case with many wetland plants, once some seedlings gained a foothold, they were able to reproduce vegetatively, spreading by way of rhizomes that could invade deeper water. If this sedge builds up a peaty substrate here, it could alter the hydrology, making the flooding briefer and shallower and displacing other plants, as well as the spotted turtles.

Other than the encroachment of beaked sedge, I haven't noticed shifts in plant growth during the eleven years I've been coming here. Nor have I detected a change in the seasonal flood cycle. But I could be missing something, and it is a mistake to think that a decade is a long time. Over a longer period this shrub swamp may change into a sedge meadow or a forested wetland dominated by red maple, then back into a shrub swamp again. Cyclic changes are inevitable over time as annual average water levels and flood periods vary and as beavers build, abandon, and return to restore their dams. Yet the same factors that transform wetland systems also perpetuate them. Although the Shrub Swamp will undergo changes, it will remain a wetland. However they may cycle and change in character, wetlands typically do not become terrestrial habitats unless a major physical force, something on the order of an earthquake or global climate shift — or human draining and filling — lowers the water levels. Under natural conditions, transition and cycle, not linear succession from wetland to upland, are the processes that prevail.

Rose pogonia (*Pogonia ophioglossoides*)

The turtles here would not die out if this shrub swamp became wet meadow grown in with beaked sedge. They would, as they always have, move on along its linking waterways and over land to other niches up or down this stream, and along the river. The spotted turtle's ecology, like the natural history of all the life of the wetland mosaic, is one of ebb and flow. Given an intact natural landscape, these turtles, and the plants and animals they live among, can adjust to transitions and cycles in their environment. But an intact natural landscape is no longer a given. It has been broken, altered, fragmented, degraded, and in large measure taken away. The takers either do not care, or they expect spotted turtles and rose pogonia to somehow find a way to continue over time, time of a dimension that the takers cannot envision.

I continue around the perimeter of the Tangle, stopping to wait and watch every few yards along the way. I surreptitiously separate branches and sedges for a look into an interior that I prefer not to enter, fearing I might trample an important spotted turtle place. I see an animated shuffling in the duff of a royal fern mound, something too rapid in its movements to be a turtle. A star-nosed mole appears, the fingerlike projections around his nose working feverishly as he tests the open air for danger or direction. These aquatic moles can see better than their woodland cousins and emerge from time to time in daylight. The shadowy depths of this section of the Shrub Swamp are tunnellike; I often feel that I am tunneling as I make my way through here. The mole slips into a shallow pool and swims away.

I move on to a foot-wide channel that still holds about nine inches of water over six inches of muck, one of the last sluiceways in the Shrub Swamp to have standing water in high summer. It cuts through a more open area, where shrubs, which grow ten to twelve feet high in the denser Tangle and its flanking alder swamp, are only four or five feet tall, have thinner crowns, and are more widely separated: slender branchings of speckled alder, silky dogwood, northern arrowwood, black chokeberry, winterberry, and sweet gale. The prolonged seasonal flooding that suppresses shrub growth here allows a broad colony of tussock sedge to flourish, and the hummocks provide footholds for other nonwoody plants. It is here that rose pogonias drift their elegant pink flowers from late June until well into July. These orchid flowers are gone now, but soft yellow spires of swamp candle glow among the sedges, and a few taller spikes of pink-purple steeplebush stand above their bowing strands. Plants flower in this shrub-meadow sector that couldn't survive the heavy shade of denser shrubs and luxuriant fern mounds. There are several blinks of blue where the earliest buds of swamp aster are beginning to open. Tiniest of the August bloomings are nodding dots of pink, the four-petaled flowers of purple-leaved willow-herb. At a far border of tussock sedge is a drift of pale fawn tufts of tawny cotton grass. These and the rose pogonia, along with the trailings of large cranberry at the interface of the Shrub Swamp and the sedge meadow, reflect the acidic nature of this area.

As I turn among the sedge mounds, I startle a little green frog into open water. He has nearly completed his metamorphosis but still trails a long tail. Green frogs and bullfrogs, unlike vernal pool–breeding wood frogs, mate and lay eggs throughout the summer. Green frog tadpoles that hatch in late spring or early summer trans-form by late summer; those that hatch later overwinter as tadpoles and undergo metamorphosis in late spring or early summer of the

Green frog (*Rana clamitans melanota*) at metamorphosis

following year. Bullfrog tadpoles may go through two or three winters before metamorphosis. I come upon young green frogs, never in great numbers, in the Shrub Swamp throughout the year, but I have never found an adult here, nor heard the calls of breeding males. I wonder where this changeling came from. The nearest permanent water in which green frogs could breed is at least 250 yards away. I cannot very well wade around the frog in our close quarters, so I wave my hands, and his quick hind legs and energetic tail take him out of sight, and possible harm's way, among the hummocks. I have read that the tails of tadpoles become useless for locomotion once the transforming frogs have devel-oped hind legs; the frogs more or less drag their tails behind them. But that does not seem to be the case with several species that I have seen at this stage, which hop and wriggle in a speedy blend of tadpole and frog.

A few sliding strides down the channel, my foot bumps against a hard object at the base of a hummock. There are no stones here or sunken logs, and even before I reach down and close my hand over his shell, I know that I have found a turtle—a very active male spotted turtle. As I pull trailings of bladderwort from his shell, I recognize the large, gnawed, spotless shapes on his carapace. This is the turtle I found all but lifeless on that chill, snow-spitting day in March and carried home in my vest. After he had regained some strength in temporary captivity, I waited until the season caught up with his indoor activity level to release him, with plenty of the mating season left. I haven't seen him again until today. The muskrat-plastered mound on which I found him is only about thirty yards from here, but I am sure this turtle, typical of the roving males of his kind, has traveled many wetland and upland paths and visited many places beyond these two points. The air temperature has been in the low nineties all afternoon. The water temperature is 68. What recollection can he have of the snow and ice, the ice-cold water, and his near-death stress when he emerged from hibernation? I can remember, can review my notes, but it is still almost impossible for me to picture that time today. This turtle may live in a more complete eternal present, the duration of his lifetime, with its cycle of seasons continually constituting "now," a present mysteriously linked to his chelonian predecessors of over 220 million years ago. With his complete inborn turtle knowledge of the world, he has a closer connection with those earliest ancestors than I have with my predecessors of two generations ago, a more direct contact with fossil *Proganochelys* of those first turtle days on earth than I have with my grandfather. This high-summer finding of the first turtle I saw this year, whom I came upon under such compelling circumstances, is one of those encounters that strike me as preternatural. But if this place holds and I can continue to be here, such meetings, with all the revelations and questions they engender, are inevitable.

After Frost

October 6, 5:43 P.M. The first burning touch of frost has brought an end to the growing season. Winterberry thickets are emblazoned with abundant scarlet fruits, all the more brilliant against maroon-black leaves that will soon be shed. Cinnamon ferns are browned and curled, and as I brush past royal ferns, bleached leaflets shower from their stems to float on black water. I find and eat some crisp, tangy, deep red cranberries that have been protected by rising water from the softening bite of frost. Some will be kept fresh enough under ice for me to eat at thaw.

At last light the daylong heavy cloud cover suddenly disperses, and an afterglow imparts a faint rosy light to the sienna, umber, and ocher of brush and sedges in the Shrub Swamp. Cold air drains down the hillsides like water. My fingertips grow numb as the air temperature drops ten degrees in half an hour, to a single degree above freezing. Daylight is quickly fading. Some plants with persistent white-haired seed heads — purple-leaved willow-herb, swamp aster, swamp goldenrod, and a few tufts of tawny cotton grass — catch a silver light.

There is little green left in the wetlands. Some remains in mats of algae spreading out from side-water pools to color sections of the channel. The algae seems to be a winter plant, spreading and becoming all the more intensely viridian as other plant life pales and wanes. The light green winter buds of flat-leaf bladderwort also lie in the channels. The last of the life in these submergents has withdrawn to these quarter-inch globes, from which channel- and pool-filling mats will unfurl when the water warms again. Plants are hibernating in their buds, roots, and rhizomes; future generations abide in seeds. The stunning silence here at twilight is as sharp as the cold air and the white moon just now rising.

Hibernaculum

November 14, 11:33 A.M. An exceptionally mild day after a siege of cold days, and nights well below freezing. Three hours ago it was 35 degrees; now it is 69. There is ice on the marsh and the shrubby borders of the brook. The Shrub Swamp is leafless. Crimson hazes of berries remain in the winterberry stands. Some years I have seen departing flocks of robins sweep through and clean out every bright berry in two or three days' time. Other years the persistent fruits are left to brighten the Shrub Swamp until thaw.

Slowly, steadily, the water is coming back. There was no sudden hurricane-season recharge this year, but historically November is the month of greatest rainfall in this region. Leafless and dormant, the plants will not be taking up any appreciable water. Cold rain, sleet, and snow will accumulate all winter long. Channels and pools are six to twelve inches deep now. Even at the approach of midday, the mounds and hummocks cast long blue-black shadows to the north, and, mild as the air may be, water in these shadows is covered with thin, clear ice. With the vegetation thinned back to bare stems and twigs and shriveled blades of sedge, and with the rising of the water, my apprehensions about the Shrub Swamp becoming too heavily grown in for spotted turtles are ameliorated.

12:15 P.M. A spring peeper calls, on one of those days that is strikingly out of sync with the season's turning. Although most of the peepers take to nooks and crannies in the upland forest floor for hibernation, I hear their sporadic sweet and plaintive end-of-season calls here often enough to think that some of them hibernate in shrub and fern mounds above the frozen waters of this brushy wetland.

12:41 P.M. As I turn into the deepest channel of the Shrub Swamp, where a foot of water now lies over six inches of soft muck, I see a spotted turtle through a window of clearest ice in a shallow edge water bordered by winterberry and tussock sedge. Her stunning carapace and brilliantly marked head bear the familiar pattern of Ariadne. Seeing me, she partially withdraws into her shell. As I record the details of this setting, she puts her head back out, nosing at the ice. She moves very slowly in water that is barely two degrees above freezing. She may be searching for a hibernaculum or, more likely, making her way back to one she knows. A turtle who has lived in this shrub swamp as long as Ariadne has knows very well where to spend the winter. She may return to the same site year after year, but since I have found her at five varied places within the Tangle at what appeared to be her earliest emergence from hibernation, I think she shifts her winter quarters around. I slowly back away and leave her to her business. She has had ample opportunity for air-breathing, perhaps even basking, during this warm spell. Days like this must have a salutory effect on turtles about to undergo the rigors of overwintering, allowing them to rewind critical physiological clocks. There have been years in her lifetime when this entire wetland has been under a solid mantle of ice for as much as a month at this point in the season. With this mild break in mid-November, the springtime opening of the Shrub Swamp does not seem so far away.

November 15, 2:30 P.M. One more day of warmth. It is 70 degrees at the Tangle. The water temperature has rebounded to 40, but an abrupt return to November is forecast for tonight, on a wind shift out of the northwest. Hoping for another late-season turtle, I search the water, sedge hummocks, and shrub mounds as I wade to where I saw Ariadne yesterday. Peepers call again from time to time. Evidently no one is in a hurry to lock in for the winter. I finger into a warm pile of leaves and fallen ferns that has collected in the nestlike hollow at the center of a cinnamon fern mound. The inviting, misleading warmth is enough to make me think I could spend the winter here. But of course spring peepers in earthen holds, and spotted turtles in waterholds, need cold, not warmth, if they are to survive winter. They must keep as close as possible to freezing, without freezing. They have adapted perfectly to the thermal margins of their environments.

At Ariadne's site I discover a rounded hollow at the base of the shrub and fern mound that appears to lead into its underwater windings of roots and stems. With my focus on her yesterday, I had not noticed this inviting entrance, which immediately makes me think it leads to her hibernaculum. From their first spring appearances in virtual icewater, I have come to know some of the niches in which the turtles here hibernate, but I have never found the precise place into which one has wedged himself for the winter. I slip my hand into a long-sleeved neoprene glove, then kneel in the water, bracing my knees against the solid mound, my feet locked in the muck of the channel floor.

I slip my gloved hand into the opening. Feeling my way through intergrown roots and stems, I find an intricate network of tunnels leading into the foundation of this island of plants. I follow one as deeply as I can, groping into the narrow spaces all along its tangled walls, but can feel no turtle shapes. Even though the day is warm and I am well insulated in waders and sleeves, I am becoming chilled by my semi-immersion in the icy water. Unable to move my arm around within the woody corridors, I must withdraw my hand and snake it into the next passageway. I am sure there are tunnels off tunnels in the labyrinthine interior, but my arm is only so long and only so flexible.

I try several passageways, probing around the tenacious roots and stems, gaining a more literal feel for the vegetative structure of a shrub swamp than I have ever had before. It is good for me to know this structure better, for it is a defining one for the plants and animals of many aquatic habitats: more than half of the wetlands in the United States are characterized by shrubs and trees. The ecology of the spotted turtle is

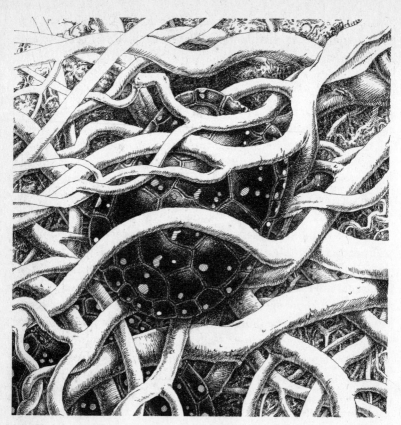

Spotted turtle (*Clemmys guttata*)

almost entirely bound up with the pit-and-mound structure of palustrine wetlands. Except for periods of upland estivation, migration, and nesting, these turtles keep to hummocks and hollows, and in some wetland habitats, the females lay their eggs on sparsely vegetated sphagnum and sedge hummocks.

Looked at from its upland margins, the Shrub Swamp could appear to be a monotonous screen of alders. But in its hollows, channels, mounds, and thickets of upreaching emergent branches, even the open space above it, this wetland provides exceptionally varied habitats. There are hollows in fern and sedge mounds, and woody branch mazes for nesting birds; spring feeding grounds for muskrats, woodcocks, ruffed grouse, and wild turkeys; migration routes for snapping turtles; summer hideouts and winter hibernacula for spotted turtles; growing spaces for rose pogonia and tawny cotton grass; hunting grounds for water snakes, mink, and raccoons; browseries for white-tailed deer and moose; berry thickets for black bears.

As my snaking, groping explorations continue, my chill deepens. I begin to think that if this is in fact Ariadne's hibernaculum, she and any comrades (spotted turtles frequently overwinter in groups) have tunneled well out of my reach. I have to force myself to thrust my hand into one more passageway. My dedication to making one last search — the key to many of my most memorable discoveries — is rewarded: I finally grasp a turtle. I know the feel at once, even through a neoprene glove, and know that I have touched the very core of a spotted turtle's overwintering. I withdraw a large female. It is not Ariadne, but I am now certain that she is here. I hastily record identifying details of this turtle, who keeps tightly within her shell, then work her back into place. Once she has wedged herself in again, she may well not move for the next four and a half to five months. She seems to have located herself safely out of the reach of otters, who would be too large to ferret their way into this recess; and it seems doubtful that mink could go without breathing long enough to nose into such a tight corner and extricate this spotted turtle. I can picture no other predator who could come close to accessing her winter sanctuary.

Finding this turtle on my "last look" renews my resolve. I straighten up for a time, to rest my back and warm my hand, then turn my attention to a tangle of underwater sweet gale stems that link a tussock sedge hummock with the main island I have been exploring. This woody roping is set in muck and winds into the sedge hummock, from which it erects aromatic sprays of branches. Among the sweet gale rhizomes set into the hummock, I feel another turtle. Ariadne again! I set her back at once. Returning to the main opening, I reach back in, twisting my way deeper than I had before, pushing to my fullest extension, armpit-deep and close to flooding my insulating sleeve. The left side of my swamp vest drapes in the water. With this effort, I recover a third turtle, a small adult male. He is packed with muck. I quickly document him, set him back in his hiding place, and decide to stop. I feel sure I could find more spotted turtles here, but now that I have documented this hibernaculum, I don't want to disturb them anymore.

4:33 P.M. Purple-gray clouds are edged with gold in the west where the sun has gone down. I could come to this wetland season after season just to watch the enormous sky space above it, a theater of ever-changing cloudscapes; but my eyes invariably become transfixed by the water and what lives within it. I have to remind myself to look up at the sky from time to time. Already the wind has shifted. True to the forecast, spring-time in November is about to end. Though I am becoming colder by the quarter hour, I sense that this will be my last tour of the year in the Shrub Swamp, and I am compelled to linger.

It is growing dark and becoming harder to see among dark mounds and into black water, but as I wade a shallow channel through tussock sedge and alder, I see a male spotted turtle prowling ahead of me, the top of his shell out of the water. There is an air of searching about his move-ments, but with the water as cold as it is, he is not looking for food. He may be looking for a hibernaculum, but I suspect he is seeking a late-season opportunity to mate. Well into fall, I have found males mounted on females inside interruption traps, with other males outside trying to get in. Although they reportedly do not breed in autumn, my observa-tions suggest that, like wood turtles and some other species, male spot-ted turtles seek a final round of mating before settling in for winter. This one seems surprisingly active in the cold water. He may well have done some solar-collecting on a warm, dry sedge mound before the sun went down. He doesn't seem aware of me until my hand is about to close over him. Picking him up, I recognize his especially brilliant and distinc-tive carapace patterns at once. I have not seen him for three years, and never before in the Shrub Swamp. Six years ago he was the first turtle of the season for me. It was the last week of March, and he was in a shrub-bordered trough of black water between a great ice sheet covering the backwater sedge marsh off Alder Brook and its deeply snow-drifted bank. By mid-April he had become a prominent member of the colony in the nearby Reedgrass Pool. For the next two years I found him at emergence in the same wetland niche, the only spotted turtle I found overwintering there. Now he has reappeared where he will surely spend this winter, some three hundred yards from his hibernaculum of three years ago. I will add him to those I look for here when I come back at thaw, for the awakening of the spotted turtles.

4:50 P.M. Two gunshots resound from the darkening hills as I wade to the southeast corner of the Shrub Swamp. My turtle season has over-lapped with deer-hunting season. I make my way to two tall white pines that mark my point of departure from the Shrub Swamp. Sharp winds have driven off the clouds and swept away the day's unusual warmth. It will be a clear, cold night in this wetland basin. There will be featherings of ice by dawn, and the ice is likely to stay this time, to deepen and hold fast through winter, an insulation for all beneath the water. When the sun went down behind the pine-crowned crest of hills to the west, in all likelihood the season of the spotted turtles went down with it.

Nesting painted turtle (*Chrysemys p. picta*)

5 THE POND

Even the seasons form a great circle in their changing,
and always come back again to where they were.

— Black Elk

First Open Water

April 1, 9:12 A.M. A sliver of water curls like a fingernail moon around the shallow cove at the north end of Bear Pond. This ribbon of meltwater, a yard or so wide, is set against acres of ice, gray-white, dark lead, and blue-gray, frozen fast to upland edgings, wetland shorelines, and ledge. It will be days until ice-out expands from this meltwater rim to the pond's deepwater core. The painted turtles that hibernate in the leatherleaf shrub-swamp compartment of the pond may not be able to bask for another week. I am chilled by the wind — though mild enough out of the southwest, it becomes refrigerated in blowing across the ice. Away from the pond the day is warmer.

As I draw near, I see a sudden surge in the placid meltwater. A pickerel flashes under the ice sheet. This is his escape cover now, as a floating ceiling of lily pads and water shield will be later in the season. Foraging chain pickerel are quick to move into the first open water, slipping into shallows that nearly expose their backs, just as herons come to fish for the likes of pickerel in such minimal margins.

The plain of frozen water is broken only by low, brushy islands of leatherleaf that has colonized floating mats of sphagnum moss. A broad-winged hawk sweeps over, rising, slicing into the face of the wind, ascending as he travels the length of Bear Pond until he becomes a dark speck against blinding white clouds. Broad-winged and marsh hawks, great blue and green herons, American bitterns, wood ducks, mallards, black ducks, hooded mergansers, and Canada geese hunt, fish, or nest among the leatherleaf islands, beneath which painted turtles and, I suspect, Blanding's turtles hibernate. Each spring I consider investigating this shrub swamp set in the pond. But I continue to be a wader, not a boatman, and there is no wading the deep water and muck between the islands and the shoreline.

With the coming of spring, the pliant marshy masses of tussock sedge and bluejoint reedgrass, dried by sun and wind, will rebound from winter's flattening. The stiffer-stemmed beaked sedge, wool-grass, soft rush, and Canada rush are bent and broken and will not rise up as the snow melts away. The shoreline hedge of meadowsweet is unbowed, but the steeplebush is mostly horizontal except for a few resilient stalks that have resisted winter's great pressing down. Ceaseless pond-chilled wind rustles through this sere garden, from which new growth will spring forth. There is a constant sound of rushing wind in bordering pines. Distant, piercing cries of killdeer penetrate the wind. They are one of the signals I've been waiting for. The sharp, plaintive calls seem to arrive

Hooded mergansers (*Lophodytes cucullatus*)

in advance of the birds themselves, gladdening cries that can fill a landscape. They come with the first crystal-melting breaths of March or early April, announcing that spring, too, is on the wing.

Hatchling

April 1, 11 A.M. The ice has withdrawn from the broad shallows of North Fen, a boglike expanse of sphagnum and sedge that has formed in an occluded, acidic backwater at the north end of Bear Pond. Adjacent to low, level land, this bay receives little of the nutrient-bearing runoff that would enrich its environment enough to support a marsh or swamp. The sphagnum-clogged shallows restrict water movement that would flush away acids and other byproducts of plant metabolism. The slow or incomplete decay of plant remains, primarily sedge and sphagnum, has allowed a peaty organic soil to build up and form a peatland, or fen. Beyond this fen, a broad island of sparkling, eroded ice with knife-thin edges lies over the deeper, more open pickerelweed marshes and water lily beds that will become floating gardens in a month or so. The dense, brooding gray of the thick central ice sheet still covers the deeper acres of the pond. No plants will emerge from those depths, which exceed six and a half feet. Such a compartment in a pond (or lake or river) is known as deepwater habitat.

At this point in the season, the open water of the pond's perimeter; the pitted, eroded band of thinner ice; and the smooth, hard-frozen central sheet map out the principal zones of the pond ecosystem. In the shallows, where open water now lies, a perennial marsh will reappear, thick with wool-grass and other emergent sedges, Canada and soft rush, white beak rush, marsh Saint Johnswort, swamp candles, rice cutgrass, rattlesnake manna grass, and bluejoint. On the verge of leafing out, emergent leatherleaf, sweet gale, and meadowsweet create an interspersion of shrub-swamp elements within this broad band of marsh, particularly along its shoreward margin. Beyond the ring of meltwater, the dissolving ice delineates aquatic bed habitat, characterized by plants that grow principally on or below the surface; floating plants like duckweed, floating-leaved species like white and yellow water lily and watershield, and submergents such as bladderwort and water-milfoil will begin to fill this space soon after its disintegrating cover of ice is gone.

Typical of the continuum of wetland types comprising the pond, a broad swath of pickerelweed will rise up in the midst of the water lilies, an emergent marsh of many square yards set in several acres of aquatic bed. Solid ice holds fast in the lacustrine depths of Bear Pond, the deepwater habitat in which plant life exists only in the form of microscopic phytoplankton. The medium for life in deepwater habitats is water; in the pond's wetlands, the medium for life is air.

As I wade into the open shallows of the fen, I find solid footing. This is an uncommon luxury here, where the layer beneath the water is a treacherous colloidal soup of submergent sphagnum and other detritus. These sediments form what is termed a false bottom. It appears as if one could wade on it, perhaps sinking in a little; but it has no more substance than water, and one slips right through it, sometimes to dangerous depths. Today this layer is still bound up with ice, and wherever I strike down with my wading stick to test the footing, I find it as hard as pavement.

Life quickens in clear water that only days ago was ice. I wade past the pond's first water striders of the season and among the first whirligig beetles. The latter enliven the surface with ceaseless high-speed whirlings that suggest a dancing of rain or riffling of wind. They spiral away in all directions across the surface as I wade among them, then close ranks to a dizzying flotilla after I have passed. Amorous red-spotted newts appear and disappear in cavernous black-green suspensions of sphagnum as banner-tailed males seek to clasp females in the weightless world beneath the surface. I move on to the outer reach of persistent emergent plants. Some eroded, granular white ice lingers in blue shadows beneath the denser clumps of tussock sedge. Spring seems to be coming to life in the tawny strands and sweeps of last year's sedge growth; the air above them wavers with radiant April heat.

Searching among swirls of sedge, I find a bit of renewed life, new to the season and to himself. Merely two yards from the retreating ice sheet is a hatchling painted turtle, lying with his eyes closed. A little over an inch long, he could be a large seed. He strikes me, in fact, as an animal seed. A part of the pond itself seems to be on the verge of rebirth in this tiny, sleeping turtle. He is smaller than some of the predacious diving beetles I have seen basking in a similar, though far more alert, fashion. They dived quickly into the water and disappeared, the way turtles do

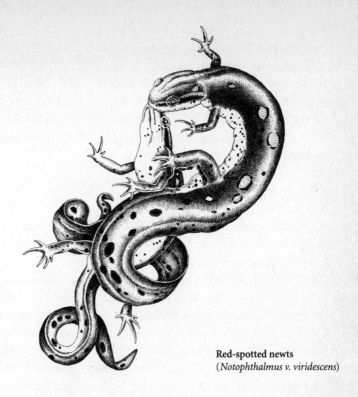

Red-spotted newts
(*Notophthalmus v. viridescens*)

once they have regained their full metabolism and active senses. It is still too early for hatchlings that overwintered in their nests to have dug out and made their nest-to-water journeys. This turtle must have left his nest last August or September and made his way to the pond then. Like the adult spotted turtle I found ten days ago, a veteran of more than twenty winters, this first-time hibernator has made it through the winter, but under great stress and with little time to spare. He read his wetland surroundings well, it appears, choosing a hibernaculum just deep enough to be beyond the ice's penetrating reach into the sphagnaceous substrate, and just in from the lingering ice sheet that would have him still sealed beneath the water. What a great struggle it must have been for this hatchling to dig his way up from a cold, lightless, muck-enclosed, vegetation-choked hibernaculum and finally crawl up into radiant sedge swirls, warm with blinding April sunlight.

The immobile hatchling seems completely unaware of my presence. In his current condition he is more than vulnerable to predation, or possibly freezing, if he is unable to get back into the water before nightfall. Although the sun can be remarkably restorative, I don't know how much he can recover with one day's basking. Faced again with a situation that is hard to walk away from, I debate for some time, than go against my customary grain and pick the turtle up. Even after several minutes in my hand, he makes no move. His eyes open briefly, then close again. For the second time this season I put a refugee from winter into the zippered pocket of my swamp vest.

Courtship Ballet

April 19, 4:30 P.M. In steady light rain I wade past the first red, curled pads of white water lilies emerging from black muck in 42-degree water. The air is only two degrees warmer than the water. Two small, buff brown ducks huddle in the drizzle, one on a log, one on a stump, at the edge of the leatherleaf islands. The distance and the rain screen preclude identifying these water birds, motionless as decoys. They are strangers here, as far as I can make out, not one of the species that frequent the pond. Both birds face me, one resting on his belly, the other standing on one leg. I have a feeling they saw me long before I noticed them, but for some reason they haven't exploded into flight as ducks usually do. I look back on them as I wade, and cannot detect a shift of foot or feather. They wait and watch. The season waits. April is a waiting month, with extended periods of darkness, cold, and rain, even snow from time to time. When the sun breaks through, life erupts in its heat and light, only to become subdued again with the inevitable return of chill cloud cover. Waiting is a part of the season's pace: crumpled water lily leaves hold in place on tightly coiled stems, not far below the surface; ducks abide within their feathers.

The rain abates; the face of the pond, at once mirror and window, becomes placid and unruffled. Able to see into the water again, I find that late in the afternoon of a day I had taken as dedicated to waiting, the season does advance, even with a stately eagerness. A large adult female painted turtle glides gracefully, effortlessly, into an open circle of water. The green-gold bars of her carapace glow softly in the near-black water; her red-orange marginals blaze. Apparently unaware of me, she passes just beneath the surface. She turns in a short arc and, with measured strokes of her forefeet and propelling flicks of her broadly webbed hind feet, swims in my direction. I hold still. Her eyes are focused forward, not upward. Cutting between us, turning directly into her yellow-streaked face, a male swims unhurriedly with a measured grace. As they come closer to each other, face to face, they slant at equal angles toward the surface and meet, with a precision that seems rehearsed. With their heads just breaking the surface, they extend their necks full length in elegant arcs and touch nose tip to nose tip. Then, with legs motionless, they sink slowly in tandem, almost to the bottom. Casually flipping her broad hind webs in reverse, the female backs away, distancing herself a foot or so from the male. She then turns around and glides off. He slides forward and follows her, keeping a foot behind.

In the center of the open pool, the male comes to a stop and hovers in suspension, halfway between the surface and the bottom. The female looks back, turns in a wide slow circle, and returns to him. As she approaches, both begin another ascent to the surface, where they meet once again, nose to nose. This is followed by another slow submersion, the female eventually turning and swimming away in the restrained ceremonial flight that is part of painted turtle courtship. The male pursues. Just as she seems about to fade out of sight in the surrounding curtains of sedge, she wheels abruptly, facing her pursuer, and holds her place, her hind feet just touching the screen of plants behind her. The male advances and, when he is close to her, extends both forelegs full length toward her face, the palms of his front feet facing outward. He suddenly vibrates his elaborately elongated foreclaws dramatically. They reflect a shivering white light that seems electric in the dark water. He repeats this at several intervals. Following this stunning accent in their rather nonchalant pas de deux, the object of the male's pursuit circles back to center stage and turns to face her suitor anew. One more time they ascend for a graceful arcing of necks and touching of nose tips. Once more the male stretches his forelegs and shivers his fully extended claws, this time on the silver-gray surface. Electric white light pulses through reflected landscapes.

Theme and variation continue until a new element is interjected into the scene. In one of her slow turnings just beneath the surface glare, the female's eyes catch mine. She freezes for a moment, then takes flight. The male, continuing his part, not anticipating any such break in the unhurried perfection of the routine, holds in confusion as his leading lady vanishes into the backdrop of water plants. It is evident that had she not wished to participate in this premating ceremony, she could have eluded the male at any point. Cocking his head, as though he had taken a cue from her, the male sees me. He, too, takes flight, disappearing not far from where his partner sought safety. I wade on, confident that these turtles will renew their courtship ballet once they feel they are without an audience.

Wading Bear Pond

April 20, 10:30 A.M. From the highest point of a granite outcropping along its eastern rim, I look down on the shimmering water of Bear Pond. This is the vista that spreads out beneath a great blue heron dropping in for a session of fishing and frogging in one of the pond's many palustrine backwaters. Few ponds of this size, much less larger ponds and lakes, are ringed by intact natural shoreline, and flanked by an undeveloped landscape. Most have been severely encroached upon by human development. Well removed from any paved road, and spared the intrusion of a single human habitation, Bear Pond is in a rare class. The rich diversity and abundance of life here are a direct reflection of its having been so left alone. This wetland-laced world lying before me in full April sun could seem a dream. How many places are there in which one can stand alone and look to the four directions without seeing roadways and rooflines, listen to the four winds over the four seasons without hearing a dog or a machine? I look across a living map, described not by ribbons and rectangles of pavement, patchwork quilts of rooftops, lawns, and agricultural fields but by natural landforms and plant communities or by shapes of clear water. At night there is no light out here save the moon and the stars.

At the southwest corner of the pond is a gray screen brushed with a crown of red — a red maple swamp, edged with the glowing gold of a tussock sedge marsh. Beyond that, sky blue water marks the aquatic bed in which lily pads are beginning to appear. The deepwater habitat lies like a dark blue stone in this setting. The eastern pond rim, beyond the gray granite of the ledge I'm standing on, is an aquamarine swath of emergent bulrush. The western margin fades into the low, umber sweep

Map of the pond

of a shrub swamp. This is flanked by the marooned screening of an alder carr, or swamp, which backs to the soft greens of upland pines. To the north, across surface water awaiting floating leaves, lies the tawny expanse of the leatherleaf shrub-swamp islands. A triangular drift of distant blue lies beyond these, and finally, at the far northern point of the pond, I can just make out the green-earth fringe of the sphagnum border of the North Fen.

The pond appears a world of water today, but in not so many warm days it will be a realm of plants. In the wetland parlance of today, it is difficult to affix a precise definition to the word "pond," but it commonly means a water body shallow enough and with enough of a silty or muddy substrate to allow rooted plants to grow from shore to shore. It can also be defined as a water-filled basin or topographical depression that supports a complex of still or slow-water wetland types in a common catchment. When one looks out across a pond, one can usually distinguish the wetlands that make it up: an aquatic bed of water lilies or emergent marsh of sedge or cattails here, a buttonbush shrub swamp or red maple swamp there. Like Bear Pond, many ponds of glacial origins have a lacustrine deepwater compartment bordered by wetland elements that have been greatly expanded by beaver dams. Ponds can also form in cutoff or slow-flowing backwaters, meanders, and oxbows along rivers, on shallower lake margins and deep marshes, as well as in well-defined basins.

Ponds vary considerably in size and depth, water chemistry, and physical makeup. They are frequently distinguished from lakes in terms of their generally shallower depth and smaller size, but the principal defining difference is water temperature. During the warm season, especially during the heat and low water typical of high summer, the upper layer of water in a pond warms up, but generally the temperature is fairly uniform from the surface to the bottom. A lake, on the other hand, has layers: a heated surface layer with currents activated by heating, cooling, and wind; a narrow transition layer; and a decidedly colder profundal zone. The temperature at the surface of a lake may reach the seventies, while its deep water is 40 degrees. In Bear Pond, bottom temperatures in summer surpass 70. The trout and salmon of cold-water lakes, which prefer temperatures of 50 to 54 degrees during July and August, could never survive there, but largemouth bass, chain pickerel, brown bullheads, pumpkinseed, and bluegills thrive. Lakes commonly feature stretches of sparsely vegetated or completely unvegetated shoreline, particularly on their leeward sides, where sandy, rocky shores are beaten by winds and washed by waves.

I make my way down the rough staircase offered by a jagged cleft in the ledge border. It is a steep and forbidding formation, on which plant succession is kept at the bare-rock stage, with spare encrustments of moss and lichen and thin holdings of ferns and grass, not by wind and waves but by the lack of soil. As I step from granite into clear water, the boundary between wet and dry is sharply delineated. Immediately, I come face to face with the day's stiff winds. The water is riffled and sparkled by its surgings out of the northwest. Though today's winds will be enough to nearly unbalance me in my wading, they are not prevailing or forceful enough to keep back the plant life that has encircled the pond so profusely.

This is the face of the open pond in the early season. It is a hard face to read. I see flashes of deep red among the rippled webbings of sunlight in the shallows, the upreaching, uncurling leaves of white water lilies on their journey to the surface. Before long, the broad green lily pads will float on calmer waters and in fact help to keep them calm. This lotus of local waters, symbol of rebirth, arises from black mud, preparing to drift its pristine white, sweetly fragrant flowers over acres of water. I seldom make my way to this end of the pond, although it lies no more than five hundred yards from my familiar haunts. Each season I vow to extend my range, to know more of the wetland mosaic here, the pond and its surrounding system of streams, marshes, and swamps; but there is barely time from thaw to freeze to keep up with my rounds of the places I have come to know and return to season after season, year after year, wanting to know them better. I am not one who is driven to cross oceans or continents. I seem to have something of an aboriginal sense of time and space. "Here and now" is a ruling concept for me, and I seldom stray far from familiar places.

The wind keeps up a reedy, whistling rush through the stiff, bleached cattail stalks of last season and the pliant green blades rising among them. Once past the cattails, I wade farther out from shore, through woolly-fruit sedge, its grasslike new growth blowing like hair in the wind, and on through water bulrush, a slender, weak-stemmed emergent that leans on the surface. This early in the season, marsh plants are as fluid as water.

Great leatherleaf islands have become established in the sedge and bulrush marsh. Many of them are fringed with sweet gale, and some have been colonized by stunted highbush blueberries and gnarled red maple saplings. The forbidding interiors of the islands, with their deep-water pockets and treacherous sediments, are home to gliding geese, wading herons, paddling ducks, prowling snapping turtles, and low-flying marsh hawks, as well as beavers and muskrats. A dulled, bronzy green is coming back into the persistent leaves of the leatherleaf. Pendant flower buds, pure white and waxy, swell along gracefully arched stems, like droplets on a candle. They are within a few mild days of opening. Sphagnum moss has crept throughout the woody rafts of the leatherleaf islands, granting a foothold to tussock sedge, stands of white beak rush and twig rush, and sprays of bog rush that drape into the water.

The sky is almost cloudless; the wind-chopped surface of the pond is given a rare blue, hard and intense. The rush of wind over the water practically tears the pages from my notebook. In turning a corner I set a scrambling of painted turtles into the water. There are hummocks out of the wind here, low to the water along the rim of a leatherleaf island, where turtles can climb from the water and tilt their shells to the sun, taking warmth from a shivering, wind-blasted day. This low-lying lee is evidently a favored spot for these inveterate baskers, who have flattened its sphagnum and sedges. One of the fleeing turtles circles my boots. The green-gold bars across the pond-bottom color of his carapace disguise him among the reticulate patterns of sunlight in the water. I had been thinking, as I tried to write with stiffened fingers on wind-fluttered pages, that it would have been better to keep to smaller wetlands cupped among the hills on a day like this. The air temperature, for all the sun, is only 57 degrees, and the wind-chill factor is menacing enough for the third week in April. I am sure sedges and grasses are rustling around spotted turtles sunning themselves in the Tangle of the Shrub Swamp and in the Reedgrass Pool; but the strongest winds pass over those places, and they receive nothing like the buffeting the pond takes.

3:15 P.M. More painted turtles drop into the water as I continue on. With no sedge mounds here, they brace themselves among shrub stems, low to the water line. Each time I turn a corner along the meandering border of the leatherleaf island, I hear turtles splashing. The wind is tremendous now, but still these turtles bask. I hear a great splash and look up in time to see an osprey rise from the water. He sweeps toward me and wheels above my head, his talons empty. I watch as he spirals beyond the ledges, high in the air, works effortlessly into the wind, then drops to the west side of the pond. With all the wind, I cannot hear him hit the water, but I see a broad spray tossed up into the sunlight. He rises again on wide wings, talons still empty, and slants off to the southern end of the pond to continue his fishing. Osprey appear here now and then, but are far more transient than marsh hawks, perhaps because the water becomes too turbid and closed over by plant growth as the season warms. These raptors must have clear water in which to sight their prey. Or perhaps the pond cannot support the fishery required of an osprey nesting site.

5:41 P.M. I turn away from Bear Pond where it begins its transition to the floating-mat aggregations of sphagnum and sedge in North Fen. Spring peepers call now from pools within this peatland, their shrill chorus piercing the unabating wind. As the sun lowers, the wind becomes even chillier, but this assembly of tiny frogs wants to keep the season going in its proper direction. Featherings and plumes of cirrus clouds, ice white and sunset rose, uncoil out of the west. If rain is to follow, as it does about half the time when these ice-crystal clouds brush the sky four miles or so above the earth, I hope it is a warm rain.

Migrations

April 29, 3:57 P.M. Tracks in the sand. It looks as if a dinosaur has passed here: two rows of deep, reptilian footprints accented by earth-puncturing claw marks, set in a plodding meander, with an incised serpentine tail-drag weaving between them. This signature in sand could hardly contrast more with the precisely spaced, straight-arrow line of red fox tracks I came upon earlier, as I read sand and sandy loam for signs of hatchling painted turtles. These prehistoric-looking tracks are another sign of spring I have been looking for, evidence that snapping turtles have begun to move from their overwintering niches along the permanent stream and its backwaters to their summer waters in Bear Pond and nearby marsh. After traveling through wet meadows and the tangles of the Shrub Swamp, some of the migrants cross sand or crumbly earth on the final overland leg of their journeys and leave a record of their passing. I look for evidence of their first crossings as I look for nest exit holes of spring-emergent painted turtles and for the hatchlings themselves on their nest-to-water journeys. The same kinds of days that inspire the snapping turtles to migrate are apt to prompt the first emergence of hatchling painted turtles from their nest chambers: those first days in late April or early May when temperatures finally reach the high seventies, or even eighties, and the earth at last begins to heat up. These movements are most likely to be triggered when the atmosphere is heavy with moisture and the year's first thunderstorm seems to be in the air.

I take up my rounds of the painted turtle nests I screened last nesting season. Each year I cover a dozen or so with screens of half-inch-square hardware cloth to prevent eggs being taken by such predators as skunks and raccoons, and to be able to document the occasional autumn emergence of hatchlings as well as the survival rates of those who overwinter in their nests. Many of the branch-pegs I used to anchor the screens have been lifted from the ground by frost heaving. I drive them back into place and replace the ones that have rotted. Some years hatchlings do not leave their nest chambers until well into May, little more than a week before their mothers begin coming back to these sandy fields to nest again.

A bit of the rear margin of a hatchling's carapace and his tiny right hind foot catch my eye as I look through the screening of a nest that had a solitary autumn emergent last September. The little turtle is not moving; he may have been exposed by last night's heavy rains and may be dead. At times when I dig into nests to record final details, I find winter-killed hatchlings so fresh-looking it seems they could walk off at any moment. I pull up a corner of the screen and touch his foot. Instantly, he pulls it into his shell. I pull up the screen and unearth the hatchling. He is tightly withdrawn into his shell, but his bright, open eyes seem to project a calm and endless patience. He seems at once newborn and half as old as time. The plastron, his lower shell, is a radiant coral. Hatchling eastern painted turtles often have rosy to red-orange plastrons that turn to the lemon or golden yellow of adults during their first growing season. I brush wet sand away from the nest and reveal the top of another carapace. This hatchling is a mere three quarters of an inch below the surface. I extract him and two more, all alive. The bottom-most eggshell fragments lie pressed into the firm floor of the nest chamber, about an inch and a half deep. Such a thin layer of earth was sufficient for these hatchling turtles to survive a northern winter.

A deepening excitement comes over me as I take in this scene. It confirms something I have suspected and have been trying to document for seven years: the emergence of both autumn and spring hatchlings from the same nest. Fragments of eggshell left behind by the solitary hatchling who dug out last September 23 are still present at the mouth of the nest. Usually the eggshells are left out of sight within the chamber, but the autumn hatchling had dragged along fragments to the surface as he made his way out. I had lifted the screen so that he could proceed on his nest-to-water journey. The dry, sandy nesting matrix had backfilled loosely after his departure, leaving a shallow crater. I did not disturb the nest to see if any living siblings remained, but refastened the screen and began a long vigil. I continued the rounds of nest checks I make from August 7 until the ground freezes. No others left the nest before frost sealed over the earth and the accrual of snow began.

I can now complete the story of this painted turtle nest. The female dug her chamber last June 6, laid five eggs, covered and camouflaged her nest, and returned to the pond at about 5:30 in the afternoon. From that time on, the developing turtles were entrusted to the keeping of the earth, to be incubated by the heat of the sun and kept from desiccation by the rain. With this elemental nurturing over the two and a half to three months of incubation, the embryo within each egg developed into a perfectly formed turtle. By late summer, each had pipped from his eggshell but remained in the nest.

Most painted turtles spend their first winter in these terrestrial chambers, but if there is an autumn emergence, usually all of the hatchlings leave. But on two other occasions I have observed the departure of a single turtle in autumn. In both instances, all the siblings who stayed behind died in the nest. I found them when I finally dug into the nests in mid-May, after none had dug out in spring. Their appearance suggested to me that had seasonal conditions not been so unfavorable — there was no insulating snow cover, and there were prolonged spells of strong, freezing winds and nights with temperatures below zero Fahrenheit — they would have survived. On the passing of summer into autumn, one

Northern water snake (*Nerodia s. sipedon*) in buttonbush (*Cephalanthus occidentalis*)

sojourner left this nest to make his journey to water for hibernation while the other four stayed behind. As September gave way to October and November, the sandy earth around them cooled down, then froze. Snow drifted over them as they hibernated. This time those who stayed behind survived the rigors of winter. Last night a wash of rain revealed one hatchling, and I opened up the closeted world of the four, who soon would have departed on their own.

May 1, 2:13 P.M. I come back to the route of returning turtles on an afternoon becoming steamy as the sun finds its way through clouds and haze in the wake of an explosive eruption of thunderstorms at midday. The moisture in the air seems to magnify the heat in the sun's brightening glare. Cloud towers build high. These conditions will surely inspire a wave of snapping turtle migrations. As I approach a deep shore-edge trough near the eastern edge of North Fen, I see an impressive snake stretched out across an old logging road. The snake is about three feet long and so dark I take him at first for a black racer, but his thick girth and faint banding tell me I am looking at a northern water snake. Our simultaneous mutual acknowledgment is to keep perfectly still for a moment, but then the snake turns with whiplike speed, surges powerfully over a narrow embankment, and slides into the densely vegetated trough. As I take several swift strides in an effort to glimpse him in the water, I see a second, smaller water snake. This one, glistening wet, turns from the outer margin of an alder stand and streaks back into the sheltering water he has just left. It is hot, even in the shade of white pines; well-heated snakes are lightning-quick in their movements.

Water snakes are clearly on the move. As I stand still in pine shadows, writing notes, a third slips by my feet, winding purposefully among sedge, grass, and fallen branches, flicking his tongue continuously. He glides into the alders, then curls out to follow the exact route taken by the first snake. Some snakes can scent-track the paths of others of their species, an adaptation that enables them to locate communal denning sites as winter approaches. Snake number three doubles back on his own route and once again nearly slides over my foot. His black-edged reddened bands and mingled fawn and umber blotches camouflage him well against the leaf litter, sedge strands, and muddy earth he travels through. At the edge of the pond I see a fourth water snake, the smallest of the lot, distinctly reddened, animatedly prowling the sphagnum and sedge shallows, then a fifth, another large, thick-bodied adult, coiled darkly among stiff upreachings of buttonbush. This one is basking, and either too absorbed in heat collecting or comfortable enough with the muck-and-water distance between us that he does not drop into the water.

I have seen more water snakes in twenty minutes than I generally see in weeks. They must be in migration, but from where and to where? Have they emerged from a common hibernaculum in the rock ledges and boulder jumbles above the pond, and made their way here en route to spreading out for the summer? Or have they overwintered right in this shrub-swamp backwater, emerged, and taken this hot day to begin dispersing outward to the streams, vernal pools, and other wetlands where they spend their active seasons? Their very name speaks of an aquatic existence, yet they often, perhaps predominantly, hibernate terrestrially. Aquatic hibernation does occur, but it apparently must take place where the snakes have access to air, as they cannot tolerate prolonged submergence without atmospheric oxygen, as turtles can.

I once found a water snake in February, still alive, though barely, after an uncommonly mild night when the temperature stayed just above freezing. The snake lay on the snowy rim of a great hollow in mud and rocks churned up by the chained tires of a skidder that had broken through the frozen crust atop an underground stream. This little feeder stream eventually erupts onto the surface and descends into a large beaver pond that has a populous colony of water snakes. It is possible that there was a communal hibernaculum close by but the one un-earthed by spinning wheels was too cold-stunned to get back into it. Snow was three feet deep all around the hollow. The snake must have been hibernating in a cavity of tree roots and stone through which the water ran, where he could hibernate aquatically and still have access to air. I took the snake home and arranged a hibernaculum in my refrigerator, hoping to get him through until spring, but his midwinter exposure had taken too great a toll, and he died within a few days.

The ditchlike section of the pond's edge, from which five water snakes seemed to have burst forth all at once, is a favored place for them when they emerge from hibernation. I find them here, often quite cryptically wound into sedge mounds, much in the manner of spotted turtles taking their first sun of the year. They are so torpid that I am able to get near enough to take close-up photos, something that is out of the question once they become active. The water snakes at this end of the pond may have a hibernation chamber under the bank. Wherever they come from, wherever they are going, they will not keep together for long.

4:40 P.M. Heat, like some accompanying presence, has intensified with the afternoon's passage. For the first time this year, stones in the shadows of pines are warm to the touch. Snapping turtles must be on the move. As I circle to the sandy old-field and the hayfields that many cross on their spring migration to the pond, I nearly walk past a small one in a flooded wheel rut on the logging road. The mud-colored turtle has found a temporary shelter, a resting place in a puddle of storm water, on his migration to the pond. I fish him out, and he fires three rapid, snapping strikes at no perceptible target. This protestation expressed, he hunkers as much of himself as he can into his shell and sullenly awaits his fate. He is three years old, young enough that his growth rings are still visible on the scutes of his carapace. With my calipers, I measure this three-year-old's carapace length at four and a quarter inches, then set him back in the reassuring turbidity of his puddle. I have found snapping turtles whose shells are barely three inches long following the same routes as their gargantuan elders. I always wonder how they accomplish this orienteering. Possibly a snakelike scent-tracking is involved, but the turtles take divergent individual paths with a common direction, rather than keeping to precise trails or closely following routes taken by those who have gone before. I see snapping turtles making the same migrations year after year, their paths crossing on occasion and even tightly overlapping for some distances, but commonly ranging over swaths that may be hundreds of feet wide. It does not appear that the travelers track one another's scents but that by employing the same acute senses and picking up the same clues in locating common destinations, they at times walk in one another's footsteps.

The degree of predictability in their seasonal migrations has made these turtles vulnerable to hunters, who can intercept and capture them with little effort. They are also easily trapped or noosed in warm weather, and in winter can be collected from hibernacula, which are often communal. Heavy taking, especially for the restaurant trade, has rendered the common snapping turtle considerably less than common in parts of its range, and game regulations have become necessary to prevent its becoming extirpated from some locales. In addition, their migrations among wetlands, and the overland travel required of nest-seeking females, put them in great jeopardy of becoming roadkill. Many snapping turtles are killed because people erroneously assume that they destroy wild waterfowl and game fish or are dangerous to human swimmers, despite abundant research findings to the contrary.

During one of my pauses in circling the hayfield, I hear a rustling in a sweetfern border and see dense, twiggy growth being shoved aside. A snapping turtle with a carapace more than a foot long is crushing toward the pond, for some reason shunning open ground and plowing through the shrub thickets crowded along the tree line. She may feel safer traveling under some cover. A few minutes later I sight another large turtle, walking-falling over ridges in the field, which has been harrowed for the first time in a decade. Huge neck stretched out full length, massive head parallel with the ground, jolting forward with uneven footfalls, this ancient reptile aims straight for the marsh-lined embayment at the beaver dam. At nearly the same moment my eyes are drawn to a far younger one, with a carapace about six inches long, who has been watching me all this while from a settled position in a tractor rut. It seems that anywhere I turn my eyes I will see a snapping turtle. I sneak among the tasseled screens of quaking and bigtooth aspens along the hayfield, then walk its northern boundary, where a slope descends to the shrub swamp, sedge marsh, and red maple swamp from which these turtles have come. I hear a sustained crunching and crackling in leaf litter and fallen branch tangles. Alarmed by the same heavy-footed treading, a snowshoe hare in brown summer dress bolts from cover and scampers by me. The hare wins this race with the tortoise, disappearing before the plodding noisemaker comes into view.

The most tremendous turtle yet labors up the last of the wooded slope and out onto the edge of the plowed field. This snapping turtle easily weighs between forty and fifty pounds. He takes a long chelonian pause to rest, or perhaps to contemplate the unfamiliar disruption of the landscape. As I approach, the turtle settles to the warm earth. In the low slant of sunlight, his smooth carapace has a dull blue sheen. His throat bellows with slow, patient breathing; his thick, studded neck folds and massive foreleg muscles bulge around his great, hook-jawed head. I kneel for a moment a few feet away, listening to his slow, steady rhythmic breathing. He has made a long and difficult journey at the end of a half year's hibernation. There is no easy cruising through the Shrub Swamp for a turtle of this size, and overland travel, with no water to buoy his ponderous weight, must be strenuous even for so well-muscled an animal. Traveling will be far easier when he reaches the water. I back away and withdraw into the alders. The turtle waits a long time. My approach added to whatever consternation he might have felt at encountering the plowed field. He has probably made this crossing eighty or one hundred times, twice each year for four or five decades, quite possibly more. A large part of the hayfield is only ten years old; it was a white-pine forest during his earlier migrations.

At length he rises and begins the final hundred yards or so of his spring journey. No matter that the earth before him has literally been turned over: he travels by signs that are constant, clear, and compelling enough that the scrambling of any one signal does not deter or disorient him. There is enough information to be gathered from the afternoon light, the larger landscape, the scents on the humid air, the position of the earth and sun — who knows what all? There must be some memory here, some recording and interpreting. He knows where the pond lies and must go there. If a four-lane highway were sliced between his wintering grounds and his summer pond, he would make the same determined, targeted attempt to cross; in all of his 220-million-year inherited turtle history there is no program for turning back. Fortunately, no paved road has divided this turtle's resident wetlands. He is safe, for now, as he resumes his tilting, high-stepping march to water. I believe all of these traveling turtles will sleep well tonight, beneath the waters of the pond.

I slip my notebook into my vest and step out into the open, inadvertently setting another traveler to flight. My focus on the snapping turtle was so intent I never saw the large doe who had moved out onto plowed ground. She tosses her head and flags her white tail in fear. She tries to bolt yet seems to be held in place. Her narrow feet sink deeply into the soggy earth. Tractor work and last night's heavy rain have turned her familiar field into a quagmire. She is something of a migrant herself, having come down from high ridges of deep hemlock cover, to which she withdrew at the advent of hunting season and the onset of snow. I rarely see deer tracks around these wetlands during winter, but I find fresh footprints every day from spring to autumn. The doe advances in slow motion, fluid and graceful even as her footing works against her. Wild-eyed, she passes in front of me, heading for the woods. How wildly her heart must be beating. And yet, in her struggle to reach cover, her every movement appears effortless. Her kind is born to move with perfect grace until the final leap.

7:37 P.M. A series of sharp, clear whistles rings out. I turn to look up at an osprey stationed on the very top of the tallest white pine along the edge of the pond. Sunlight from the west slants full on his breast, lighting up its brilliant white. The osprey's illumined breast is as sharp an accent in the landscape as are his piercing calls. He has stayed at the pond longer than I thought he might, but will soon be on his way. In the more distant sky, a softer white goes peach and rose, as cloud remnants of the day's earlier storms pass on to the east. The clouds in their endless passing make their own migrations. I watch a great white anvil cloud, shaded with lavender, ride out of the west and make a slow, stately passage, low on the northern horizon. Its billowing contours are etched by the lowering sun. High above the still earth, ten miles or more in the air, the cloud's mountainous crest is wind-sheared to a flat plateau, extruding eastward. Trailing in the wake of the last of the towering thunderheads, this perfect cumulonimbus capillatus formation signals the end of rain. These clouds have the exact appearance of those that drifted across these wetlands a year ago, bringing the thunder, lightning, and torrential rain of the first thunderstorms of the season. I could think that the same clouds come back each year to bring a final awakening to spring and announce that another season, summer, is somewhere on the move.

Migrations great and small have a mystery about them, even in the face of the advanced knowledge and sophisticated field-study technology of the day. Departures and returns, the dimensions of time and distance, and the routes taken between the comings and the goings, puzzle the mind and excite the imagination. We can track messages from sea turtles and whales over oceanic depths and distances or follow migrating whooping cranes in airplanes, plotting with impressive precision times, distances, and routes taken, and still wonder at these movements of life over the planet. Individuals follow pathways taken by their contemporaries and by countless preceding generations, even by different, preceding life forms, without any communication we can perceive having passed among them, any sign we can read having been left along the way. We are able to track, but in the end we cannot follow. It is enough to travel along with these movements, to keep appointments with those who leave and return. I am well enough aware of turnings I cannot follow. I rejoice in the meetings along moments in time.

Pond in the Making

May 19, midday. I follow a stream course to a series of long-abandoned beaver ponds. The dams that created these impoundments have been eroded over time by water and ice and by what Robert Frost termed "the slow, smokeless burning of decay." Deep-muck sediments collect in the lingering ruins of the beavers' work, and here wetland gardens grow. The afternoon air is scented by the leaves of wild mint I crush in traversing the bottom pilings of a dam. Spring-blue and brightly golden-eyed, uncoiling wands of forget-me-not, another plant that finds a niche on woodland beaver dams, edge the green mint clusters. Beaver dams that have fallen into desuetude become profuse botanical gardens of wetland plants not adapted to flooded ponds or the saturated muck of drained ones.

In the first beaver pond the water is shallow, a little less than two feet at the deepest, and clear. It escapes in murmuring rushes and whispering trickles over and through the ancient dam. If the beavers were still active here, the sound of this much water rushing through their dam would quickly bring them to the site with branches, root clumps, mud plaster, stones, and other implements of repair. With legendary engineering, beavers maintain a precise and constant water level, usually two to three feet deep, gauging it to lie even with the floorings of their lodges at all times, in all seasons. In doing so, they stabilize the water level over extensive wetland areas. The beavers' response to the sound of escaping water is well known to trappers, who will open a leak in a dam to draw them into a trap.

It is possible that beavers were trapped out of this pond, although it appears more likely that the natural cycle of beaver dams is being played out: after the supply of preferred food plants — aspen, willow, birch, and maple — ran out, the beavers had to move on. Duckweed is beginning the division upon division that will cover much of this pond, and the floating leaves of yellow and white water lilies expand on the surface to begin their claim on the sun-flooded water. Every shift of my wading stick sends green frog and bullfrog tadpoles darting in all directions. The muck is so soft that they sink into it a bit when they settle on the bottom. It is too shallow here for beavers, but painted turtles, finders and keepers of ponds in almost any state imaginable, stay on.

There is little standing water in the next pond upstream, which was abandoned earlier. Downed trees lie in a tall wet meadow of bluejoint reedgrass, joe-pye weed, boneset, spotted jewelweed, wool-grass, fringed sedge, and soft rush. A number of persistent trunks stand here and there, bereft of the spreading crowns of dead branches that once held great blue heron nests, but persevering as bleached pillars riddled with entrance openings of tree swallows, woodpeckers, and other cavity nesters. The dam is almost entirely breached, and the stream run that had become lost in the broadening depths of the pond is once more cutting its way through the sediments of this gradually draining beaver basin. After the beavers abandoned this dead-tree swamp, the dam eroded in stages, and its impoundment became first deep marsh, then shallower marsh and shrub swamp. The extensive backwaters converted to wet meadow as the level of standing water steadily dropped. Over time, as the final impediments to stream flow give way, drained wet meadow will convert to upland old-field, forest will replace old-field, and a redefined woodland-bordered brook will run where acres of ponded water once stood. And then one day a two-year-old beaver, who voluntarily left or was forcefully driven from his parents' lodge and pond, will journey up the brook. His bright eyes will judge the reestablished food supplies and the topographical setting to be right, and he will begin cutting saplings and dragging them to the streaming water, setting them in place and packing them with mud. The cycle will begin again. Impounded trees will drown, and great blue herons will come back to establish a rookery. A fringing of shoreline marsh will arise anew; water lilies, pondweeds, and duckweeds will spread great beds of floating leaves over the surface of the reclaimed pond as aquatic plants seed in or sprout from long-dormant seeds. Ducks will swim and turtles bask where white-pine forest had stood for a time.

Newly constructed beaver dams are generally ten to thirty-five feet long, depending on the terrain. As a colony expands, it builds and maintains multiple dams, converting a free-flowing stream reach into a staircaselike descent of ponds. These impoundments, and their associated beaver channels, canals, and backwaters, maintain extensive acreages of shallow, productive, species-rich marsh, shrub swamp, swamp, and peatland habitat. In a low-gradient, nearly level landscape, beaver colonies may occupy a drainage for centuries and build a dam a mile and a quarter long. Core samplings beneath historic beaver-pond sites often reveal that the cycle of colonization, abandonment, and recolonization has been repeated many times. Beavers influence virtually every small river and stream within the tremendous territory the species occupies. Other than humankind, no animal plays a greater role in determining the fate of wetlands than the beaver.

I return to my car, drive higher into the hills, and walk into the woods, looking for the beaver brook four miles above the abandoned dams. Entering a flooded meadow, I stand in water up to my thighs on a submarine shelf that not long ago was the bank of a stream. The water level is out of sync with its resident plants. Spring flood levels have fallen away; royal ferns ought not to be submerged at this point in the season. I am ever watchful of water lines in relation to vegetation. If the lines are above the seasonal high-water marks (indicated by such signs as the crowns of fern and sedge mounds and water stains on woody plants) or if upland plants have been inundated, I surmise that the area has been flooded or, if there has not been sufficient rain for a flood, that beavers have built a dam. These signs are not cause for alarm. But if water has drained away or dropped disproportionately low for the season, it is likely that people have done some ditching and draining or, more commonly, have torn out a beaver dam. The natural disintegration of a beaver dam is a gradual process that usually allows time for its ecological community to adjust.

Here the water is rising, and it won't be receding. I can tell that I am present at the making of a pond: beavers must be putting in a dam downstream. The process here will be the reverse of that taking place in the abandoned ponds downstream. Plants will be drowned out, and animals dependent on the flow and depth of the free-running brook will have to relocate up or downstream. Once the beavers get the water level even with the floor of their lodge, animals and plants will redistribute themselves at their favored depths and flow rates throughout the resultant wetlands. For now, sensitive fern is under water, and black-nosed dace dart where damselflies flitted among streamside sprays of woodland grass last fall. Before long, wild brook trout will move in. Beavers are often blamed for destroying trout habitat, yet they are in fact great enhancers and extenders of trout waters if one views the beaver-dam cycle at the watershed level. Brook trout prosper during the early years of a beaver pond, typically growing much larger and reproducing more successfully than they can in undammed wooded streams. They are able to breed in spring-fed beaver ponds. Deep impoundments provide refuges for trout during summer's low, warm waters and winter's floods and ice scour. Some older ponds do become too silted in and warm for brook trout. But the constant renewal of meadow ponds and wooded-stream impoundments and the seasonal maintenance of water levels are of enormous benefit to wild brook trout, as they are to a host of plants and animals.

The beavers are making great use of alders here. Many have been cut away. Often they build with the same shrubs and trees that they eat, but they certainly do not restrict themselves to aspens, willows, alders, and red maples. I have seen them girdle enormous upland red oaks and beech and fell and drag away everything from staghorn sumac to white pine. One of the architects of this new pond glides out to eye me himself. All of his plans, his architectural renderings and maps, his hydrological calculations, are in his head. He floats, looks at me for a time, then glides away without the customary warning slap of his broad tail. Of all the wetland startlings I undergo, the night-shattering explosion of an unseen beaver's tail-slap in silent, pitch-black waterways is one of the most attention-getting. I wonder if he will be allowed to keep his pond. There are danger signs: a paved road is not far away (though well enough above the evident high-water mark), and the lower margins of a nearby hayfield may be within reach of rising water. Concern about the flooding of either road or field, whether real or imagined, is enough for execution orders to be drawn up and dam-removal permits to be signed. Not everybody loves nature's engineer. As the human species continues to breed itself into every corner, there is little room for the likes of the beaver.

Beaver
(*Castor canadensis*)

A sudden, surging wake in the water tells me that a beaver has caught sight of me and gone down, though still swimming in my direction. Large and umber, with tawny tinges, the beaver churns by me, his broad tail and powerful webbed hind feet powering him through the water with little outward display of effort. His mouth is full of mud and fern roots, and he trails a long, smokelike brown plume downstream. Across the water, another beaver arranges a leafy cutting of red maple atop a newly plastered lodge. As far as the beavers are concerned, their dam is here to stay, and there is a new pond in the world.

Raccoon and Painted Turtle

June 22, 5:17 P.M. Midsummer's Eve. Scanning for nesting turtles, I make out a tawny mammal crouched low to the ground, so absorbed in what he is doing that he has not detected my approach along the bracken border. As he shifts position, I instantaneously recognize that he is a raccoon and that he has a painted turtle in his paws. Turtle-nesting continues at its height. It is nearly solstice, the longest day of the year; I rarely encounter raccoons out in the open with so much light left in the day. My first thought is that this may be a rabid animal, as rabies is taking a heavy toll on raccoons this year. But he is full-bodied and full-furred and appears to be in excellent health. He has settled on his haunches, bearlike, and is rapidly turning the turtle in his paws, gnawing alternately at the fore and hind edges of her shell. He turns the turtle, undoubtedly a female out to nest, around and around, feverishly grinding away. I hear teeth working on bone. At frequent intervals he holds her with one paw and his teeth, bows his head, and furiously rubs his free paw over his ears and black-masked face. The black flies are murderous, and the raccoon is as heavily besieged as I am. I check my immediate reaction, which is to rush at the predator. I am here as an observer. In all the years that I have been following nesting turtles, I have heard accounts of predation on them but have only once or twice found evidence of it and have never witnessed it in my own study areas. Scenarios recounted by colleagues who have noted predation with some frequency typically depict headless females or empty carapaces found later in the season, commonly in woods not far from open nesting grounds, usually only one or two, but sometimes a dozen or more.

The turtle holds tight within her shell. I can sense her pulling in as deeply as possible at the corner being assaulted by grinding teeth. The raccoon then demonstrates his unique predatory advantage, and the gravest threat to the turtle. He holds her with one paw, seeming to balance her on his lap, while deftly digging at the fore edge of her shell, thrusting and clawing with his handlike paw into the narrow opening between her carapace and plastron, seeking to pull out one of her forelegs or her head. Were this a fox or any other mammalian predator with cursorial feet adapted to a life of running, the contest would be limited to bone against teeth; but the specialized, manipulative forefoot of the raccoon adds another dimension to a struggle with a long evolutionary history. The turtle's fortress, and her resolute maneuverings within it to keep limbs and, above all, head, from tooth and claw, frustrate the raccoon's relentless efforts. It must take great strength on the turtle's part to keep a leg from being pulled out of her shell.

After seven minutes of furious gnawing, thrusting, and pulling, a telling crunch sounds loudly in late afternoon stillness, and all four legs of the painted turtle dangle from her shell. The raccoon has worked her head from the bony recess of her shell and bitten through her skull. At the penetrating sound of the killing bite, I take an involuntary half-step forward. The raccoon sees me at once. Unwilling to relinquish his hard-won meal, he sets off toward the woods, the turtle in his jaws, her lifeless legs flailing with his running gait.

I see that even if I had intervened earlier, I would not have been able to spare the turtle. The raccoon would have taken her with him to continue his work under cover, perhaps high in a tree. Despite the difficulties of the predatory work I witnessed, it seems that raccoons can prey on nesting females at will. Turtles, with their better than 220-million-year history, may seem like outmoded reptilian relics in a world dominated by warm-blooded, fast-paced mammals. But coevolution is at work. The original, exceptionally successful turtle design has doubtless been adjusted over the time that raccoons and other contemporary predators have evolved. All of these things are still being worked on out here: the form and function of the raccoon's dextrous forefoot, the design of the opening between the turtle's carapace and plastron, the mode of withdrawal of neck and head into the shell, adaptive points and counterpoints of which we have scant knowledge.

The floodplain

6 THE FLOODPLAIN

Red trees followed by red trees;
    hardly aware of distance . . .
Green streams, many curves,
    then cloud-forests

— Wang Wei

Cobblebars, Sandbars, and Riverbanks

September 4, 10:32 A.M. Morning light flickers from a shallow slide of river over cobblestones and gravel as I walk a cobblebar after wading a riffle. In the bluejoint reedgrass and shrubby hedges of willow that crown the smooth-stoned bar, I come face to face with one who has recently come up out of a deeper run of the river. A wood turtle, an old male, his carapace worn as smooth as a river stone, has halted in midstep in his progress along an animal trail through the tall grass. When I pick him up, he feels like an oversized cobblestone in my hands. His carapace's faceted, geometric sculpturing has been reworked to Inuit-carving smoothness, perhaps by many seasons in a stony river, perhaps by age. It is easy to see how one living along a stream reach floored with sand, gravel, and cobblestone could have a smooth-worn plastron, but I am not sure how the top shell of an old male like this would come to resemble sea glass. Wet green algae is caught in the large salmon-and-black scales on his broad, powerful forelegs. Probably he has been foraging in the thick beds of filamentous algae in a nearby backwater. How well he must know this river, probably for a mile or more above and below this cobblebar. Over the course of his life he may have traveled more of the river than that and even well up into some of its tributary brooks. He appears to be in the range of a half century old, though I can only guess. Strong and restless, difficult to manage as I look him over and record him in my notebook, he reassumes a freeze-frame pose the moment I set him back down. Were he closer to the edge of the water, he might make a wood-turtle run for it. But under the circumstances, he will keep statue-still until I am out of sight, then bolt for the river, lie low for a time, then resume his morning.

I move on up the cobblebar, among the bluejoint and willow stands. The distinctly shimmering, long-pointed leaves of the shining willow gleam in the morning sun. Long hedges of black willow are kept to a brushy shrub stage on this site by the harsh annual prunings of ice scour. Black willows, in shrub or tree habit, are elegant and often dramatic accents along the banks of streams and rivers. Especially well adapted to life on the edge of a stream, they readily put forth new roots and branches following floods, establishing belts that help stabilize streambanks. There is a third species here, possibly sandbar willow, but I can't be positive; it is difficult to identify some willows precisely. The leaves of these sallows, willow sprouts that have risen from river-sheared roots, are a favored food of the wood turtle. The three willows, one grass, and silky dogwood are the entire botany of this cobblebar. Few plant species are capable of taking hold on such a flood-swept mounding of stones.

There is little in the shallow water of this September morning to suggest the great depth and wild force of the swirling whitewater currents that rage down this river at other times of year. But if I look up to the high crest of the undercut bank on the opposite side, four or five feet above my head, then raise my eyes another three to four feet to the massive red maples holding the bank against the river's cutting curl, I see gouged trunk wounds, deep bark scars, and shattered wood, testimony to the crushing, cutting impacts of blocks of ice swept along on the forceful floods of winter's fitful transition to spring. It looks as though the wing of a snowplow had bashed a line of roadside trees. Such evidence speaks of the extremes to which the wood turtle, bluejoint grass, and willows must be adapted in order to inhabit the river. The open channel itself, shallow and almost completely devoid of cover at low water, all but impossibly swift and scoured at flood, is home to a comparatively small percentage of the river's life, and that for generally short periods. Plants and animals proliferate in edge-water and backwater niches along the river's channel and throughout the riparian corridor.

Typically dense and diverse, with its floodplain forests, back swamps, pools, ridges, and swales, riparian habitat is broadly defined as the wetland zone lying between the water's edge and the beginning of uplands.

I wade another streaming riffle and walk the cobbled edge of the water's present margin. Strong currents continually reshape the river's banks and its bed and associated sand- and cobblebars, ever rearranging the rock collection the river keeps, except for its most steadfast boulders. Moving water sifts and sorts and shifts the components of its mineral bed by size and weight, working with a range of weights and measures. Cobbles are rock fragments on the order of ten to three inches in diameter, typically smoothed by the river's flow, polished by its washings of sand and gravel. Gravel ranges in size from three inches to eight-tenths of an inch in diameter; smaller rock fragments are considered sand. On down the scale from the smallest diameter of sand, which is marked at a near-immeasurable seventy-four thousandths of a millimeter, is mud. Smaller yet, clay particles are in the range of a thousandth of a millimeter in diameter. Once disturbed, these particles settle very slowly, about one foot per year in still water. Suspended particles known as soil colloids are even more minute and may take more than fifty years to sink one foot in completely still water. Up the scale from cobble, rock fragments from ten to twenty-four inches in diameter are considered stones; anything larger is called a boulder. In varied sortings, jumbles, and deposits, the river holds all of these classes, from clay to boulders. In a matter of several strides along this reach I experience footings that run the gamut from jarrings on unyielding, if sometimes slippery, boulders to midshin sinkings in muck.

Among wet cobblestones and washings of sand and gravel at the water's edge I find mats of creeping spearwort, diminutive green threadings with flowers that, although barely a quarter of an inch in diameter, are distinctively showy. They are the brightest yellow, highlighted with the same eye-catching sharp white gleam as their relatives the buttercups of meadows and fields. Stems a fraction of an inch in diameter creep and arch over cobble and gravel, rooting in wet sand spaces. The fine leaves are barely twice as thick as the stems. This is a plant adapted to living on the edge, on wet and stony shores between the turfy, vegetated bank (where it could never gain a footing and compete with ranker growth) and the retreating water line. A living, linear script, spearwort takes its place in the time of low water. This plant is minute by nature, but not far above it, in gravel deposits in the cobble, is a botanical garden of little wetland plants dwarfed not by evolution and adaptation but by environment: miniaturized specimen plants of blue vervain, nodding bur-marigold, marsh skullcap, cardinal flower, lance-leaved goldenrod, joe-pye weed, and boneset. All are flowering at heights from a few inches to a foot, far shorter than their normal habit. I have been dwarfed by many of these same plants in rich wet meadows. Blue vervain flowers at seven inches here, but not far downriver, on a sediment-enriched floodplain banking, its indigo spires reach heights of seven feet. These plants reflect the river's giving and its taking away. Here, enriching detritus is washed away; where the tall plants grow, nutrient-laden deposits are laid down, flood after flood.

I move on to a peninsular sandbar, another of the restless river's shapings of its mineral bed. Here, too, the crowning vegetation is kept to bonsai status by unforgiving conditions. Reed canary grass, the plant that towers over my head in the Reedgrass Pool and other richer settings, is barely knee-high. Wool-grass, a sedge that commonly grows to four feet in marsh substrates, is not quite a foot and a half high. Only a few of these sedge clumps have managed to flower. Among tufts of canary grass and wool-grass are four-to-six-inch blunt spikerushes, low cudweed, and strawcolor flat-sedges that typically grow to a foot or two. I begin to feel like Gulliver and tread as lightly as I can among the tiny plants.

Careful treading is advised: I come upon a wood turtle, its shell little more than an inch long, appropriately scaled to this Lilliputian setting only because he is a hatchling. By contrast, the old male I found upriver would seem like a Galápagos tortoise on this sandbar. Still possessed of his egg tooth, this turtle is not long out of the nest, and perhaps not far from it, though even newly hatched wood turtles can be great wanderers. As I reach for my notebook and pen (by touch and feel, in their familiar places in my swamp vest, for my eyes are always scanning), I catch sight of a second hatchling in shallows along the backwater side of the small peninsula. This day, this time of year, and this habitat are just right for hatchling wood turtles; I anticipate encountering one at every turn. Yet I could search for years under these same conditions without seeing

Studies of a hatchling snapping turtle
(*Chelydra s. serpentina*)

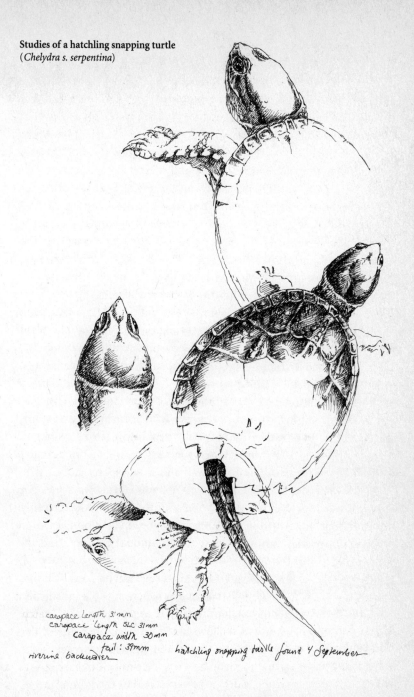

carapace length 31mm
carapace length SLC 31mm
carapace width 30mm
tail: 39mm
riverine backwater

hatchling snapping turtle found 4 September

one. Finding these two confirms my theory that wood turtles nest somewhere along this reach of the river. They could well be siblings, though the second one proves noticeably smaller upon close inspection and features the salmon-pink plastron typical of hatchlings, whereas the first had a dark umbery bottom shell.

Turning back upriver, I search the shallows that border a long, broad pool some thirty-five yards across. Where a lazy eddy forms at the constricted tail of the pool, a narrow band of the river turns back upon itself to form a stream within a stream, drifting slowly against the current until it becomes caught in the riffle at the head of the pool and is redirected back downstream. The shoreward shallows through which the eddy circles harbor beds of deep green algae. One of the small, bubbly eruptions in the algae mats catches my eye, and I make out the head of a hatchling snapping turtle. Moving closer, I see that he still carries an egg tooth on the pointed snout of his tiny black head. This is how the turtles of the river get their starts, on pebbly shores and sandbars with scatterings of aquatic plants and in backwaters and the margins of quiet shallow pools that for now hold a soup of algae and countless crustaceans, insect larvae, and invisible clouds of phytoplankton and zooplankton.

This seems a perfect world for nascent turtles and for blue vervain, bur-marigold, cardinal flowers, and sweeps of algae. But it is such a temporary world. Surging whitewater currents with battering ice and scouring gravel will become the order of things here before spring eventually erupts on the far side of winter. Much will be swept away or rearranged, but millions of seeds will lodge in sand and gravel spaces and in gripping backwater muck, and resilient woody stems and stalwart bankside root-holds will survive the raging flood and its scourings. Remarkably, overwintering wood turtles, from hatchlings on up, will find places in the river where they can hold on through winter's icy water and the early-spring fury of the flood.

Musk turtles, green frogs, bullfrogs and their tadpoles, brook trout, black-nosed dace, fallfish; the larvae of crayfish, caddis flies, stoneflies, dragonflies, and damselflies — many forms of aquatic life will find their places as floating drifts and sunken packs of blazing autumn leaves burn out in the river. With the intensifying cold of winter's approach, some creatures will migrate to deeper pools in the channel; others will take refuge in twistings of tree roots or in undercut banks and mammal burrows. Still others will descend into spaces among stones or tunnel into sand and gravel. Many painted turtles, snapping turtles, and frogs will leave the volatile channel to hibernate in outlying pools. All will reappear with the budbreak of the willows, the warming and quieting of the river and its edge-water wetlands, and the return of the sun to its high, warm-season rounds.

I wade back across the riffle to the west bank, the clear water sparkling over cobble washing away the sand, silt, and muck that have sifted into my sneakers and plastered my pant legs and socks. The water has begun to cool. It is 58 degrees, nearly too chill for uninsulated wading, but tolerable enough on a day with strong, full sun and an air temperature in the low eighties. As the season progresses, and the water becomes colder and deeper, I will go from sneakers to hip boots and finally to neoprene chest waders, reversing this sequence in the spring.

Once across the riffle, I begin to acquire a new floodplain coating as I walk wet and dry sand, leaf and littler layers on a great bar that has built up on the inside of a bend in the river. Flowing water runs swiftly around the outside of a bend, cutting away at banks and scouring out beds; along the inside, where sediments build up, forming jutting mounds called point bars, it is slower. In time a point bar will rise high enough for plants to colonize it, stabilizing it against erosion, and eventually the bar will be added to the floodplain. Rivers and streams are ever cutting down the earth along the outsides of bends, building it up along the insides.

I remember a late-winter visit to this bend, when the flood surge of snowmelt and late-winter rain was strengthening and ice was beginning to break up. The river was running a wild race, loud with roaring water, grinding and crashing ice, grating cobble, and the sound of vegetation being torn away. It seemed that the unruly water and ice were conspiring against the earth. The flood surge was reclaiming ice floes that had set hard and fast into vegetation in the wake of bank overflows throughout the winter and been left suspended in the air as the water dropped away. These heavy sheets of ice tilted downslope into the channel, where the insistent, raging river pulled at them, demanding that ice follow water in its rush to the sea. The ice, in turn, would not relinquish its hold on earth and plants, ripping grasses and willows from the riverbank. In places, the earth itself was being peeled away, as though the bank were being skinned. The scouring and the cooler microclimate maintained by the late-melting ice pack favor the establishment of plants that are characteristic of this bend in the river: sweet gale, willows, silky dogwood, and spikerushes along its edge; little bluestem and deertongue grasses, meadowsweet, sweetfern, beaked and American hazelnut, virgin's-bower, flat-topped white aster, and woodland sunflower upslope to drier ground.

The river is a fluid landscape element, and it creates a fluid environment. In the river's channel and along its riparian corridor, landforms are shifted and reshaped over and over by the workings of water. Plants are obliged to shift with the rearrangements of silt and mud, sand, gravel, and stone. Plant species change places and at times replace one another along the river corridor; and the abundant and richly varied animal life supported by a healthy river moves with them. Shifts in structure and vegetation change the locations where black bear, moose, and white-tailed deer feed, neotropical migrant birds and woodcocks nest, wood turtles hibernate, brook trout spawn; where ebony jewelwings, stoneflies, caddis, and mayflies complete metamorphosis, and freshwater mussels burrow.

The point bar I ascend is heavily grown in now, but when I came here at the end of May I saw wood turtle trails meandering over its dunelike moundings of fine white sand, and found foot scrapings suggesting the presence of nest-seeking females. At that point in the season, this sandy promontory had areas open and extensive enough to provide the hours of sunlight requisite for the incubation of turtle eggs, but once the water dropped deeper into the channel, the sandy bar burst forth with luxuriant growth. Today I find a few open places but no sign of turtle-hatching. Clearings kept by washouts or heavy deposits of pure sand are too limited, too closely circummured by rank, shading growth to allow incubation. I will have to look elsewhere for the nest sites of the hatchlings I saw upriver.

Leaving the point bar, I wade another riffle back across the river, walk and wade a line of cobblebars, then cross a broad, shallow pool in which the water barely moves to another buildup of sand and stone. The movement of the water is so tranquil, so gradual here that a film of tannin-colored sediments has settled on the sandy river bottom. I leave a long, smokelike cloud of disturbed sediments behind me. These eventually settle out to the sides of the footsteps that stirred them up, leaving a path of cleared sand to mark my crossing. Even in drought times I am obliged to cross the river many times, because of deep troughs and pools along outer bends. As I head for another zone of mound-building, I cross the path of a wader who has forded the river before me: a clear line of great blue heron tracks is registered in the sediment layer. It is indicative of the range of the river's moods that such a delicate tracery can persist for days in a channel where at other times great sandbars have been pushed around and trees torn loose from their moorings.

The low sand and cobblebar along which the heron stalked has been stabilized by an entrenchment of silky dogwood, one of the very few plants that can establish itself in the active channel of a river. This wetland shrub, which is extremely important to wood turtles along the banks of brooks, is critical to them in riverine habitats, commonly providing the only vegetative cover for hundreds of yards. Many silky dogwood barrier islands off steeper riverbanks lie under water through the winter. I am certain these provide wood turtles with hibernation holdfasts and protective cover from otters. As water levels drop in spring, it is in these near-impenetrable tangles that I frequently find the first basking wood turtles. Over the course of the seasons, these barrier islands provide food and shelter for bullfrogs and their tadpoles, green frogs, musk turtles, minnows; for innumerable insects, aquatic snails, and other aquatic invertebrates; and for butterflies, birds, and mammals of the floodplains and bordering uplands.

I struggle along the dogwood-crowded edge of this bar, another configuration of the river's unceasing shiftings of substrates. Riverine corridors have a constancy within their flux. Riffles, pools, runs, point bars, gravelly islands, and levees, which are subject to wildly varying flows and flood pulses, change places over time, but the arrangement of these elements remains much the same along the river's course. This patterning plays a major role in the ecology of flowing waters, among other things assuring that brook trout will always find riffles feeding into pools that flow on into runs, however these complexes may be transposed from one stream reach to another.

The dogwood bar tapers to an unvegetated ridge of wet sand. A great school of little fish flees the shallows as my shadow passes over them. Their silvery streaming, so much like the element in which they live, constricts in narrow canals among exposed sandbars at the river's edge, then fans out into a broad drifting cloud in the main channel, flickering with metallic flashes as individuals tilt on their sides in the sunlit amber water. Silver-scaled minnows can catch and reflect such glinting lights in the darkest waters on the darkest days. These appear to be black-nosed dace, but in the confusion of their multitude, movement, and staccato glimmerings, I cannot get a good enough look to say for sure.

Along the river margin stand abandoned pebbled nesting mounds of fallfish, rough pyramids that suggest the majestic stone buildings of ancient human civilizations. I once watched a school of fallfish, as industrious as an ant colony, constructing a mound in a slower edge water off the brisk central run of a brook in April. In what struck me as an exceptionally well-planned, well-coordinated effort, each gleaming fish was ever on the move, placing his small piece of stone on the mound and darting quickly away to pick up another in his mouth and swim back to the stonework, hovering over it until the proper place to set a new pebble had been determined. Standing out of water now, the fallfish mounds have been colonized by plant seedlings that have no future, for the islands will be destroyed by the river's deep and scouring incarnation.

Becoming a levee at the time of low water, the shrub-tangled bar and its tapering extension of sand have isolated a muck-bottomed pond of about half an acre, shingled with water lily pads and still covered with white and yellow blooms. The pond is ringed with emergent growth highlighted by a final blue-purple flowering of pickerelweed. Rather than scouring sediments away from this backwater depression, the river deposits them here. Part of the river at flood, this seasonally separated wetland now harbors perennial plants more aquatic than those of the riverbanks and cobblebars. It teems with green frogs and bullfrogs. Dragonflies and damselflies hunt like jeweled darts in the open air above the lily pads and throughout the surrounding spear-leaved forests of rushes and sedges. Painted and snapping turtles bask and prowl. This is a favorite fishing and frogging place for great blue and green herons, who daily wing up and down the river, making their rounds of such niches, which are few and far between. The fact that such top-of-the-food-chain predators as herons and snapping turtles come to forage in this wetland attest to its abundance and diversity of plant and animal species, and to its significant role in the riverine ecosystem.

I pick a passage around the higher, sandier margin of the pool, dodging muck and skirting the thick swales of rice cut-grass, which can tear clothing and cut skin. I walk through tufts and sweeps of spikerush, soft rush, and sedges, laced with delicate and highly poisonous bulbet-bearing water-hemlock and spotted water-hemlock. Mingled with these toxic plants is the deceptively similar water parsnip, a plant whose roots can be boiled and eaten, if one chooses carefully. In my boyhood I ate the tubers of broad-leaf arrowhead, known as duck potatoes, boiling them on swampside twig fires in autumn, and in spring I boiled up streamside marsh marigold leaves. Other than that, I have not looked to the wetlands for my food. Scattered arrowheads grow here, but I leave their potatoes for the ducks. Among them are beds of blue flag, setting heavy seeds in heavy pods. Fine-flowered clusters of mild water pepper make intense pink hazes among the wetland greens. The closely related swamp smartweed grows sturdily erect on the higher wet bank and sits as an aquatic, floating-leaved plant in the marshy shallows. Both forms have large, showy heads, with clubs of tightly packed, tiny pink flowers and buds. A few pale yellow spires of the last swamp candles of the season glow in grass and sedge, candles about to be put out by the turning of the year. I am lulled by the warmth of the day, the full-blown profusion of wild wetland growth, and the generous late-season flowerings. But I mark the date in my notebook and see that a cardinal flower is down to the last crimson bloom and bud on its tall stalk of faded flowers. Any night now, one hard frost, riding a river of cold air down this riverine corridor, will extinguish all these colors, all these living lights.

Ascending to the crest of the riverbank, where tree roots help solidify the damp floodplain soil, I enter yet another botanical realm. Throughout my floodplain excursions, I feel I am walking in the house of plants. House and garden are all the same here. The structure of this section of the banking is one of the most architectonic I encounter, with screens and weavings of herbaceous stems, leaves, and vines, ropes and cables of woody vines, tremendous walls of shrub tangles, and beams and roofs of towering silver maple trees. From a narrow strip of open bank just outside the walls of this city of plants, I can look back down on the slow slide of the river, with its brushy hedges of sallows and silky dogwood, its aquatic bed and accompanying backwater marsh and shrub swamp, open and variously vegetated niches that are habitat islands, wetlands within the river. Taken together with the deepwater channel and the pool sections, such wetlands are considered riverine habitat. In leaving the river channel (which often involves a steep climb), I have moved from riverine to riparian habitat, which extends from the edge of a river or stream channel to the margins of its flanking uplands.

Because they follow the routes of waterways, riparian corridors are typically linear in form. They are highly variable in width, composed of elements as diverse as floodplain swamps, wetland forests half a mile wide, broad or narrow bands of shrub swamp, borders of emergent marsh, and wet meadows that may be only a yard wide or may cover many acres. Along an abrupt upland rise or at the base of a river-hugging valley wall, riparian wetlands may consist of a single file of willows, eastern cottonwoods, or red maples. Although riparian habitats are commonly defined as lying between the water's edge and the beginning of the uplands, a more ecologically comprehensive definition would embrace all surrounding habitats that influence a river, stream, or wetland. Under this view, a forested upland ridge set back from wetland borders but whose nutrient-bearing leaf-fall reaches the water would be considered part of the riparian habitat.

I continue along a grassy bank edge, skirting the outer wall of vegetation, an extended thicket of silky dogwood all bound up in river bank grape. There is enough light along the edge of the river for all these floodplain layerings; the silky dogwood flourishes despite being all but laminated by broad grape leaves. Vines are entwined among vines, as wild mock-cucumber trails over the grape and dogwood and threads its way into a stand of American elderberry. Virgin's-bower weaves through tall deertongue grass and rough-stemmed goldenrod and tangles over the leafy surface of the grapevine-draped thickets. Virginia creeper ascends some thirty feet into a long-dead American elm on the bank, transforming a bleached, skeletal tree into a tower of leaves showing the first crimson flickerings of the autumn blaze they will become. The flood surge annually clears out great reaches of riverbank, opening it up for the development of vine communities that are not able to flourish in shaded upland forests. Poison ivy is common along floodplain riverbanks, where it spreads as a winding, upreaching ground cover and ascends high into massive sycamores and silver maples. Herbaceous vines such as groundnut, hog peanut, bedstraw, arrow-leaved tearthumb, and climbing false buckwheat wind throughout the sedgy, grassy swales of shadier floodplain forests.

Following a deer passage, I bow and enter the vine-covered shrub thicket. Its heavily shaded interior is open enough that I can walk upright beneath domes of branches, vines, and leaves along a sand levee that is barren of ground cover, then move into nearby silted swales choked with false nettle, wood nettle, clearweed, and spotted touch-me-not. These annuals, like the vines, are adapted to flooding and silting. Thriving in disturbed wet areas, they are quick to fill soils kept bare of more permanent growth by the rigors of the river's flood pulse. More stable ridges and higher terraces, in contrast, support perennial wildflowers like Carolina spring beauty, trout lily, wood anemone, bluets, and dog violet. Keeping an eye on the plants of the ground cover, I come to the buttress rootings of an impressive American elm, and look up to see a tree at least eighteen inches in diameter at breast height, ascending high above the shrub layer to take its place in the high canopy of red and silver maples. This tree appears vigorous and well past the point at which Dutch elm disease almost always kills the trees back to sprout clumps, which may linger for years before finally dying off. Maybe a resistant elm has risen here, one not destined to become another of the dead giants whose bone white trunks and branches, some still standing, many fallen, have been a feature of the floodplain for decades. Perhaps in time this riparian species, which now lives on primarily as sprout-clump saplings and seedlings of struggling diebacks, will reclaim its former arching majesty in the floodplain forest.

Downriver

2:37 P.M. Downriver with the afternoon, I walk a high bank where a broad meander cuts against upland forest. Rivers and streams that cut through mountainous or hilly terrain are often bordered for considerable extents by elevations not subject to flooding and high enough above the water table that they do not support wetlands. In these settings the riparian zone is composed of upland habitats, typically high banks of well-drained woods. The plants around me now are upland plants. Eastern hemlock, a tree that takes to well-drained soils as well as moist ones and even grows on sphagnaceous mounds in forested wetlands, here, in its dry-footed mode, crowds sections of the high riverbank as well as the steep slope above it. Little is able to grow in the heavy shade of these trees, but I see one carpet of shinleaf, shimmering in the dim, green-black light of the shadowing hemlocks. In openings among the conifers are stands of American beech, with parasitic beechdrops thrusting up among the smooth-barked, snakelike roots. Sugar maples and red, white, and scarlet oaks mingle with white pines; shrubby sprays of witch hazel, low late blueberry, and black huckleberry provide intermittent understory; and there is a scattered ground cover of spotted wintergreen, trailing arbutus, and tree clubmoss. Sweeps of white wood aster flower in sun-washed openings along the lip of the dry riverbank. My sodden sneakers seem out of place, making squishing sounds as they rustle through the dry leaves that carpet this upland forest. Unfortunately, habitat of this nature that borders on streams, rivers, larger ponds, and lakes is exempt from wetland regulations. The land is commonly cleared to the water's edge for residential or commercial development, providing expansive views and golf-course lawns (if not actual golf courses), or is manicured for parks or campgrounds.

The high, forested bank descends to a broad, low area, where I again walk layerings of fine sand and leaf pack, silty alluvial soil, the familiar footing of the floodplain. Deep flooding occurs throughout this bottomland at least once a year. A line of immense and rigorously rooted silver maples holds the riverbank. Their massive roots in the bank and among themselves would seem to make them unassailable, but one of them has fallen across the river's thirty-five-foot-wide channel, its crown embracing the ranks of a companion row of silver maples on the opposite shore. The tree has been toppled but has not been ripped from its moorings. It lives on, recumbent, heavily in leaf. Silver maple is so well adapted to the erosive life of a riverbank that it can grow horizontally. Even when these massive trees are undermined along runs too broad to allow them to reach support on the other side, their extraordinary root-holds can suspend their great mass well out over the water, nearly parallel with, and at times touching, its surface. Such resolute last-stand entrenchments may hold for decades, with branches along their inclined trunks rising vertically, attaining the stature of mature trees. This defiance of gravity is remarkable enough in thin air, but these trees can hold on even in the face of the powerful sweep of flood surges deep enough to engulf them. Eventually, living or dead, they do let go or are torn loose, to become one with the river, massive submarine deadfalls branching beneath as well as above the water, providing structures and refuges as critical to life in riverine habitats as standing, leaning, and fallen trees are in upland forests.

My continuing descent brings me to a sandy, river-bordering terrace, and I find myself back in dense thickets. I can walk open forest floor along a stream or river on comfortably high and dry ground, be eased by imperceptible degrees down into relatively open forested wetland glades of fern and grass, and then, before I am fully conscious of it, be directed by the meandering water's edge into an all but impassable maze of intergrown branches wound with vines. No doubt it is places like this that have given rise to the word "trackless." Not long ago I walked upright, with long strides, among widespread pines and oak. Now I inch forward. The insistent vegetation compels me to move in a crouch, to use my hands and arms as much as my feet and legs to make forward progress. The vines and branches all but take me by the head and shoulders and drive me to the ground.

Bends in a river, meanderings in a brook, intricate windings and doublings back: waterways have a way of measuring the earth and so possess a geometry, but one that has little to do with straight lines or the shortest distance between two points. It appears to be some living form of mathematics, as changeable, even willful, as it is reckonable, involving measuring, depths, distances, flow rates, degrees of heat and cold; perhaps it is an organic geometry whose forms resist the pure triangle, circle, and square. Water has its own way of mapping the earth, without reference to fixed points. And so many living things, moving on belly, feet, or wings, or traveling as seeds or broken bits of stem capable of rooting, follow its endless, shifting traceries over the time and space of the earth.

On hands and knees I tunnel toward light, coming to a place where I can stand up in a clearing along the river's edge. It is drifted with fine

Wild-rye (*Elymus riparius*)

white sand and filled with waist- to shoulder-high sedges, grasses, and goldenrod, many wound with virgin's-bower. This wild clematis, approaching its feathery, silver-swirled, "old-man's-beard" seeding stage, is also entwined among outreaching thickets of riverbank alders and tall meadow rue, which still bears a few flowers on eight-foot stalks. I stand shoulder to shoulder with one of the more distinctive plant forms of floodplain clearings, riverbank wild-rye. The stiff, upright bristles of this tuft-forming grass have already yellowed with the season. Before the land clearing that followed European settlement, many native inland grasses were limited in the Northeast to clearings created by blowdowns, fires, and floods. Species adapted to wetlands, like this wild-rye, find niches in openings provided by marshes, swamps, stream- and riverbanks, and old beaver dams. The light that rivers bring into the forest provides growing places for plants that cannot live in unbroken shade.

The riverbank features networks of animal trails and sandy troughs cut by streaming floodwaters. These water cuts and animal paths, which often overlap, provide welcome passageways, but walking here is not without its perils. This stretch of riverbank is riddled with burrows, some rather cavernous and undoubtedly the work of the beaver, others just big enough for my foot to slip into. Many tunnels go deep and have well-concealed entrances. Having once dropped, in a jarring instant, rib cage–deep into a beavers' bank burrow among the massive roots of a silver maple, right to the watery floor of the beavers' entrance hall, I am extremely cautious in traveling such well-tunneled banks.

I discover a large, round hole in sandy sod among root gnarls at the base of a stump carved by tree-cutting beavers. Reinforcing branches, beaver-chewed, are worked into the earth and among root crevices. Other branches are scattered crisscross over what I take to be the roof of a bank burrow. The higher reach of the river here, with its extreme flood pulse and periods of swift water, is not conducive to the beavers' building a stick-and-mud dam, so they have taken up residence in a riverbank. To keep their dens above the reach of floods, beavers may build them so high in the banks that the roof is just a shallow layer of sod and roots. Should the roof collapse, the beavers are likely to repair it with branches and earth. If the river does flood their den, they abandon it until the water goes down. Beavers may also build dens in the banks of ponds deep enough to meet their needs. The tunnels they dig from these dens to the pond may be fifty feet long.

Along the populated sections of this river, where beaver dams are repeatedly destroyed and the animals themselves shot or trapped, they may take to living in the riverbanks in response to human measures to eliminate them. A species of beaver native to Europe that had been trapped to near-extinction abandoned dam building completely and instead dug lodges in riverbanks. When, after many years, legislation was enacted to protect these animals, they resumed their historic way of life almost at once, building dams and constructing lodges on their impoundments. It was as though the beavers had representatives in the halls of legislatures, who reported the good news to them. I can report no such good news to the beavers of this river. There are no assurances for any of the animals and plants that live along it. Among other things, a golf course has been proposed that would take a mile of the riverbank in a town downstream, cutting it clear to the very edge of the water. With ever-increasing economic pressures and demands for places for humans to live, work, and play in the region, critical habitat and riparian buffer zones could vanish in less than a decade along the whole length of this river, as it has along so many brooks, streams, and rivers throughout the country.

But here, for now, habitat abounds. I could pass within a couple of yards of a black bear or moose and never know it. Beavers appear to be entrenched and in charge, something I take as one of the best signs in a wetland ecosystem. These remarkable mammals are landscape architects as well as engineers; they have much to do with the clearing I have come to. The beavers influence this reach of the river nearly as much as the flood pulse does. Every few years they cut back woody growth, forestalling the development of heavily shading canopy and allowing open meadow and lightly shaded glades, small fields and swales of fern, sedge, grass, and goldenrod, stands of sweetfern and bracken, brushy hedges of meadowsweet, and thickets of blackberry and red raspberry to flourish. Clearings like this on higher banks, beyond flood reach, may have a beaver-thinned canopy of shrubs and saplings of species that spread quickly to deforested sites following some natural or human disturbance: beaked hazelnut, staghorn sumac, quaking and bigtooth aspens, black and pin cherries, gray birch and white pine. Virgin's-bower commonly winds through such riparian niches, which I have come to think of as wood turtle parks, for I find all age classes of these turtles, sometimes several at a time, frequenting them. These clearings appear to be of especial importance to hatchlings and juveniles. I could almost think that beavers manage them specifically for wood turtles, but many other animals visit and inhabit them as well. In particular, woodcocks appear as at home as wood turtles. I once came upon a heavily spotted, recently born white-tailed deer fawn, hidden on a knoll in a bed of grass and goldenrod. The fawn never so much as flicked an ear the whole time I searched about him for wood turtles.

Woodcock (*Scolopax minor*)

Beavers extend habitats of this nature to riparian sites that are out of reach of rising streams and rivers or only rarely influenced by their flood pulses. These wild coppices appear to support plant associations that are, as things go, stable. The beaver-cut knolls I have visited for eleven years along my two primary wood turtle streams have changed very little over that time in terms of species composition and vegetative structure. With their judicious upland riparian cuttings and their far more extensive workings in riverine and wetland riparian habitats, beavers can be thought of as consummate wildlife managers. The term "wildlife management," often used in the environmental polemics of the day in reference to human manipulations, is an oxymoron. We should have learned long ago to simply leave the proper natural space, to respectfully withdraw and let wildlife manage wildlife.

As I travel along the river, I hear the sweet-sad singing of goldfinches and look into the masked face of a yellowthroat, the incessant singer of spring and summer, who has taken his autumnal vow of silence. Stream and river corridors are of critical importance to migrating birds, providing refuges for resting as well as abundant forage on their long seasonal journeys. Many migratory avian species end up nesting in riparian environments. Often the only extensive, reasonably wild places remaining, these corridors offer not only the last holdouts for many plants and animals, but the final links connecting isolated niches in the fragmented modern landscape. Where they are intact throughout a watershed, they enable species movement and gene flow, helping to offset the island effect, the physical and genetic cutting off of populations and colonies

Wood turtle (*Clemmys insculpta*) in speckled alder (*Alnus rugosa*)

from one another. Such separation is already the dominating feature in a much-divided world.

However, some of the greatest pressures from people are brought to bear along streams and rivers. All too often the compromises reached to protect streamsides and riversides from full development, though they may protect water quality for human purposes, fail to provide for viable habitat margins and involve heavy concessions to access and recreation agendas. I have found "compromise" to be routinely tantamount to "sellout" in terms of preserving natural habitats.

Leaving the little wood turtle park, I have to crawl again, through silky dogwood and northern arrowwood, enmeshed in riverbank grape. The growth habit of wetland shrubs is frequently more horizontal than vertical and so low to the ground it seems that even a mink would have to slither on his belly to pass beneath them. There is barely enough clearance for a wood turtle's shell in the silky dogwood stand before me. I take up the next leg of my journey with a climb through springy weavings of prostrate and horizontal branches, hoping always that my eyes will not be caught by the whiplash of one of the innumerable in-my-face twigs, which can snap back more quickly than the blink of an eye.

The Oxbow

I slant through the maroon outermost mazes of dogwood branches, extricate myself from a final snarling of grapevines, and turn from the river for a time, walking beneath silver maples with trunks some three feet in diameter and broad, arching crowns forty to fifty feet above my head. An expanse of herbaceous vegetation luxuriates in the dim, greened light of this cathedral-like forest. The setting is as close to William Henry Hudson's Amazonian, rain-forested *Green Mansions* as I am ever likely to wander in the glaciated Northeast. I pass through a great glade of ostrich ferns whose impressive plumes rise shoulder-high, spraying from ascendant, trunklike rhizomes, then closing over my head as I cross the hollow they have colonized. I have gone from feeling like Gulliver among the knee-high plants of this morning's sunlit sandbars to feeling like one of his Lilliputian friends in this outsized forest of ferns. These deep-rooted plants may be more durable, and perhaps older, than the trees high above them. Their tropical appearance belies their northern distribution. Ostrich ferns grace forested floodplains, river bottomlands, and swamps from Labrador to the Arctic Circle in Alaska. The great, feathery plumes of their sterile fronds crumble with the first frosts, but the lyre-shaped fertile fronds persist well into the cold season. Winter's crushing water and ice and the sweeping floods at thaw flatten and clear out the engulfing fern glades and viny jungles that arise so profusely each growing season. After the floods and before new growth, this glade and much of the floodplain are an open world, flooded not with water, but with the beckoning sunlight of April and early May.

Today the glade is flooded with leafy darkness. Adumbrated by silver maples, tall ferns create shade within shadow. I no longer have the contours of the river to guide me. With few glimpses of the sky and few distinct directional shadows, I rely on my pocket compass to keep the eastern bearing that will lead me to the oxbow. It is a little less than a hundred yards away, but I have on occasion walked in circles in dense interior swampland. I remember once following what I thought was a fresh animal trail in sedge-choked alder thickets for some distance before realizing that I had doubled back on my own pathway of half an hour before. I suppose it was a fresh animal path after all, and an intriguing way to lose oneself and find oneself in a wetland.

There has been barely an inch of rainfall over the past six weeks, but this fern glade is dank. I can walk as quietly as a black bear on its damp-silted flooring. I sink in some places, but the roots and rhizomes of the ostrich ferns and the widespread root systems of the silver maples form a supportive, if springy, turf. Beyond the ferns I come to an ankle-deep trough, slickly silt-bottomed along most of its length, but with a gravelly washout that serves as a ford. A well-worn trail at each end shows this to be a major animal crossing. The trough, which links the oxbow with the river, is the last trace of what was once a segment of the river. Flooding and draining exchanges between the river and the oxbow keep this shallow remaining sluiceway from becoming completely plugged with clay or other fine deposits. Oxbows are crescent-shaped river sections left behind when floodwater, following its tendency to erode a shortcut where it can, over time cuts a straighter channel and connects with the downstream bend of the meander. The meander's entrance and exit become plugged as deposits from the new, straighter run form a levee, and a bend in the river becomes an oxbow. The river has rerouted itself a number of times and will do so again in the future. As rivers grow older they often transform narrow, V-shaped cuts in the landscape into broad, U-shaped valleys, in which they build wide floodplains of sand and silt. In their lateral meanderings through these river valleys, they alter their courses again and again, creating levees, oxbows, and scroll ponds (curvilinear cutoff channel sections that are analogous to oxbows). Although it is reclaimed by the river for a time during floods, the oxbow I approach is no longer a part of it; it is a still-water wetland that harbors an array of plants and animals that cannot live in the active channel. The shallow trough I ford was once a deep riverine channel.

Within the oxbow's arc is a moist terrain of ridges and swales tracing some of the river's migrations across its floodplain. Silver maples grow along the present channel, and red maples around the oxbow and its flanking back swamps. Beneath their high canopy grow copses of ironwood, tangled swales of grass and sedge wound with bedstraw and tearthumb, more open hollows of false nettle and jewelweed. Like the hummock-and-hollow microtopography of the Shrub Swamp and Red Maple Swamp, the high and low points of this ridge and swale topography differ by only a foot or two, but this is sufficient to create gradients of wetness along which different plants arrange themselves. Some of the snaking hollows, and the deeper pockets within them, are deep enough or in close enough contact with the water table to collect standing water for varying periods of time.

I circle a deep hollow that is plastered with black leaves and ringed with stately cinnamon ferns and the not-so-stately disintegrating remains of skunk cabbage, spent with the season. This silent, waterless bowl in the floodplain forest was brimful and raucous with wood frogs when I came here the second week of April. For weeks before, floodwaters from a foot or two to five feet deep swept through the entire riparian zone, and there was no way to distinguish river channel from oxbow, or surrounding marsh and swamp from either, other than by the winding rows of silver maples or red maples that lined their submersed banks. With the passing of the flood, water dropped back into its channels and pools and the shapes of the floodplain's individual waterholds reemerged: the river's silvered run, glimmering vernal pools, scroll ponds like ribbons of sky fallen to earth, and the deep, horseshoe-shaped oxbow, bristling with emergent shrubs yet to leaf out, tawny jumbles of standing and crushed cattails awaiting the greening of their arundinaceous beds, and cloud-reflecting open water on the verge of being covered with lily pads.

A week later, however, following three days of heavy rain, those individual identities were immersed once again in an encompassing flood. The river and its associated wetlands, from headwaters to the sea, were at full charge and immediately spilled over their banks. Surrounding uplands, many of them steep, were saturated and so contributed heavy runoff to the lowland floodplain. With so much water in the wetlands and in the upland soil, only the floodplain could contain the flood. Although its fury posed challenges for many plants and animals, the return of flood here in mid-April was a consequence of natural forces and was acted out in a natural arena, with an ecologically built-in give and take. Along many rivers and streams, flood damage to humans and wildlife is greatly exacerbated by runoff from acres of roofs and paved surfaces, and by human alteration and conversion of floodplain wetlands that disrupt their natural regimen and greatly reduce their flood-storage capacity.

Here, green frogs relocated well up the terrace of uplands that borders the floodplain. Painted turtles basked placidly on the trunk and tipped-up root mound of a tall red maple, glowingly in bud, that had been taken down by the flood. Things did not go so well for the wood frogs. Their vernal pool was lost at sea, one to three hundred yards from the floodwater shores. The frogs could take to high ground, but any egg masses they had committed to the pool were surely lost to the sweep of the flood or to predatory fish, to whom every inch of the floodplain was given for a time. Banded sunfish and redfin pickerel, small fish of the vegetation-choked backwaters, must have kept low in the emergent plants that for the time being lay deep under dangerous open water, where big fish could quickly capture little fish. Just beginning to bloom, flowers of the floodplain forest and flanking woodlands — Carolina spring beauty, trout lily, wood anemone, and bluets — had to get by for a time as water plants.

Four days later the flood had passed, and the wetlands, riparian, and riverine habitats had all found their places once again and reassumed their usual ecological forms and functions. Green frogs, ubiquitous amphibians of every water edge and puddle, followed the retreating water lines back to more customary settings. None the worse for wear, the spring beauties, trout lilies, wood anemones, and bluets went on with their flowering. I neither heard nor saw wood frogs, nor did I find any egg masses in the several floodplain vernal pools I searched. The rains that brought apparent devastation to the floodplain wood frogs benefited their upland cousins, filling their woodland pools to maximum depths and breadths. I thought of scroll ponds, many of them quite small and seasonal, in some of the most active flood regions of the river; I had found fairy shrimp in them, and I marveled that such minute, fragile crustaceans could persist in the face of such hydrologic extremes and environmental uncertainty. The flood pulse is the major force controlling plant and animal life in floodplains, the flux and force to which all riverine and riparian species must be well adapted.

Although there is evidence of this year's flood history all about me, great wracks composed of everything from tree trunks to blades of straw, tangles of drift caught in branches above my head, and silt stains high up on the trunks of the maples, it is hard to picture flood times as I walk the floodplain on this tranquil low-water September day. Approaching the oxbow, I find that the thickets of northern arrowwood crowding the margins of its inner arc have been crushed down to the ground, bent and broken. Leaves have not been stripped, nor twigs browsed, but all the berries are gone. Chipmunks and ruffed grouse eat the fruits of this wetland shrub, but this can hardly be their doing. I search the sedgy turf for a footprint, but find none, not even in the black mud at the rim of the oxbow. Still, I have the strong feeling that a black bear has foraged here. I set to work, untangling and freeing unbroken stems that spring back to full height, gratefully, it seems. Some whip back to full height immediately, straight and even, like the shafts of arrows into which they were once fashioned by Native Americans. Other stems, older, thicker, and twisted, rise more slowly to their place in the middle canopy.

Northern arrowwood grows, black bears feed, and I walk in a wetland garden created by a meandering river, on earth restructured and ruled by water. The river will change its mind, or have its mind changed, time and again by flood years, drought years, giant fallen trees and the water-deflecting debris dams they create, hard winters with flood and scour, massive ice dams, and the slow, steady cutting of clay and stone by water and washes of sand. Every shift in the river is a change in the floodplain, an expression of the ongoing dynamic between water and earth, a continual balancing between structure being built up and structure taken away.

With shatterings of water and plaintive calls, wood ducks explode from a far corner of the oxbow as I step from alders bordering the arrowwood thicket and wade into the oxbow's emergent buttonbush. I am announced far and near: at my second step into the water, green frogs take off screaming in all directions, skipping over the surface as though someone were skimming stones. Owing to its deep muck, the oxbow is on the whole unwadeable, but by carefully bracing my feet at the snaking basal stems of the buttonbush, and with the help of a wading stick, I can make some progress out into the water. This is one of those places that is better for watching from than for wading in. The buttonbush is surrounded by beds of bur reed, pickerelweed, and three-way sedge, scatterings of tussock sedge, and isolated stands of arrow arum and wool-grass. Among these are aquatic-bed pools and canals, with white and yellow water lilies, watershield, and common bladderwort. There are expanses of open water in the middle of the oxbow. This bend in the river has undergone an ecological transformation since the river left it behind.

As I stand still, the frogs quiet down, and in time painted turtles appear, browsing at the surface, grazing in the trailings of fountain moss on the underwater buttonbush stems. One, close by me, surges from the surface over and again, thrusting from the water with forelegs flailing as though trying to swim in the air. He bites at a pickerelweed's flower head and holds on, then drops back into water. He may be catching insects from the emergent plants, as I have seen these turtles do, sometimes half a dozen of them at a time, when there is a hatch or some other concentration of insects among marsh plants. While he is under water, I alter my position for a better look. He bursts forth again and latches onto a bowing flower head. This time I see that he has set his sharp jaws on a ripening seed. Cutting and twisting, he tears loose the seed and drops back into the water to eat it.

A water snake winds by. Green frogs again scream off in all directions. I continue to wait and watch, hoping for a spotted turtle to appear, though I have never seen one here. The flood pulse evidently excludes this species from this area, which is inhabited by painted, snapping, musk, Blanding's, and wood turtles.

Using binoculars to scan some farther reaches of buttonbush screens and water lily beds for the bright yellow chins of Blanding's turtles, I think back to my only sighting of them here, near sunset on a chill, wind-blasted April day three springs ago. I suddenly made out not one but two of of these exceptionally elusive turtles, one basking atop the other, on a log well screened by leafless buttonbush. Such a startling and fulfilling sighting becomes riveted in my mind's eye, a clearly catalogued picture to go by, encompassing seasonal conditions and habitat parameters, as I seek further insights into the natural history of turtles and their wetlands. As I admired the long-necked turtles, I picked up the sound of vegetation being torn. An animal, evidently of considerable size, was roughly ripping away at some plant, not browsing or gnawing but shredding. I tracked the distant but distinct sound to the opposite bank of the oxbow, a levee well fortified by red maples. Beneath their canopy, spring beauty and trout lily were in bloom, skunk cabbages were opening, and cinnamon ferns unfurling. I made out a tremendous snapping turtle, black with wetness, lurching out of the water, forefeet planted firmly on the bank, rocking his head this way and that, tearing at a skunk cabbage plant, bending it back and forth. Skunk cabbage is an important early-season plant for black bears; here it provided one of the first dinners of the year for a snapping turtle not long out of hibernation. I thought at once of photographs a friend had sent me, of several large snapping turtles just up from overwintering in a pond she watches over, wrestling water lily tubers from deep muck, digging them out, and eating them as though they were giant potatoes. The tough fibers of the skunk cabbage resisted the determined efforts of the powerful turtle. He employed his capable jaws more as a vise grip than as a shearing tool, until the twistings of his massive head and tuggings of his muscular, bulging neck at last ripped the plant stalk free. He then backed down into the water and submerged. Leaves and stems, bright green in the dark water, floated to the surface. I watched as he ate his spring salad, cutting it up with razor-sharp jaws and submerging to swallow unchewed mouthfuls. These turtles, who consume great quantities of plants, and in many habitats are largely herbivorous, cannot eat out of the water.

Black bears come down from the forest to gather floodplain berries in autumn, snapping turtles come out of floodplain water to harvest greens in the spring. I believe that coyotes of forest and field search wintry wetlands for snapping turtles. One January a friend found coyote scat on a forested ridge above beaver wetlands. The scat contained reptile skin that looked to her like snakeskin, but upon investigating, I found that the pieces bore the unmistakable foreleg scales of a large snapping turtle. The next year I saw the cleaned-out shell of a good-sized snapping turtle that had been found well away from water by a deer hunter late in November. A coyote may have carried away and finished off a turtle that had been wrested from its aquatic hibernaculum by the arch-predator of wetlands, the river otter. But in the prairie pothole region, members of the dog family are skillful at digging snapping turtles from hideouts in the mud of dried-up sloughs and marshes in drought years, and it appears to me that if ice cover does not prevent it, coyotes will extricate snapping turtles from their hibernacula, which are often located in relatively shallow backwaters. Such predator-prey relationships are representative of the continual interactions among wetland, riparian, and upland ecosystems.

I make no particularly startling observations today, but I see sunlight, shadows, and cloud reflections on the water, emergent and mirrored plant forms, skimmings of dragonflies, unblinking stares of green frogs,

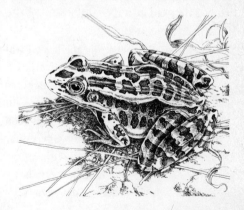

Pickerel frog (*Rana palustris*)

and leisurely cruisings of painted turtles, and I hear the occasional calling of birds. I am present for the orchestration of a wetlands day in its passing, a moment in its season. The wordless but infinitely evocative dialogue of living and nonliving elements of a wetland is always a vision, always a revelation, always worth my being here.

The Levee and the River Channel

Leaving my watch at the oxbow, I turn back to the river, crossing sunlit, uncanopied wet meadow that grows eyebrow-high and higher and passing through shaded ironwood glades with low-growing ferns, sedges, and grass. Coming to a levee fashioned by the river itself, I follow its narrow crest downstream. Overbank flooding deposits heavier, coarser material along banks, creating ridges that drop sharply, almost perpendicularly, toward the water and slope more gradually away from the channel. These levees are often the highest points in the floodplain, providing a footing for plants as varied as massive sycamores and tiny northern white violets. Finer sediments, suspended in sweeping floodwaters, are carried well beyond the immediate banks to settle out over the broader floodplain. Some are transported far from the river channel to places where the water meets an upland rise, such as a valley wall, or a high terrace formed by alluvial deposits put down far back in the river's history, an abandoned floodplain no longer linked with the river's hydrology. Back swamps, like the alder, meadowsweet, sweet gale, and leatherleaf shrub swamp and the red maple swamp that lie between the oxbow and the uplands, arise in floodplain depressions lying between natural levees and valley walls or terraces, where these finer sediments have been deposited.

Silver maples grow along the levee I walk, paralleling the river's flow. Silver maple, so well adapted to riverbank and floodplain life, is unable to compete with other species in other environments, except in artificial settings, such as urban streets, where human manipulation excludes trees that would shade them out. This ecology is shared by another alluvial tree species, the sycamore. Silver maples line the banks of a considerable stretch of this river, with an occasional sycamore and more frequent stands of red maple, trees that take root and hold along the shifting, dynamic borderline between water and land. For as long as they are able, these floodplain trees anchor earth against the cutting edge of wild and restless water. As the river shifts and ancient trees go down, seedlings arise in the spaces left along the reconfigured banks.

On down the tree-lined levee, I brush through thick growths of herbaceous plants that surge forth after the river's own surging abates. Two plants known familiarly as devil's needles proliferate: the showy bur-marigold and the inconspicuous nodding beggar-ticks, their ripening nutlets armed with barbed awns that will stick tight to otters and mink, muskrats, deer, ducks, and me and be transported all along this river, as well as to rivers and wetlands far away. Barnyard grass is bristly with seedheads, almost lurid in their blendings of red-purple and lime green. Two aquatic polygonums, swamp smartweed and marshpepper smartweed, drift their pink and pinky white flowers along the lower slope of the levee. A crowning of swamp milkweed, at this time of year bearing a candelabra of graceful, narrow green seedpods, stands over a tangle of grass and sedge draped with bedstraw. There are deep gold stands of lance-leaved and late goldenrods, pale purple sprays of swamp aster borne on wine red and deeply purpled stems, purplings of joe-pye weed, occasional crimson accents of cardinal flower, and the varied shapes and greens of water parsnip, false nettle, and royal and sensitive ferns, along with fringed, hop, bladder, and porcupine sedges and woolgrass. The river and its floodplain are the keepers of endless botanies, through which a rich and multifaceted zoology is ever on the move.

The levee ends abruptly at a channel only a few strides across but too deep to wade, flowing through a tussock marsh into the river. I circle the backwater embayment of the tussock marsh to where beavers have built a dam across this stream that feeds the river. This broad dam has an especially heavy mud component and is richly vegetated with many of the same plants that grow on the levee. After crossing the dam, I walk a narrow belt of damp-earthed, seasonally flooded red maple swamp that has not been under water since the great flood of April, before turning back to the river.

4:11 P.M. I ease my way through a broad, waist-high belt of poison ivy and down a slippery washout in the wet, clayey riverbank to a wadeable run. At low water the river barely moves through this reach. A swath of late afternoon sunlight lies low across the water, coming through an opening in the riverside canopy created by the toppling of a silver maple. About seven feet below the main banking, there is a narrow, sloping shelf along the channel, against which the present water level lies. Green frogs are populous here, screaming and leaping in typical fashion as I wade by. These frogs live "between the devil and the deep blue sea": there are more than enough predators working the banks for them, yet if they leap into the river, they are at once in smallmouth bass and chain pickerel country. Aware of the thin line they walk, or hop, they leap into the river when something threatens ashore, but often cut back toward shore the moment they hit the water, scrambling back up onto the bank without a pause. As they zigzag frantically back and forth between these realms, they alternate between flight and concealment, hiding in clumps of riverbank vegetation or scurrying under a pack of sunken leaves in the water for a moment, only to leave one for the other, like someone changing hiding places repeatedly, seeking the safest hideout before the one who is "it" has counted to ten.

Cardinal flowers are aflame in shafts of sunlight at the frog-enlivened water's edge, and pink masses of amphibious smartweed glow in muddy pockets along the generally unvegetated, silty bank. Cardinal flowers also stand like sentinels along the poison ivy–crested higher bank. I wade the channel, skirting depressions that even at this season are five feet deep. The silt-bottomed stretches are treacherously slick, so wherever I can I wade on clean-swept sand and gravel. Having walked and crawled through floodplain forest, riparian thickets, glades, and swales, I now enter a water garden of floating leaves tethered in a gentle drift. Great billowings of submersed plants are motionless in still-water side pockets or slowly waver in the gradual snaking of the central current. There are large beds of floating-leaf pondweed, mingled with a smaller, finer pondweed with few floating leaves, bright green larger water-starwort, delicate plants with masses of slender underwater leaves and floating rosettes of broader, rounded leaves. Dense, black-green beds of water crowfoot are thickly matted just beneath the water surface. Throughout these submarine greens are sheetings of what appears to be a brown algae. Schools of minnows appear and disappear as I stir the plants with my wading stick. Young smallmouth bass streak by me like high-speed shadows, a crayfish jets backward down an open water column. Long, pale green ribbons of wild celery undulate slowly, ceaselessly, in the central cut of the channel.

Common musk turtle
(*Sternotherus odoratus*)

Searching among the water plants, separating their pliant, under-water ropings with my hands or wading stick, I make out the top of a musk turtle's shell, barely breaking the surface. Verging on invisible, the black turtle, with his algae-decorated shell, basks in warm surface water on a near-black matting of water crowfoot. Sunlight comes late to, and does not linger long on, this north-south, tree-lined run of the river. Although musk turtles are highly aquatic, and much of their activity occurs at dawn, dusk, and after dark, they have the basic turtle need for basking, and along tree-shaded rivers like this, they must take advantage of the sun when it is on the water. At times they may bask like this, with their shells just beneath the water or barely breaking the surface. At other times they seem to be trying to get closer to the sun, climbing, with surprising agility, six feet or more into deadfalls. In their tree-basking mode, musk turtles typically adopt a pose quite in contrast with that of the heads-up, ever-watchful painted turtles: they droop their long necks and pointed-nosed heads close against the stumps or logs on which they rest, masquerading as knobs or stubs of wood. At any menacing movement, these turtles plummet, like the river stones they resemble, to the safety of the water.

Their wariness, even as they keep their heads down, includes attention to the sky. Bald eagles will carry a musk turtle off to a feeding tree, rip off the plastron, and eat the flesh like an oyster on the half shell. The turtle I pluck from his solarium at once lives up to his common and Latin names — musk turtle, stinkpot, *Sternotherus odoratus* — projecting a noxious smell from glands under the border of his carapace, along the bridge between it and his plastron. For good measure, he makes threatening open-mouthed gestures and awkwardly attempts to bite. Though not as proficient and powerful a self-defender as the snapping turtle (who frequently creates a malodorous ambience around his much larger self that is only slightly less penetrating than that of the musk turtle), these small turtles can inflict a determined and painful bite on the unwary captor. As with snapping turtles, I have never met a musk turtle who did not appear heavily overfed. Her glossy flesh bulges roundly from beneath her carapace as she tries to pull her head and limbs into her shell. The little freshwater clams, mussels, snails, crayfish, and insect larvae of this plant-choked stretch of the river provide ample forage, and there are dead fish and such to scavenge.

I stir and grope through dark entanglements of water crowfoot, now raising their last white flowers of the season above the surface, and turn up another musk turtle. This one, a female, has a heavier growth of algae than the male all over her carapace; such growths are common on the shells of this species and add greatly to the difficulty of finding them. Just upstream there are some rock and boulder piles on the gravelly bottom, a substrate musk turtles favor, along with deadfalls and debris dams. As is the case with edge-water pockets of emergent marsh and shrub swamp, aquatic-bed habitats are relatively small and widely separated in many rivers. In lieu of those habitats, with their vegetative cover, numerous river animals find shelter in deadfalls, rock jumbles, and burrowable gravelly substrates.

As I set the musk turtles back in their submersed beds, I hear a turtle drop into the river from a deadfall thirty yards upstream. I start wading, the river growing deeper as I approach a fallen red maple with many branches and twigs remaining in its toppled crown. Its leafless, gracefully bony fingers have collected rafts and pileups of drifting bark and branches, stems and leaves, and two plastic bottles that gleam deceptively in the tangle, imitating the shells of basking painted turtles. I wade on tiptoe now, waist-deep, too low in the water to be able to see into it very well. There are no rooted plants here, but the tree provides a forest of cover. I see no turtle, but discover colonies of big duckweed that have found moorings in the protection of the deadfall. These tenth-of-an-inch plants, which blanket ponds and other still waters, are able to inhabit a flowing river by colonizing deadwater surface areas backed up by fallen trees and debris dams. There is something animallike in the way duckweed takes to these microhabitats within an overall environment so challenging to plant life and so different from the placid beaver ponds and nonflowing marshes for which it seems perfectly suited. I suspect the first of these plants came to the river on duck feathers or on muskrat or beaver fur. Washed off, drifting on the surface, the plants were transported by wind and water to quiet areas of the stream, where they multiplied into floating mats. They fare well not only in niches out of the wind and current but in raftings of ensnared drift held in place by sweepers, the overhanging branches that dip into the river. Such floats are a favorite feeding place for brook trout and other river animals.

Nearly waist-deep, tiptoeing along a ridge of coarse sand, I skirt the deadfall, holding on to its outer twigs as though they were a steadying comrade's extended fingertips. The riverbed ascends, and I, emerging from deeper water, wade on upstream to a low beaver dam and its frothy, murmuring spillways. In this time of low water, the river has been silent along nearly all of the reach I have walked. It is quite shallow here. The dam, little more than a foot high, backs water up in a long, broad, gradually deepening pool. Low dams like this create staircases of water up the gradual gradient of a riverbed. When the river becomes too shallow for the beavers, the dams probably serve purposes of safety and transport, like the canals these animals trench to reach food and building materials away from waterways. But I suspect the major purpose of these step-dams is to assure that underwater entrances to bank burrows do not become exposed during dry seasons. They appear to be temporary structures, engineered for times of low water. They do not look as though they could withstand the towering torrents that rush through here in flood season. With water levels so reduced, the spillways of these low dams create the only turbulence along several miles of the river. The

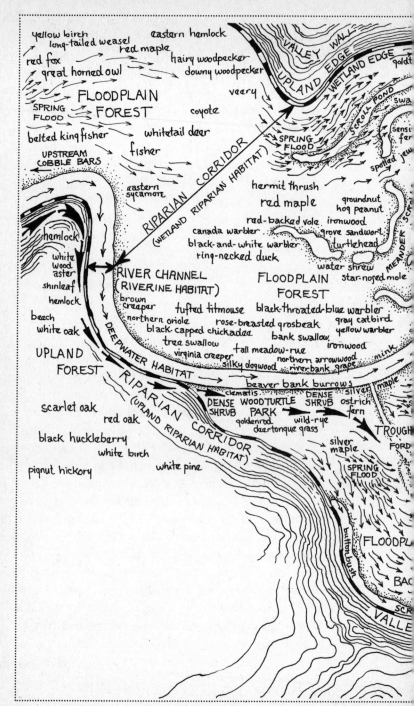

Map of the floodplain

bubbling escapes from this dam no doubt help to aerate the water and aid fish and other gill-breathers in the pool beneath the deadfall and on downstream. If brook trout have not abandoned this section of the river, they may well depend upon this aeration to meet their relatively high need for dissolved oxygen.

Big duckweed has established colonies along the upstream margin of the dam, where it seems to huddle, backing away from the several over-flows. But some of these floating plants surely are washed downstream to start new colonies in other deadwater niches. Frothy buildups of foam have also collected against the dam. Although they might appear to be some form of pollution, these bubbly mixtures are composed of chemicals from fallen leaves and other natural organic matter, as well as enormous numbers of spores from fungi and bacteria. They drift to surface spillways, foaming up all the more as they tumble to lower water, then ride on down the river in cloudlike flotillas.

Even the modest extra depth provided by this backed-up water greatly benefits aquatic animals, from ducks to black-nosed dace, cray-fish, and dragonfly larvae. Like the beaver-pruned riparian glades that wood turtles favor, beaver impoundments are so habitat-enhancing and life-influencing that I could be tempted to think of them as being pur-poseful. But anything in nature that might resemble altruism comes not from intent but from the broad existential design of coevolution. In the web of life that spins through the black universe on this blue planet, the water planet, the duty of each species is only to its own species. Yet what a study it would take, and what a catalog it would generate, if one were to attempt to understand and chronicle all the effects of the beavers' water-impounding behavior on the life of these riverine and riparian ecosystems. The dimensions of coevolution that have arisen in and af-fected life in freshwater wetlands since the day the first beaver built the first dam must be incalculable.

Near dark, I depart the river at the beaver dam, making my way up the argillaceous bank with the help of handgrips and footholds provided by exposed roots. I pass through a brushy edging of ironwood and ascend a rise of upland forest. Standing on a beaver-cleared knoll, I look back down on parts of the river's gleaming run and the wetland mosaic of swamp, red-maple-bordered oxbow, beaver-dammed drainage stream, ponds, marsh, and shrub swamp, all backing to a red maple swamp. I think again of the great flood of last April, when, from this same promontory, I surveyed what seemed an inland sea. A series of *Hooo'-hoo-hooo*'s, low and distant but profoundly penetrating, breaks the silence. The call of a great horned owl evokes a lingering wildness and defiance. The hills are darkening now. The river is a silver slide in riparian darkness. I am always reluctant to leave. All that falls away from me as I enter the wetlands through the outer screens of reedgrass, sedge, fern, and shrub carr threatens to overtake me again as I come back out. But as I leave, the calls of the great horned owl carry down the river corridor once more.

American larch (*Larix laricina*)

7 BOGS AND FENS

As if individual speculators were to be allowed
to export the clouds out of the sky or the stars out
of the firmament.

— Henry David Thoreau

Black Fox Bog

June 23, 3:37 P.M. Summer solstice. The heat of the day drops away noticeably as I pick my way through a final thin band of red maples and approach the open mat of Black Fox Bog. The peat, a deep, waterlogged accretion of dead sphagnum moss underlying this forest-surrounded wetland, creates its own separate climate. Even when the surface layer thaws, the insulating peat holds ice well into the growing season; after it thaws completely, it continually wicks up and releases moisture to its immediate surroundings, maintaining boreal root zones and cooling and moistening the air that settles into this boggy hollow. This spongy moss accounts for the presence of northern, even tundra, plants far south of where one would expect to find them. I walk a progressively mossier world as I move through the outer limit of red maples and cinnamon ferns, heading toward the light of the open bog mat.

I am forced to detour by a long channel of shallow water, abundantly crisscrossed with the creeping rootstocks of wild calla, raising their white spathes and heart-shaped leaves from a bed of black muck. This is one of those wetland plants that signals where not to tread, as it invariably settles in treacherously deep deposits of the most gripping organic soils. I find no steady footing. The trees themselves are tipsy. In this sodden, edge-of-peatland setting, their roots are restricted to broad discs even shallower than those of most swamps. Many trees have been toppled by wind. Some of these become my bridges. In the dark pools formed in the craters left by tipped-up tree roots, wild calla and green

Pale laurel (*Kalmia polifolia*)

frogs find lodgings. Even the red maple, so well adapted to wetlands, is kept from advancing beyond this point by the acidic, oxygen-deprived, cold, saturated substrate of this sphagneous peatland. The maples are widely scattered and severely stunted; their miniaturized leaves already show flashes of autumn orange and red, a premature coloring that reflects the harshness of their environment.

Red maples fade out completely as I move over the open sphagnum. Some two hundred yards short of the bog's central pond, I already find places where I can thrust my walking stick out of sight in dark water and deep muck. Low-mounded sphagnum moss rolls on ahead of me, a plush carpet of dark yellow-greens splashed with rosy accents, set with specimen sedges and neat, knee-high ericaceous shrubs. There are trees here, but they are widely scattered, standing as individuals or as isolated stands of three to half a dozen or so, branchy little forest islands in a sea of low-growing shrubs and sedges. Only two tree species can grow in such saturated acidic peat: black spruce and American larch, or tamarack. The habitat they have found here is similar to that of the northern tree limits and vast tundra beyond, where they are dominant species.

The lacy, ornamentally twisted larch and the black-green, stiffly upright black spruce are distinctive accents on a Persian carpet of bog colors, forms, and details: blue-green drifts of bog rosemary, Labrador tea with white clusters of flowers at its branch tips, shrubby spreads of ocher-tinged leatherleaf, aromatic sweet gale, scattered sprays of tawny green sedges, and the rosy blushes, rich deep greens, and radiant yellow-greens of the various sphagnum mosses. The profuse archings of waxy white leatherleaf flowers have gone by, but at midsummer's eve the boggy background is decorated with the pale and deep pink flowers of pale laurel, sheep laurel, and bog rosemary. As summer deepens and these flowers fade, the soft yet vibrant magenta-pink of rose pogonia or-

Horned bladderwort (*Utricularia cornuta*), **small cranberry** (*Vaccinium oxycoccus*), **round-leaved sundew** (*Drosera rotundifolia*), **and sphagnum moss** (*Sphagnum* sp.)

chids will blink among the sedges; rust and maroon-red caps of pitcher plants will rise above their red-veined, yellow-green, insect-trapping leaves; and tawny white tufts of hare's tail will drift above ripening cranberries. All about my feet in this richly ornamented bog-garden are miniaturist details: rosettes of sphagnum moss, threadings of creeping snowberry and horned bladderwort, trailings of large and small cranberry. A bog is an unforgiving habitat for most plants; its harsh terms of existence protect its well-adapted flora from invasion by other species. While relatively low in plant diversity, an acidic peatland is a unique and irreplaceable botanic garden, one more wetland gift of the glaciers.

The bog mat yields but bears my weight. I choose each step with care, as much for the plants' sake as for my own. The only paths worn in this remote peatland are the narrow trails of white-tailed deer along its perimeter. As I come close to the edge of the blackwater pond the sphagnum mat encircles, I rely more and more on stands of leatherleaf for my footing. Their entangled roots and rhizomes provide some stability in the peat. In less than an hour I have crossed a distance that these sphagnum mosses took thousands of years to cover, since the first encroachings upon the open water of a deep glacial waterhold. That encroachment may be continuing today, with the time-defying insistence and cell-by-cell patience of living things, or it may have been arrested by a consortium of hydrology, water chemistry, and other abiotic and biotic factors. Such a stasis could hold in place for centuries. In walking from the swamp border of Black Fox Bog to its open-water core, I walk the history of its plants, the history of the peatland they have formed, and the water and earth in which it is set.

Leatherleaf (*Chamaedaphne calyculata*)

Sedges bow and rise in the winds that sweep across the bog pond and the low, open outermost edging of the surrounding mat. There is a constant low swishing sound, not quite a whistling, in the scattered stands of spruce and larch. Like the encircling sphagnum that may or may not advance farther upon the water, the black spruce and larch may expand to form a broad belt around the mat or be kept to the crescent-moon arc they occupy at present. The afternoon wind has driven the black flies back into the ferny thickets at the edge of the swamp, but the deer flies are undeterred. There always seems to be a stirring, a restlessness in the air over these moss-mounded peatlands, as though a northern wind must tend their boreal plantings. More keenly than in other remote wetlands, I feel these boggy niches to be places unto themselves.

I ease my way among blooming bog rosemary and pale laurel, approaching the water's edge. The soggy peat mat quakes beneath me now, as I walk a floating world of living and nonliving plants. Leatherleaf stands several feet away shake with my footsteps, and I can rock the immediate landscape simply by transferring my weight from one foot to the other. This leading edge of sphagnum is suspended over deep water, but the roots and stems of woody plants that have made their own advance over the sphagnum provide enough resilience to keep me from sinking deeper into the peat and the water beneath it. Soils underlying other wetlands generally contain a great deal of clay or organic silts; bogs or fens typically rest on accumulations of nearly pure organic deposits.

Beyond the raftings of leatherleaf and sweet gale, the bog mat undulates like water. Descriptively named "quaking bogs," peatlands like Black Fox Bog form in small — usually less than two hundred acres — deep glacial kettle holes or lakes with severely restricted inflow and outflow. The water in these kettles is typically cold, acidic, and nutrient-impoverished. Floating mats, initiated by colonies of sphagnum mosses, which in turn become colonized by other plants, develop along the shoreline and gradually spread out over the water. In time, and under the right environmental circumstances, the mat may cover the entire surface or may leave a central opening in the pond. The advancing sphagnum mat, which becomes settled by sedges and shrubs adapted to boglike environments, generates a slow, steady rain of dead plant material. Decomposition is arrested in the cold, acidic, anoxic water, and incompletely decayed plant remains accumulate on the bottom as a less decayed fibrous layer of peat deepens just beneath the living sphagnum at the water surface. Eventually the peat deposits building up from the bottom connect with the floating mat. Given enough time (perhaps millennia) under the requisite ambient conditions, the entire kettle may become filled with waterlogged peat. In some places the peat may become dense enough to support the weight of a person, black bear, or moose. But where the mat is suspended over looser peat or water, a creature as light as a fox could slip through the mat into the depths below.

Among the plants reaching out for open water are the arching, inter-twining, woody branches of water willow, or swamp loosestrife. This wetland shrub can more or less walk on water, as it arcs out from wet soils along a shoreline or from the leading edge of a sphagnum mat. Where its specialized branch tips touch the water surface, they sprout roots. Spongy, air-filled tissue called aerenchyma develops at these con-tacts, swelling and buoying the branch tips, establishing floats from which new stems arise to arch over the water. Water willow may estab-lish a living framework of roots and branches upon which sphagnum mosses continue their march across the water, and accretions of sphag-num on water-willow raftings can then become colonized by sedges and heaths, setting the stage for the growth upon growth at the water's sur-face that initiates development of a bog habitat.

Several fleshy plants with succulent green growth that would seem more at home in a marsh stand out against the terse forms and dusky, restrained tones of the mosses, heaths, and sedges. Buckbean, or bog-bean, is one of the few plants that extends functioning roots deep into the anaerobic layer of the peat. The active roots of most bog and fen vegetation are restricted to the comparatively thin, somewhat aerated upper layer. The presence of bogbean is a sign that a peatland receives at least a degree of mineral enrichment from the surrounding uplands, a trickling inlet stream or slight groundwater feed, an indication that it is not a true bog.

By strictest definition, a bog is a peatland that receives no input of water other than precipitation; there is no runoff from surround-ing surfaces, no seepage or stream feed. Nor does a true bog have any outlet: obtaining their water only from rain and snow, mists and fog, these harshest of wetland habitats are known as ombrogenous (rain-originating) or ombrotrophic (rain-fed) peatlands. The extreme condi-tions required for an ombrotrophic bog are not widely found; where they are, the sphagnum peat builds up to completely fill the glacial basin in which the bog originated, then mounds above the rim of its catch-ment to stand somewhat higher than the surroundings, as well as above the reach of groundwater. This aspect of their ecology gives these peat-lands yet another name, raised bogs. True bogs may form atop moun-tains or in stony cradles on high ridges. In the northeastern United

States, they are found only in coastal and northern Maine and the northern Adirondack Mountains.

Technically speaking, because it receives some incoming water, however slight, in addition to precipitation and has some outflow, Black Fox Bog is not a bog but a poor fen. Conditions in the densest interior regions of its mat are so boglike that it could properly be called a very poor fen, or harsh fen. Fens are defined as geogenous (earth-originating) or minerotrophic (mineral-fed or mineral-nourished) peatlands. The most acidic, least mineral-enriched fens closely resemble bogs; the neutral to alkaline fens with the most mineral enrichment are meadowy, sedge-filled wetlands closely aligned with wet meadows and marshes. Most peatlands fall on a gradient between sphagnum moss–dominated true bogs and sedge-dominated rich, or calcareous, fens, which feature little or no sphagnum. In terms of plant life, poor fens are very similar to true bogs and have almost nothing in common with calcareous fens; some peatland ecologists use "bog" to refer to peatlands that have an extensive carpet of moss dominated by sphagnum. Though it might technically be called a fen, Black Fox Bog has ecological characteristics that closely approximate those of a pure rain-fed bog; the use of the word "bog" in its name (as is common with sphagnaceous fens in the glaciated Northeast) is understandable, and a practice not likely to be revised.

Thrusting my walking stick a foot and a half into the mat, I bring its tip into contact with a layer of peat that is probably more than a thousand years old. In the hollow of a pure rain-fed bog at that same depth, I could touch a point in time over two thousand years past. In the most nutrient-impoverished settings, it can take a hundred years for one inch of peat to build up. Some bogs and harsh fens are still in the early stages of development after ten thousand years. Globally, vast areas of northern peatland ecosystems have vanished, because in recent times sphagnum peat, the stuff of millennia, has been dug up by the cubic mile. In many countries, small-scale hand cutting of peat has been going on for centuries, primarily for fuel, but today's mechanized operations remove peat at a prodigious rate for fuel and landscaping. In the early 1990s an effort to preserve existing natural bogs in Ireland was abandoned, because it was found that in essence none remained. Vegetation can regenerate in peat-mined sites, but it does not appear possible to replicate the peatland's original ecological status.

The plants here yield an exceedingly sparse harvest over the years. Dead fragments of sphagnum mosses, withered strands of sedge, and small, reluctantly yielded leaves, bits of bark, and twigs of ericaceous shrubs amount to very little compared with the heavy plant production in a marsh or swamp, the annual autumn leaf fall that a vernal pool or woodland brook receives, or the cascades of leaves that enrich the floors of upland forests. But in the decay-resistant catchment of a bog or fen, even the least sheddings of detritus outpace the rate of decomposition, resulting in a steady, if annually minute, gain in plant material. A peatland develops in wetlands in which the accumulation of organic matter exceeds the rate of decay. In contrast with the more completely broken-down organic muck, or the clay and other mineral soils of marshes and swamps, the soil of bogs and fens is a fibrous, spongy matrix of incompletely decayed plant, and even some animal, remains that has built up in a waterlogged environment.

My knees sink into the soggy mat as I kneel to take a close look at the bright red rosettes of one sphagnum mound, the green, starlike clusters of another. Worldwide, there are some 250 species of sphagnum moss, adapted to various boggy growing conditions. In northern realms, this cosmopolitan, unique nonflowering plant covers vast areas, including, in Canada and Alaska, endless miles of muskeg, the saturated expanses of mosses, dwarf shrubs, and stands of conifers. So similar in form and function as to seem a single species, sphagnum mosses are ecologically diverse enough that fifty different species may find their requisite habitats within a single bog. Some grow on drier hummocks, modest inches above the fully saturated mat; others flourish in adjacent sodden hollows that are inundated from time to time. Each species has a tremendous water-holding capacity. The leaflike stems of the growing moss can hold fifteen to twenty times their weight in water. They are one cell layer thick, with two types of cells: small, chlorophyll-containing cells that produce food and give the plant its color and large, water-holding cells that retain water long after they die. Riddled with large pores through which water can pass easily in all directions, the cells of these mosses continually pull water up to the living layer through capillary action.

Constant evaporation of this wicked-up water contributes to the cooler temperatures at the surface of a bog or poor fen even in summer.

Sphagnum mosses have an ancient lineage on earth and an enduring link with the planet's water. Sphagnum has followed water, settled where it collects, blanketing shores, edging along flowing runs, moving into impounded depths, and spreading over still surfaces. Few species are known to produce spores on a seasonal basis; most of the time they spread vegetatively. When I finger into the sphagnum, it is cold and wet immediately beneath the surface, as though another season were being kept there, just out of reach of the flooding June sunlight. Any small bog creature, a redbelly snake or masked shrew, traveling over the wet, plushly mossed bog mat would experience an ambience closer to that of the first day of spring than its last, belying the climate above the sphagnum or in the dry, heated uplands around it.

From a firm spot near the edge of the mat I can look down into the black water of the open pond. Its darkness results largely from humic acids that form as plant tissue is broken down. Bogs and fens typically do not harbor an abundance or great diversity of animal life, in large part because of their acidity. As acids — the byproducts of respiration associated with slow and incomplete decay — accrue, the water becomes inhospitable, in some cases lethal, to fish and amphibians. Their eggs

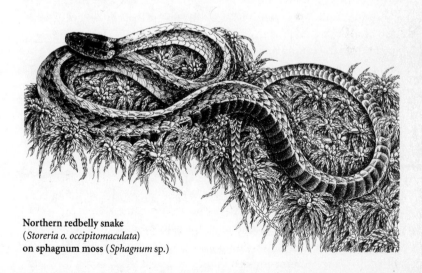

Northern redbelly snake
(*Storeria o. occipitomaculata*)
on sphagnum moss (*Sphagnum* sp.)

cannot survive in waters with a low pH; levels below 6.0 cause severe deformities, and those below 4.0 prove fatal to most species. The pH of bogs ranges below 4.2, and in harsh fens it may not reach much higher than 4.8 or so. Since the acidic waters inhibit aquatic life, the food chain is very limited. As one goes up the scale from true bogs to the most mineral-enriched fens, the abundance and diversity of animal species increase.

Birds flit in and out of peatlands in pursuit of dragonflies and other insects that are able to live there, and they come for blueberries and huckleberries, as do black bears. White-throated and Savannah sparrows keep to the shrubby heaths and open sphagnum, and Lincoln's sparrow and palm warblers nest at times in the shrubs or on moss hummocks. Tree swallows wing over all manner of wetlands, including bogs and fens. Marsh hawks, in half-hovering flights, drift low in quest of two mammals that do live in boggy habitats: southern bog lemmings and red-backed voles. Brown creepers and several species of warblers and flycatchers inhabit bogs and harsh fens in which heavy coniferous cover has become established. White-tailed deer and moose browse in peatlands, although the ericaceous shrubs that dominate these habitats are for the most part unpalatable. The more acidic and nutrient-impoverished habitats are difficult for amphibians, but the four-toed salamander commonly broods its eggs in sphagnum moss, and mink frogs, with their tolerance for acidic environments, appear in northern bogs.

South of the tundra and muskeg of the far north, bogs and poor fens are generally limited, widely spaced outposts from another geologic time set in an entirely different landscape. For all the miles that may divide them from one another, these haunting places possess a mysterious commonality that one becomes aware of the moment one enters any of their inner circles: the kinship of bog and acidic fen.

The Moat Bog

October 15, 12:27 P.M. Though it is no more than six to eight strides across, there is no wading across the four- to six-foot-deep dark waters of the Lagg, a muck-bottomed moat that surrounds the seventeen-acre Moat Bog, a sphagnum-mossed island. I weave my way along the Lagg's forbidding margins, over, around, and through buttressing red maple roots, windthrows, shrub tangles, fern, and sedge. Walking, wading, clinging, I come to a narrow, treacherous bridge, the bleached trunk of one of the largest red maples to have grown in the swamp that abuts the moat. This fallen tree, slow to die after being brought down by a storm, bridges two different worlds. Its upended disk of roots still grips the mud of the swamp; its crown is lodged in the heath shrubs and engulfing mosses at the edge of a sphagnum mat.

Not uncommonly, wetlands are bordered by a moat, or lagg, along their landward margins. Sometimes the wetland is completely encircled, in true medieval-moat fashion. Such a moat is commonly so uniform in width as to appear man-made. In my first encounters with these often impassable barriers I wondered why they had been dug, but they are formed not by the hands of humans or the paws and mouths of beavers, but by runoff from upland rises collecting around the rim of a wetland basin and pooling deeply against a central peat mass. Trapped between the basin rim and the dense floating island of peat, the water may develop a gradual circling flow. The ring of dark water characteristically sits on treacherous deposits of muck. The laggs of boglike peatlands are particularly forbidding, but I have also come to such watery boundaries around extensive buttonbush or leatherleaf shrub swamps; after arduously circling their landward margins, seeking a place to cross, I have been denied entrance, though the water is not wide. The moats that surround many peatlands seem an intentional bar to heavy-footed passage within their easily trampled interiors, keeping them "exempt from public haunt."

Lining the edge of the swamp where the fallen red maple once stood are autumn-bleached sprays of bluejoint grass, black-stemmed winterberry emblazoned with brilliant red berries, and mounds of highbush blueberry, still burning with a few fire-bright leaves. Beyond this screening, mazes of alder and dominating stands of red maple extend up to drier ground. A ribbon snake winds out of sight in mats of bluejoint and tussock sedge as I take a footing on my one-log bridge. I possess nothing of the balance of a tightrope walker and am all the more awkward in hip-high wading boots, but the tree trunk is sturdy and broad enough, and enough deadfall branches offer reassuring hand holds that I am able to cross the moat.

On the other side of the Lagg, I step down into that other wetland world. It is a constant delight to me in my swampwalking that such small crossings, or similarly slight turnings in watery pathways, can lead to markedly different places. Plants again delineate a transition in ecologies. There are some sprays of bluejoint growing on this side of the moat, but they are smaller and fewer in number, widely scattered among dense edgings of sweet gale flanked by leatherleaf. Tussock sedge hummocks maintain solitary holds along inlets lined with leatherleaf and red chokeberry. Winterberry is present in occasional dwarfed clumps. The few red maple saplings, buttonbushes, and royal ferns along the island's outer rim are not faring well in this harsh-fen environment although they flourished in the wetlands on the other side of the Lagg. Similarly, only a few species of bog plants, represented by scattered, struggling individuals, appear in the outer margins of the red maple swamp. The hydrology of the lagg, by its distribution of nutrients and flushing of acids, tempers the development of peatland along this wetland frontier and maintains a stasis.

I have gone from mire to quagmire, from the swamp margins, in whose mucky hollows I could become entrapped, to the springy peat and shrub raftings of the moat-bog border, which yields beneath my footsteps but bears my weight. All about me there are openings into water, scattered pools, twisting channels, startlingly dark and doubtless deep. I probe five feet or so with my walking stick and arm without touching anything of substance. Along the moat fringe, the sphagnum has not built up anything approaching the dense peat of its central mat.

Flying in tandem, a pair of ruby meadowflies, the last of the dragonflies to be killed by frost, dips to the surface of the moat. While eight wings work individually, with intricate synchronization, to keep the coupled dragonflies in place, the female lowers her abdomen into the water, just off outreaches of sedge and black chokeberry, and begins to deposit eggs. Keeping his hold behind her head, the male buzzes his wings vigorously. Suddenly the female's wings become entrapped, spread flat and held fast on the water's surface. His blur of wings loud in the peatland quiet, the male struggles valiantly but fails to lift her free from the water's hold. His glistening wings slow, then vibrate furiously. At length he relinquishes his hold and darts away. Alone now in her struggle, the female rests on the water, her wings still glued to the surface. Her head and thorax are above water, but her abdomen, with its breathing pores, is submerged. Her small, wiry black legs work in the water, but this once gill-breathing, completely aquatic insect is now, in the aerial manifestation of her life, out of her element. A terrific vibration of wings sends ripples across the inlet. With this concentrated effort, she frees her forewings, and it seems she will take to the air. But the surface tension's relentless hold on her hind wings is enough to keep her imprisoned. Her days are numbered enough by the season. I extend the tip of my walking stick. She clasps it, and I lift her to a warming, drying rest on a red chokeberry branch.

Not far from the wet-winged dragonfly's recovering place are several once-stately arrow arums that have been destroyed by the first touches of frost. Their large, lush arrowhead leaves have gone black and disintegrated into shapeless masses. Although found in boglike habitats, arrow arum is more typical of shallow marshes, swamps, and ponds, and the edge waters of sluggish rivers. The several that have taken hold at the outer margins of the moat bog reveal a degree of mineral enrichment and oxygenation that drops off sharply beyond the island's sphagnum rim and is completely excluded from its boglike heart. The Lagg has neither inlet or outlet, but it does receive a measure of upland runoff, so its water quality is very different from that of the blockaded water in the island core. If a moat has an inlet and/or an outlet or receives generous seepage and percolated ground flow, it can support a diversity of plant and animal life equal to that found in a marsh. Should beavers colonize such a lagg, deepening it by means of a dam, the moat bog can rise with the water, preserving its separate, self-contained peatland existence.

The increasing acidity of the peat is marked by the plants I encounter as I move to the interior of the Moat Bog. The water willow, red chokeberry, occasional arrow arums, and red maples of the moat fringe may have their roots in water with a pH as high as 5.75. The dwarfed black spruce near the central peat zone are rooted in waterlogged sphagnum that has a pH on the order of 4.38. Just as acidification rises along a gradient from the moat fringe to the center of the peat island, saturation, stagnation, oxygen deprivation, and nutrient impoverishment become more extreme. Sphagnaceous peatlands tend to develop either from the shoreline of a kettle hole toward the center or from a central floating mat outward toward a moat, so the surrounding vegetation is typically in concentric bands. Changes in the species composition reflect transitions in growing conditions in the peat.

The next zone I come to is one of tall shrubs growing in dense thickets. I shoulder my way into thickly grown bog thickets with only rare, small glimmers of water. For the first time since I came onto the island, I am moving among shrubs that are taller than I am. I also brush among my first larches, or tamaracks, trees that are few in number and widely spaced in this shrub-favoring zone. In the distance I see a stand of taller larches, part of the golden-crowned ring that seems a guardian gate for the Moat Bog's innermost circle. Black huckleberry, black highbush blueberry, and highbush blueberry proliferate here, their snarled growth forming a woody barrier that is nearly as impassable as the Lagg. They, too, would seem to shield the heart of the bog from intrusion. These heaths prosper in acid peatlands but also grow in nonsphagnaceous wetlands, weaving some of the most backbreaking shrub swamps I wade. Related ericaceous shrubs, leatherleaf and sweet gale, grow in small openings among the huckleberry and blueberry. Wishing I possessed something more supple than my human form, I twist my way through the shrubs' nearly immovable twistings. Huckleberry and blueberry seem to have fingers, as they wind into my hair and snag my shirt, holding me in place, painfully at times. Do they mean to prevent my going any farther? For all their wild and untamed growth, these thickets and hedgerows are set on the mat in such an orderly-looking fashion that they could make one wonder whether they were planted by unseen bog people.

Breaking free from the last clutching holds of the bog thicket, I lurch into an agreeable, open passage with a flooring of sphagnum mosses set with specimen shrubs and trees. The abundant ten- to fifteen-foot tamaracks, intermittent clusters of smaller black spruce, and studdings of black highbush blueberry, black huckleberry, leatherleaf, and sheep laurel appear to grow by the grace of the moss. The needles of larch, a conifer that sheds its foliage every fall, have gone to their October gold. I have entered a golden circle set on an emerald carpet. The stillness and silence of this moment heighten my awareness that I am in a plant world. As far as I can tell, I am the only living thing here that is not a plant. I stand still for a time, as though I were a shrub or tree among shrubs and trees. There is a compelling kinship among the plants of a peatland, as if long ago they conspired to create their unique wetland ambience and ecologies. They have traveled together along routes roughed out by glaciers, shifting with transformations in climate, topography, and hydrology, finding and occupying their special places for millennia at a time.

Swishing through pliant branch-gates and bowing under arches a little less than head-high, I advance among the larch, whose growth habit grants me a passage as favored as the shrubs' was unwelcoming. I could imagine that the shrubs' seemingly willful obstruction was some sort of test or initiation, and that having passed through it, I am now openly conducted toward the heart of the moat bog. One final screen, a far less intimidating maze of shrubs, separates me from the center. I slip through it and peer into another variation of the shrub-tree-forest theme, a truly miniature forest in which larch falls away and black spruce proliferates. With a few shoulder-high exceptions, the trees and shrubs here are less than waist-high. The few larches that have managed to spring up struggle as red maples do back out on the moat fringe. Their ecological horizons sharply restricted, those seedlings that do sprout here can live on only as knee-high natural bonsai.

Conditions in the heart of the moat bog closely parallel those of a pure rain-fed bog, and the plants here are the essence of bogs: drifts of pale laurel, stands of leatherleaf, Labrador tea, and sheep laurel, dwarfed tufts of hare's tail, cotton grass, few-flowered sedge, and other small-to-tiny sedges, northern pitcher plant, round-leaved sundew, vinings of small cranberry and snowberry, all interspersed among the black spruce and occasional larch. I have come as close as I can to the heart of a peatland, an ancient and present core of silence and solitude, a self-contained temple of integrated living and nonliving forces. In the pervading sense of ecological isolation here I come closer to an understanding of the completely nonhuman.

Calcareous Fen

June 6, 8:27 A.M. *Che-beck'!* . . . *che-beck'!* The repeated two-note calls of a least flycatcher, so reminiscent of speckled-alder swamps and riparian thickets in my home wetlands, sound assertively from a stand of smooth alder in southwestern New England. An alder flycatcher taking insects on the wing darts back and forth between an alder stand and a willow screen, over sprays of sedge and spreads of shrubby cinquefoil. A rivulet sparkles by as I stand in the cover of its borderline of autumn and hoary willows. I look out over a low, treeless, wet meadow of grass and sedge. There are occasional shrubby stands of swamp birch and streamlet-lining hedges of alder and willow. Gently sloping sedge meadow rises gradually to the west, to wooded kame terraces that roll up to the footings of steep forested mountains, their topmost peaks over two thousand feet high. Water drains off this long, north–south-running mountainhold, cascading down boulders, sliding over bedrock, and percolating through deposits of sand and gravel, then seeping through the sedge peat on the broad, low-gradient slope that descends to the valley floor. As the water moves over the marble and limestone bedrock of the basin, it becomes charged with calcium carbonate. The bedrock underlying any wetland and the surrounding landforms from which its groundwater flows influence its hydrology and water chemistry; these in turn shape the plant and animal associations that come to populate the wetland. The granitic base of my home wetlands imparts to them their acidic nature. The marble and limestone base of this valley enriches the groundwater with calcium, making it neutral to alkaline, and enables the establishment of calcareous fens. These peatlands, in contrast with bogs and poor fens, feature continually moving, mineral-rich alkaline water. The distinct hydrologies of these two peatland types are reflected in their dominant vegetation: sphagnum in bogs and poor fens, sedges in calcareous, or rich, fens. The scattered fens of this valley slope are relatively small, ranging in size from twenty to fifty acres. They are set in a greater complex that includes calcareous seepage swamps dominated by trees, principally larch and red maple, and an extensive range of marsh, shrub swamp, and riparian habitats bordering the valley's central brook and its tributaries. As in the calcareous fen, the water in all of these is enriched (in varying degrees) with calcium.

I step in and out of the narrow stream, crossing it in two half-strides, then brush through waist-high willow and pass on into shrubby cinquefoil now opening the first bright yellow flowers of its long flowering season. At a collection of pools and channels in a swalelike sweep of fen sedge, I begin to look in earnest for bog turtles, the prime inspiration for my journey here. This site, with its unique ecology, has been purchased and set aside for its resident bog turtles and unique botany. The habitat is not suited to repeated foot traffic, and it will be closed even to researchers for five to ten years following this season. At this northern limit of its disjunct, localized range, the severely declining bog turtle is restricted to a few widely scattered calcareous fens. I wade narrow, ankle-deep watery corridors through a knee- to waist-high meadow of sedges, grasses, and rushes. This fen includes many calcium-loving plants not found in the more acid boreal wetlands I am familiar with: muhly grass, yellow sedge, and knotted rush. Grass-of-Parnassus, which I have never seen before, and rose pogonia, which I know well, will begin to bloom among the sedges in a matter of weeks.

I kneel in a channel of placid water, in a layer of mud atop a springy but walkable sedge peat. Most of the low sedge hummocks that fill this meadowy fen have turtle tunnels bored through them. Groping at the bases of the hummocks, I finger into tunnels the height and width of the turtles I am looking for. They may well create some of their own subterranean corridors, but much of the bog turtles' wetland subway system has probably been reworked from the widespread tunnelings of mammals such as meadow voles and star-nosed moles. Resilient plant growth itself forms the structure of some tunnels, as do the hummocks of the open meadow and the twisted roots of alders and willows along deeper streamlets. Some of these latter shrubs serve as hibernacula, much as red maple, alder, leatherleaf, and sweet gale do for spotted turtles in the Shrub Swamp. Bog turtles require shallow, treeless wetlands with soft peat floorings that they can burrow into.

In the midst of my groping search, I turn my head to see a bog turtle looking up at me from beneath a sedge mound a few feet away. Dark-eyed, the umber face of an adult male, flecked with subtle browned oranges and set off by a resplendent golden-orange blotch on each side, has emerged from shallow water at the base of a tussock. He could disappear as suddenly as he appeared, traveling the hidden passageways that have served generations of his kind in this fen. I work the turtle out from his sedgy hideaway and set him in my right hand. Fully mature, with a carapace a little over three and a quarter inches long, he seems a living toy as he turns and walks on the platform of my palm and extended fingers. It is easy to see why bog turtles in particular have had such appeal that over the years people have carried them away in

Bog turtle (*Clemmys muhlenbergii*)

tremendous numbers, to be kept as pets. In more recent times this turtle has been hunted in earnest by commercial collectors as a result of the high prices it brings. The pet trade is now illegal, but that does not mean it doesn't continue. The species' rarity has only escalated the prices collectors are willing to pay, and increasing collecting pressure in turn has made bog turtles rarer, creating a vicious cycle that has extirpated many populations.

As is generally the case, however, a principal cause of the species' precipitous crash has been loss of habitat. There is no telling how much habitat has been lost and population thus diminished since Europeans first colonized the eastern United States. The practice of extensive ditching and draining for agriculture and pasturage goes back to a time prior to any cataloging of this turtle and its habitats. As the expansion of agriculture and grazing and the conversion of land for human development continue, the destruction of bog turtle habitats proceeds. As the species comes closer to being more fully protected (if that is the correct word for heavy-management, late-in-the-day attempts to keep final populations from disappearing and the species from becoming extinct) its plight becomes all the more severe. The very prospect that bog turtles will be designated as endangered under the Endangered Species Act has led some landowners to quietly drain habitat on their property, effectively eliminating the turtles and thereby circumventing the restrictions.

My feelings of excitement at this first encounter with a bog turtle in his native realm are tempered by the realization that I may be holding a vanishing species in my hand. I think of a place from which the bog turtles disappeared when a private bird sanctuary was converted to grazing land. When I asked a researcher friend how the turtles he studied there were doing, he replied that the property was "ditched and drained and going to hell." The restless male in my palm is anxious to get back to his bog-turtle way of life in the peatland to which he is so perfectly adapted. Animals and plants simply go on as long as they can, no matter whether the worlds to which they have become adapted are challenged or taken by glaciers or humans. As soon as I set him down, he crawls into a watery tunnel, out of sight.

In the northern part of their range, bog turtles seldom wander beyond treeless, low-meadow peatlands like this except to migrate to similar habitats or on occasion to nest. More typically, females lay their eggs atop the very sedge hummocks beneath which they spend so much of their lives. These semiaquatic turtles stay within a water regime considerably more minimalist than that of spotted turtles, which often swim just beneath the surface. Bog turtles typically forage and travel with the domes of their carapaces just above the surface in water that wouldn't cover my ankles. Like me, they are waders, not swimmers.

Scanning the network of narrow channels about me, I see a small mound of glistening mud raised just above the surface, a mud shape extremely suggestive of the carapace I so recently admired in the palm of my hand. I wade carefully over, gently close my hand on the mud hump, and feel the wonderful form of another bog turtle. There is just enough water in the channel for me to rinse away the mud and admire a female only slightly larger than the male I found earlier. Each scute of her deep mahogany carapace bears radiating patterns of narrow, broken bands of umber-glazed orange. Her time of nesting is at hand. Bog turtles lay from one to six eggs; with a carapace length a bit under three and a half inches, this female will probably lay at least three eggs, the typical number for her species.

Like spotted turtles, bog turtles are most active in spring. During the low water of summertime, these reclusive turtles settle into hideaways and become all the more cryptic. The continuous seep of water through the saturated surface soil that supports the unique plant associations of these fens provides the tunneling turtles with damp to watery burrows and lodging places in high summer. Although unventuresome during this phase, they are not exactly dormant. Researchers studying bog turtles have affixed tiny spools of thread to them. The resulting gossamer weavings reveal movements on the order of thirty yards in less than twenty-four hours, all within a refuge of about four square yards.

Throughout much of their range, particularly in Virginia, the Carolinas, and the eastern tip of Tennessee, these turtles inhabit boglike acidic sphagnum peatlands, but in the stricter sense they are "fen" turtles rather than "bog" turtles. Their northernmost limit, in north-central New York and northwestern Massachusetts, falls far south of the boreal latitudes at which most true bogs develop. The hydrology of a peatland and the presence of a peat substrate, be it sphagnum or sedge, appear to be more critical habitat criteria for bog turtles than the acidity or alkalinity of the water. They require a water regime that limits shrub growth and almost entirely excludes trees.

Beaver and deer are important in providing these requisite wetland spaces. Many of the nonsphagnaceous bog turtle habitats that do remain are used for cattle grazing. This activity may keep a wet meadow from becoming overgrown with trees, but it brings about long-term heavy trampling. In addition, nutrients from fertilizer and cattle feces alter the water chemistry and cause a proliferation of vegetation that displaces the native calcareous fen plants and the bog turtles along with them. The natural seepage through calcareous fens is mineral-rich but nutrient-poor, deficient in phosphorus and nitrogen. This condition plays a key role in preserving peatland vegetation and hence the structure of the bog turtle's world.

Calcareous fens are one of the specialized environments that are termed, in the vernacular of the day, "fragile" or "delicate," inspiring implorations for the protection of remnant examples. But these words seem misapplied to ecosystems possessed of long natural histories that would continue at least many centuries into the future if their landscape and hydrology were free from human impact. Had people never come to rework their historic settings, calcareous fens, and the more widespread acidic sphagnum fens, would still be intact and considerably more extensive than they are today. On a planet where even continents shift over time, it is hard to characterize an ecosystem that has been functioning vibrantly since the retreat of the glaciers as anything less than enduring. This valley fen I wade in search of bog turtles is made of landforms, after all, is built from mountains, kames, bedrock depressions, and from water that will not cease its seasonal flowings and floodings unless there is a major climate shift or some restructuring of the bedrock itself. We continually miss the irony of such human terms as "fragile," with the implication that ecosystems could not exist without us. They have gone on and would go on without us. The only thing we need to protect them from is ourselves.

Shifting my focus for a moment, I look up from my sustained concentration on the network of silvery threads of water and black ribbons of mud among hummocks of bowing sedges in a meadow of green June growth to look at the grouped, druidlike personages of larch and red maple in the surrounding landscape. I look back up the broad slope of the valley that harbors this calcareous fen, surveying the glacier-sculpted topography, with its unique waterworks, that has created a habitat for particular plants and animals, an ecology found nowhere else for great distances. This place seems to me a valley lost in time and space, or possessed of its own time and space, with parallels to the Galápagos Islands, otherworldly evolutionary outposts exemplified by the giant tortoises for which they are named. Here in this valley fen, at the opposite end of the size scale, three-and-a-half-inch bog turtles embody the specialized habitat that nurtures them. At the same time, I cannot overlook another parallel, the unsettling fact that discovery often leads to ecological extinction. Whatever might have come to pass here over a broader time has been circumscribed by human activity and presence. Even with rigorous preservation of pieces and parts of this landscape, the time that might have been here has been brought to an end. As I set the bog turtles back in place in their now precarious peatland, I again feel that I have visited one of the last places.

Tamarack Bog

October 18, 2 P.M. Larch in autumn, a radiant gold visible beyond a gray screen of leafless red maple. I head for the glowing open space, evading increasingly soupy pockets, until I link up with a boardwalk that winds into the quaking-bog heart of this peatland. In my descent to this kettle hole cupped among steep, rocky hills, I passed from an upland forest's drifts of dry, curled leaves of beech, white birch, and sugar maple to a soggy shore of sphagnum with thickets of winterberry, stands of blue-joint, and mounds of tussock sedge and royal fern. At this spot, a millennium and a half or so ago, I would have been standing at the gravelly edge of a deep, clear kettle-hole lake. At the right moment I would have seen the first few fingerings of sphagnum moss among the wet stones and gravel of the shoreline.

The kettle hole was formed by the melting of a tremendous chunk of glacial ice buried beneath tons of rock, gravel, and sand. When the ice melted, the water it yielded, supplemented by floods of glacial melt-water, filled the cavernous space left in the landscape. Over thousands of years, mosses from the stony shore crept across the water and filled the depths with peat. Under the straggling red maples on the bog's margin the sphagnum peat may be ten to twenty feet deep; in the central mat, forty to fifty.

As I pass through the fringe of red maple, I encounter the dark, crisp-needled shapes of black spruce. Over their blue-black shoulders, tama-racks stand golden and vibrant against the sky's deep October blue. Like huddled, cloaked figures, the black spruces thrust up among these bright, open-branched, ethereal trees. Far more shade-tolerant than tamarack, black spruce can grow up among them and eventually supplant them. These two conifers are widespread in boreal forests, near the northern limits of growth of any tree. Far to the south they find footholds in harsh fens, where similarly stringent conditions favor these species and keep other trees at bay. At the beginning of glacial retreat, larch and spruce were widespread, but as the climate grew warmer and drier they re-treated farther to the north, except for habitats such as Tamarack Bog, set among rocky rises in central New Hampshire.

As I near the center of this peatland, the tamaracks dwindle to a little less than human height, twisting arabesquely, like dwarfed, dancing fig-ures holding poses. Closer yet to the open mat they become horizontal, almost creeping on the sphagnum, as though growing on a sparse, wind-swept mountain ledge. Black spruce too become progressively shorter, as if they were descending a staircase, until they stand less than knee high and become ever more sparse. Many of their short, horizontal, stiffly drooping branches have died; the diminished, tufted black-green crowns keep their life going. Growth can be so slow in bogs and harsh fens that a thirty-year-old scrubby black spruce may have a trunk only one inch in diameter.

Under some ecological conditions, plants may fill in and eventually turn a peatland basin into a terrestrial environment, or a rise in water level may shift it to swamp or marsh. But unless a major change occurs in the landscape or prevailing climate, or the activities of beavers or humans intervene, a bog or fen can remain impervious to transformation for great spans of time. Trees other than larch and black spruce may move in over protracted periods of drought, but they will be drowned back when years of abundant precipitation return. Trees that die off and topple will be reclaimed by the patient sphagnum. Similarly, the seemingly inexorable advance of peatland vegetation on the open water of a pond or lake may be held in check by such factors as the water regime and its chemistry. A peatland's ecology is not controlled by abiotic factors alone. Once established among the physical gradients of a peatland basin, plants (especially sphagnum mosses) do much to shape their own environments. By influencing the distribution and chemistry of the water and the nature of substrates, they affect the composition and distribution of the plant communities. Unless there is a major perturbation, these peatland systems remain ecologically intact for thousands of years. The classic concept of an inevitable succession from open water to peatland to grown-in wetland and finally upland forest appears to represent a most uncommon scenario. The dynamics of peatland ecology are marked by an interchange of vegetative advancement and recession along a body of water; it is not likely that a peatland basin is destined to become a forest. The bog's dual faces of change and permanence play upon my own sense of time, both confounding and consoling me. When we look for constancy in nature, we cannot use human lifetimes as a measure. We are barely on track when we think in terms of the life spans of glaciers.

At the fringe of the last low larches, I can see that the moss is moving up the squat, twisted trunks and stems of the outermost conifers and heaths. All of this woody vegetation becomes movement arrested, fixed in place. The growth of trees and shrubs, every twisting reach of stem and branch for light, every inching of root for water, nutrients, and stability, becomes locked in lignified form. Movement is rendered architecturally, in a construct the eye can trace. Beneath the twisted trees, the mosses that move on water and carry water with them are inexorably engulfing a colony of pitcher plants. The sphagnum has reached their very throats. I didn't notice at first how many of these signal carnivorous bog plants there are around me, for they are little more than open mouths in the encroaching peat. A living sea is rising, a deepening sea of moss coming to drown all plants that cannot manage to keep above it. The pitcher plants have little chance for photosynthesis now, and their roots must literally be in deep trouble, as the upper peat layer buries them more deeply with each season. They will need to be successful at trapping insects; they have little other means to sustain themselves. I make out now that some have died in the mat, buried alive by living growth.

Backtracking a few steps into the waist- to shoulder-high forest of spruce and larch, I find pitcher plants that have perished by another mode, at the hands — or, rather, the roots and foliage — of advancing vegetation. The darkly shading spruce have taken the sky away from the woody vines, low-mounded shrubs, sedges, and pitcher plants. These last may be insectivores, but they are green plants and cannot live without sunlight. Their persistent pale gray ghosts stand at full height in the shaded moss. But the species lives on, flourishing in tall-cupped colonies that crown emerald hummocks of sphagnum farther out on the open mat. These pitcher plants could well have arisen from seeds dispersed from the final flowerings of the ghosts beneath the spruce.

Even within the deep shade of the conifers, the mosses are at work, reaching for everything that rises from them. But the black spruce responds to this encroachment. As sphagnum moves up the trunks to reach the lowest drooping branches, the branches develop adventitious roots within the moss. These help support and nourish the tree in the yielding peat. As these roots spread, buds on the outer tips of the branches grow upward to become the trunks of new trees, a botanical process termed layering. These young sprouts commonly form a ring around the parent tree, appearing more vigorous than the beleaguered elder they encircle, whose roots are more deeply embedded in an increasingly anoxic and nutrient-impoverished layer of peat. Away from the peatlands, in the cool, moist soils of the boreal forest, black spruces often effect layering when their lower branches are pressed to the earth by snow.

The harsh-fen conditions around the landward perimeter of Tamarack Bog have been ameliorated over time by neutralizing and enriching leaf fall and other detritus from surrounding forests, and the bog's rim has become a red maple swamp. But sphagnum remains the conquering force: slight increase in annual precipitation or decrease in temperatures could turn the moss back against the encroaching ring of red maples. In some regions and climate epochs, mosses conquer trees and bogs overtake forests. Because sphagnum mosses pull water along with them by capillary action, conditions that favor their advancement, the roots of upland vegetation can become so saturated that they suffocate; the diminutive growth of a bog is capable of drowning a forest. This process is termed paludification. Geological shifts and global climate changes can turn the water tables, so to speak, on the plants of drier footing. Although bogs that have developed from the encroachment of plants on deep, steep-sided kettle holes, lakes, or ponds are generally the most familiar, they may be much less common globally than peatlands resulting from paludification.

Close to the center of the bog I feel I am witness to the water's final closing over, the putting out of a ten-thousand-year reflecting light. But for a few small pools, themselves so laced with creepings of moss they cannot manage a proper reflection, the sphagnum that set out so long ago from the shoreline of a glacial lake has claimed its water. My own brief time coincides with the blinking out of the last open waters of this ancient peatland. By a long route of life, growth, and death, Tamarack Bog has come to this point of transition. All things being equal, it may hold in place for another ten thousand years. In scanning the living and dead plants, I can envision the long-ago time when the glacial lake filled in, can imagine it as an ice-space, then water-space, and finally a peatland plant-space. Bogs and fens are laboratories of time, representing freeze-frames of the workings of earth, air, fire, and water, together with plant life, over centuries and millennia. The march of the tiny mosses on the water from every point around it has been completed. Now they will build upon themselves, and in varying degrees and cycles other plants will follow in their wake.

The deep peat of bogs contains a decipherable record, a history written in a woven cuneiform of plant, and some animal, fragments. I finger down into the sphagnum past the rather thin skin of the living layer and the slender zone beneath it, in which some oxygen is available and some decay occurs. A few soggy inches deeper I am in the profundal realm in which decay is virtually arrested and from which I can extract recognizable bits of plants: the ever-present sphagnum mosses, twigs and pieces of heath and sedge leaves that I could probably identify to the species with the aid of a microscope. I pull out a bit of stiff, blackened stem that might be a remnant of bog rosemary that bloomed here two hundred years before I was born. But this is very recent history in peatland terms. It does not even represent yesterday. Cores extracted from depths of twenty to forty feet, examined with powerful microscopes and aged by such techniques as radiocarbon dating, would reveal pollen from plants that lived here ten thousand years ago, in many cases identifiable to species. Core samples from clay beneath the peat would contain pollen loosed by grasses, sedges, and shrubby tundra plants of fifteen to twenty thousand years ago, bearing witness to the first vegetation after the glaciers receded northward. Some animal history is also revealed, in remains ranging from the exoskeletons of insects to the bones of such extinct animals as woolly mammoths and mastodons. Human bodies have been kept remarkably intact in European peat bogs for two thousand years. Bodies buried in Florida peatlands seven thousand years ago have yielded the earliest known examples of human DNA in their brain tissues.

The bog is impartial, as all of nature is impartial. Its records, in underlying clays or once-living peat, read as they were written. If a smoke of pollen drifts down upon the mat, it is covered and sealed in the ongoing growth of the sphagnum. A dusting of ash from a volcanic eruption halfway around the world becomes incorporated into the time line of its day, its layer in the stratified peat. Charcoal from searing bog fires is stratified at relatively regular two-century intervals.

The peatlands of the current day in earth's history are recording a strangely high-speed chapter of actions and perturbations associated not with the comings and goings of ice sheets or geologic upheavals but with the unprecedented environmental manipulations of *Homo sapiens*. Three hundred years or so deep in northeastern American peatlands lies a sudden break in the pollen record. Deposits of pollen from native forest trees, which had been accumulating for centuries, suddenly give way to the pollen of field plants. Some of these are native to the region, but most, like plantain, are exotics brought across an ocean by colonizers who interrupted the tree-pollen record by cutting away forests for building and agriculture. A little over two centuries later, lead suddenly appears in the peat record, testimony to the invention of the automobile. Lead may have left its final traces now, but new substances appear for periods of years, as the inventors of the automobile go on with other experiments. Many of these substances are restructurings that have no link to the natural history of things on earth, artificial materials with initials like DDT and PCB, a litany of man-made marvels that have come to be called pollutants. One of the most recent additions to the peat record has a persistence that challenges even a bog's time: radioactive fallout, with its lethal persistence of half a million years.

A new chapter takes its place in the annals of the bog, as it does in other vaults of history on the planet. It is the story of the only species to adapt the earth to its own ends, rather than adapting itself to the terms of existence on the planet. This story is being written in the libraries of peat, inorganic soils, stone, water, and air, alongside glacier scratches on mountainsides, dinosaur tracks, vapors of volcanoes above the clouds, and fossilized bacteria from the dawn of life. It is being written in footprints and scraps and scratches on the earth's solitary moon, on other planets and their moons, in bits of rubble drifting in outer space. Traces and markings, records and evidence, a history being written whether or not there will be a reader.

EPILOGUE

With *Swampwalker's Journal* I complete my "wet-sneaker trilogy," books of writings and drawings centered on turtles, trout, and wetlands, respectively. The seeds of these volumes go back to my youth. Originally I simply wanted to celebrate and share the natural world I had been so lucky to find and come to know more deeply over the years. But as time went by and I was compelled to move as wetlands vanished around me, I inescapably came to see a landscape of loss, and I must report this as well. A century and a half ago, Thoreau wrote in dismay and anger of his realization that he was attempting to read the book of nature, only to find that his ancestors had torn out so many pages. How many more pages have been torn away since then?

I did not want to overwhelm readers of this book with laments and tirades, but each wetland I wrote about evoked vivid scenes of habitat degradation, alteration, fragmentation, and loss. A primary reason that this book took me more than seven years to complete is that I became involved along the way with efforts to prevent the loss of some wetlands I had come to know. Nearly all of those endeavors were, or soon will prove to be, losing battles, a reality familiar to anyone working for the preservation of wild places.

There are so many issues under the general heading of environmental concerns that I had to curtail or leave out some deep and divisive considerations in order not to overburden this book. Thus I could not properly treat such vital concerns as the sorry business of wetland mitigation, in which people presume to replicate or replace in kind wetland habitats taken for development, road building, and the like. It is my contention that ethical and aesthetic, as well as ecological, considerations render this a failed policy.

For all the rising awareness and increased sounding of environmental alarms, we do not, on the whole, truly grasp the enormity of global habitat loss and its consequences for nonhuman life and, in the end, for ourselves. Nor do we seem to recognize the role of individual human lives in the intensification of this loss. We are, as a species, environmental racists. I do not mean the issue of the "haves" visiting their castings, hazardous waste, and such upon the neighborhoods of the "have-nots." Rather I refer to the unchecked global population we so arrogantly allow ourselves and to the remorselessly human-centered tenor of global economics and politics. We use the words "environment" and "environmental protection" too exclusively in reference to human environments, human service: clean air for us to breathe, clean water for us to drink, swim in, stock and catch fish in. Mountains are there for us to climb and ski and hold our communication towers; their sheerest rock faces are for us to scale. Deserts and wetlands exist to provide challenges and arenas for our equipment, technology, and all-terrain vehicles. Or they are all no more than agreeable backgrounds, something to look at out our windows, over cleared spaces that were once rich in habitats and species. In conservation debates, we cannot use the phrase "in perpetuity" without putting it in terms of our own future generations, our children's children's children. The depth of our anthropocentric behavior reveals explicitly the extent to which we think of ourselves as owning all living things, along with the very earth, air, and water in which they live, as if we possessed some divinely mandated dominion over all creation. As we will learn in time, none of this belongs to us.

The one species that most affects the earth and all other species, having set itself apart from them, and evidently considering itself capable of living outside of the strictures governing all the others, must come to heed the voices that express the ecological ethic and aesthetic. It is these voices that speak to the inescapable awareness that the human being and human spirit do not exist outside of the coevolutionary design, the framework of the natural world.

LIST OF COMMON
AND SCIENTIFIC NAMES

SELECTED BIBLIOGRAPHY

INDEX

LIST OF COMMON AND SCIENTIFIC NAMES

PLANTS

Alder, speckled	*Alnus rugosa*
Anemone, wood	*Anemone quinquefolia*
Arbutus, trailing	*Epigaea repens*
Arrowhead, broad-leaf	*Sagittaria latifolia*
Arrowwood, northern	*Viburnum recognitum*
Arum, arrow	*Peltandra virginica*
Ash, black	*Fraxinus nigra*
Ash, green	*Fraxinus pennsylvanica*
Ash, white	*Fraxinus americana*
Aspen, bigtooth	*Populus grandidentata*
Aspen, quaking	*Populus tremuloides*
Aster, flat-topped white	*Aster umbellatus*
Aster, swamp	*Aster puniceus*
Aster, white wood	*Aster divaricatus*
Azalea, swamp	*Rhododendron viscosum*
Bald cypress	*Taxodium distichum*
Beak rush, white	*Rhyncospora alba*
Bedstraw, rough	*Galium asperellum*
Beech, American	*Fagus grandifolia*
Beechdrops	*Epifagus virginiana*
Birch, gray	*Betula populifolia*
Birch, swamp	*Betula pumila*
Birch, white (paper)	*Betula papyrifera*
Birch, yellow	*Betula alleghaniensis*
Blackberry	*Rubus allegheniensis*
Bladderwort, common	*Utricularia macrorhiza*

Bladderwort, flat-leaf	*Utricularia intermedia*
Bladderwort, horned	*Utricularia cornuta*
Bladderwort, purple	*Utricularia purpurea*
Blueberry, black highbush	*Vaccinium atrococcum*
Blueberry, highbush	*Vaccinium corymbosum*
Blueberry, late low	*Vaccinium vacillans*
Blue flag, larger	*Iris versicolor*
Bluet	*Houstonia caerula*
Boneset	*Eupatorium perfoliatum*
Broom-sedge, pointed	*Carex scoparia*
Buckbean (bogbean)	*Menyanthes trifoliata*
Buckwheat, climbing false	*Polygonum scandens*
Bulrush, green	*Scirpus atrovirens*
Bulrush, soft-stem	*Scirpus validus*
Bulrush, water	*Scirpus subterminalis*
Bur-marigold	*Bidens laevis*
Bur-reed, American	*Sparganium americanum*
Buttonbush	*Cephalanthus occidentalis*
Calla, wild	*Calla palustris*
Cardinal flower	*Lobelia cardinalis*
Cattail, broad-leaved	*Typha latifolia*
Cattail, narrow-leaved	*Typha angustifolia*
Cherry, black	*Prunus serotina*
Cherry, pin (fire)	*Prunus pensylvanica*
Chokeberry, black	*Aronia (Pyrus) melanocarpa*
Chokeberry, red	*Aronia (Pyrus) arbutifolia*
Clearweed	*Pilea pumila*
Clubmoss, tree	*Lycopodium obscurum*
Cotton grass, few-nerved	*Eriophorum tenellum*
Cotton grass, tawny	*Eriophorum virginicum*
Cottonwood, eastern	*Populus deltoides*
Cranberry, large	*Vaccinium macrocarpon*
Cranberry, small	*Vaccinium oxycoccus*
Crowfoot, water	*Ranunculus trichophylla*
Cudweed, low	*Gnaphalium uliginosum*
Dewberry	*Rubus flagellarus*
Dewberry, swamp	*Rubus hispidus*
Dogwood, silky	*Cornus amomum*
Duckweed, big	*Spirodella polyrhiza*
Duckweed, lesser	*Lemna minor*
Elderberry, common	*Sambucus canadensis*
Elm, American	*Ulmus americana*
False-hellebore, American	*Veratrum viride*

Fern, bracken	*Pteridium aquilinum*
Fern, cinnamon	*Osmunda cinnamomea*
Fern, crested shield	*Dryopteris cristata*
Fern, interrupted	*Osmunda claytoniana*
Fern, marsh	*Thelypteris palustris*
Fern, ostrich	*Matteuccia struthiopteris*
Fern, polypody, common	*Polypodium virginianum*
Fern, royal	*Osmunda regalis*
Fern, sensitive	*Onoclea sensibilis*
Flat-sedge, strawcolor	*Cyperus strigosus*
Forget-me-not	*Myosotis scorpioides*
Fountain moss	*Fontinalis* species
Goldenrod, gray	*Solidago nemoralis*
Goldenrod, lance-leaved	*Solidago graminifolia*
Goldenrod, late	*Solidago gigantea*
Goldenrod, rough-leaved	*Solidago patula*
Goldenrod, rough-stemmed	*Solidago rugosa*
Goldenrod, swamp	*Solidago uliginosa*
Goldthread	*Coptis groenlandica*
Grape, riverbank	*Vitis riparia*
Grass, barnyard	*Echinochloa pungens*
Grass, deertongue	*Panicum clandestinum*
Grass, fowl manna	*Glyceria striata*
Grass, little bluestem	*Schizachyrium scoparium*
Grass, rattlesnake manna	*Glyceria canadensis*
Grass, reed canary	*Phalaris arundinacea*
Groundnut	*Apios americana*
Gum, black (tupelo)	*Nyssa sylvatica*
Hare's tail	*Eriophorum spissum*
Hazelnut, American	*Corylus americana*
Hazelnut, beaked	*Corylus cornuta*
Hemlock, eastern	*Tsuga canadensis*
Hickory, pignut	*Carya glabra*
Hickory, shagbark	*Carya ovata*
Hickory, water	*Carya aquatica*
Hog-peanut, American	*Amphicarpa bracteata*
Huckleberry, black	*Gaylussacia baccata*
Jack-in-the-pulpit, swamp	*Arisaema triphyllis*
Jewelweed, spotted (touch-me-not)	*Impatiens capensis*
Joe-pye weed, spotted	*Eupatorium maculatum*
Labrador tea	*Ledum groenlandicum*
Ladies'-tresses, nodding	*Spiranthes cernua*
Larch, American (tamarack)	*Larix laricina*

Laurel, pale	*Kalmia polifolia*
Laurel, sheep	*Kalmia angustifolia*
Leatherleaf	*Chamaedaphne calyculata*
Loosestrife, purple	*Lythrum salicaria*
Maleberry	*Lyonia ligustrina*
Maple, red	*Acer rubrum*
Maple, silver	*Acer saccharinum*
Maple, sugar	*Acer saccharum*
Marsh-marigold, common	*Caltha palustris*
Meadow rue, tall	*Thalictrum pubescens*
Mermaidweed, marsh	*Proserpinaca palustris*
Milkweed, swamp	*Asclepias incarnata*
Mint, wild	*Mentha arvensis*
Mock-cucumber, wild	*Echinocystis lobata*
Moss, haircap	*Polystichum commune*
Moss, sphagnum	*Sphagnum* species
Nettle, false (bog hemp)	*Boehmeria cylindrica*
Oak, overcup	*Quercus lyrata*
Oak, red	*Quercus rubra*
Oak, scarlet	*Quercus coccinea*
Oak, swamp white	*Quercus bicolor*
Oak, white	*Quercus alba*
Pickerelweed	*Pontederia cordata*
Pine, white	*Pinus strobus*
Pipewort	*Eriocaulon septangulare*
Pitcher plant	*Sarracenia purpurea*
Pogonia, rose	*Pogonia ophioglossoides*
Pondweed	*Potamogetan* species
Pondweed, floating-leaf	*Potamogetan natans*
Raspberry, common red	*Rubus idaeus*
Reed, giant	*Phragmites communis*
Reedgrass, bluejoint	*Calamagrostis canadensis*
Riccia, purple-fringed	*Ricciocarpus natans*
Riccia, slender	*Riccia fluitans*
Rose, swamp	*Rosa palustris*
Rosemary, bog	*Andromeda glaucophylla*
Rush, soft	*Juncus effusus*
Saint Johnswort, dwarf	*Hypericum mutilum*
Saint Johnswort, marsh	*Triadenum virginicum*
Sedge, beaked	*Carex rostrata*
Sedge, bladder	*Carex intumescens*
Sedge, fox	*Carex vulpinoidea*
Sedge, fringed	*Carex crinita*

Sedge, hop	*Carex lupulina*
Sedge, inflated	*Carex inflata*
Sedge, porcupine	*Carex hystricina*
Sedge, tussock	*Carex stricta*
Sedge, woolly-fruit	*Carex lasiocarpa*
Sedge, yellow-nut	*Cyperus esculentus*
Shinleaf	*Pyrola elliptica*
Skullcap, marsh	*Scutellaria galericulata*
Skunk cabbage	*Symplocarpus foetida*
Smartweed, marshpepper	*Polygonum hydropiper*
Smartweed, swamp	*Polygonum coccineum*
Snowberry, creeping	*Gaultheria hispidula*
Spearwort, creeping	*Ranunculus reptans*
Spicebush, northern	*Lindera benzoin*
Spikerush, blunt	*Eleocharis obtusa*
Spikerush, slender	*Eleocharis tenuis*
Spring beauty, Carolina	*Claytonia caroliniana*
Spruce, black	*Picea mariana*
Spruce, red	*Picea rubens*
Sumac, staghorn	*Rhus typhina*
Sundew, round-leaved	*Drosera rotundifolia*
Sunflower, woodland	*Helianthus divaricatus*
Swamp candles	*Lysimachia terrestris*
Swamp-loosestrife, hairy (water willow)	*Decodon verticillatus*
Sweetfern	*Comptonia peregrina*
Sweet gale	*Myrica gale*
Sycamore	*Platanus occidentalis*
Tamarack (American larch)	*Larix laricina*
Tearthumb, arrow-leaved	*Polygonum sagittatum*
Tearthumb, halberd-leaved	*Polygonum arifolium*
Trout lily	*Erythronium americanum*
Turtlehead	*Chelone glabra*
Vervain, blue	*Verbena hastata*
Violet, dog	*Viola conspersa*
Violet, lance-leaved	*Viola lanceolata*
Violet, marsh Blue	*Viola cucullata*
Violet, northern white	*Viola pallens*
Virgin's-bower, Virginia	*Clematis virginiana*
Water-hemlock, bulbet-bearing	*Cicuta bulbifera*
Water-hemlock, spotted	*Cicuta maculata*
Water lily, white	*Nymphaea odorata*
Water lily, yellow	*Nuphar variegatum*

Water locust	*Nyssa aquatica*
Watermeal	*Wolffia columbiana*
Water-milfoil	*Myriophyllum* species
Water parsnip	*Sium suave*
Watershield	*Brasenia schreberi*
Water-starwort, larger	*Callitriche heterophylla*
White cedar, Atlantic	*Chamaecyperis thyoides*
White cedar, northern	*Thuja occidentalis*
Wild celery	*Vallisneria americana*
Wild-rye, riverbank	*Elymus riparia*
Willow, autumn	*Salix serissima*
Willow, black	*Salix nigra*
Willow, hoary	*Salix candida*
Willow, pussy	*Salix discolor*
Willow, sandbar	*Salix interior*
Willow, shining	*Salix lucida*
Willow, silky	*Salix sericea*
Willow-herb, purple-leaved	*Epilobium coloratum*
Winterberry, common	*Ilex verticillatus*
Wintergreen, spotted	*Chimaphila maculata*
Wood-nettle, Canada	*Laportea canadensis*
Wool-grass	*Scirpus cyperinus*

INVERTEBRATES

Amphipods	Amphipoda (order)
Backswimmer, common	*Notonecta undulata*
Beetle, predaceous diving	Dytiscidae (family)
Beetle, whirligig	Gyrinidae (family)
Blowfly	Calliphoridae (family)
Caddis fly	Trichoptera (order)
Cicada, periodical	*Magicada* species
Clam, fingernail	Sphaeriidae (family)
Crayfish	*Cambarus* species
Cricket	Grillidae (family)
Damselfly	Zygoptera (suborder)
Dragonfly	Anisoptera (suborder)
Fly, black	*Simulium* species
Fly, deer	*Chrysops* species
Grasshopper, meadow	Conocephalinae (subfamily)
Green-jacket	*Erythemis simplicicollis*
Isopods	Isopoda (order)
Jewelwing, ebony	*Calopterix maculata*

Katydid, true (northern)	*Pterophylla camellifolia*
Leech	*Placobdella* species
Mayfly	Ephemeroptera (order)
Meadowfly, ruby	*Sympetrum rubicundulum*
Mosquito	Culicidae (family)
Shrimp, fairy	*Eubranchipus vernalis*
Stonefly, common	Perlidae (family)
Tenspot	*Libellula pulchella*
Water bug, giant	*Lethocerus americanus*
Waterscorpion	*Ranatra* species
Water strider	Gerridae (family)
Water tiger (larva)	Dytiscidae (family)

FISH

Bass, largemouth	*Micropterus salmoides*
Bass, smallmouth	*Micropterus dolomieu*
Bluegill	*Lepomus macrochirus*
Bullhead, brown	*Ictalurus nebulosa*
Dace, black-nosed	*Rhinichthys atralatus*
Fallfish	*Semotilus corporalis*
Perch, yellow	*Perca flavescens*
Pickerel, chain	*Esox niger*
Pickerel, redfin	*Esox americana*
Pumpkinseed	*Lepomus gibbosus*
Sucker, white	*Catostomus commersoni*
Sunfish, banded	*Enneacanthus obesus*
Trout, brook	*Salvelinus fontinalis*

AMPHIBIANS

Bullfrog	*Rana catesbeiana*
Frog, green	*Rana clamitans melanota*
Frog, mink	*Rana septentrionalis*
Frog, northern leopard	*Rana pipiens*
Frog, pickerel	*Rana palustris*
Frog, wood	*Rana sylvatica*
Newt, red-spotted (eastern)	*Notophthalmus v. viridescens*
Peeper, spring	*Pseudacris crucifer*
Salamander, blue-spotted	*Ambystoma laterale*
Salamander, four-toed	*Hemidactylium scutatum*
Salamander, Jefferson	*Ambystoma jeffersonianum*
Salamander, marbled	*Ambystoma opacum*

Salamander, spotted	*Ambystoma maculatum*
Toad, eastern American	*Bufo a. americanus*
Treefrog, gray	*Hyla versicolor*

REPTILES

Slider, red-eared	*Trachemys scripta elegans*
Snake, eastern garter	*Thamnophis s. sirtalis*
Snake, eastern ribbon	*Thamnophis s. sauritis*
Snake, northern water	*Nerodia s. sipedon*
Snake, redbelly	*Storeria o. occipitomaculata*
Turtle, Blanding's	*Emydoidea blandingii*
Turtle, bog	*Clemmys muhlenbergii*
Turtle, common musk (stinkpot)	*Sternotherus odoratus*
Turtle, common snapping	*Chelydra s. serpentina*
Turtle, eastern box	*Terrapene c. carolina*
Turtle, eastern painted	*Chrysemys p. picta*
Turtle, red-bellied	*Pseudemys rubiventris*
Turtle, spotted	*Clemmys guttata*
Turtle, wood	*Clemmys insculpta*

BIRDS

Bittern, American	*Botaurus lentiginosus*
Blackbird, red-winged	*Agelaius phoeniceus*
Catbird, gray	*Dumetella carolinensis*
Chickadee, black-capped	*Parus atricapillus*
Creeper, brown	*Certhia americana*
Dove, mourning	*Zenaida macroura*
Duck, American black	*Anas rubripes*
Duck, ring-necked	*Aythya collaris*
Duck, wood	*Aix sponsa*
Eagle, bald	*Haliaeetus leucocephalis*
Flycatcher, alder	*Empidonax alnorum*
Flycatcher, great-crested	*Myiarchus crinitus*
Flycatcher, least	*Empidonax minimus*
Flycatcher, willow	*Empidonax trailii*
Goldeneye, common (American)	*Bucephela clangula*
Goldfinch, American	*Carduelis tristas*
Goose, Canada	*Branta canadensis*
Grackle, common	*Quiscalus quiscula*
Grouse, ruffed	*Bonasa umbellus*
Hawk, broad-winged	*Buteo platypterus*

Hawk, marsh (northern harrier)	*Circus cyaneus*
Heron, great blue	*Ardea herodius*
Heron, green	*Butorides virescens*
Killdeer	*Charadrius vociferus*
Kingbird, eastern	*Tyrannus tyrannus*
Kingfisher, belted	*Ceryle alcyon*
Kinglet, ruby-crowned	*Regulus calendula*
Merganser, hooded	*Lophodytes cucullatus*
Oriole, northern (Baltimore)	*Ictarus galbula*
Osprey	*Pandion haliaetus*
Owl, barred	*Strix varia*
Owl, great horned	*Bubo virginianus*
Phoebe, eastern	*Sayornis phoebe*
Rail, Virginia	*Rallus limicola*
Robin, American	*Turdus migratorius*
Sandpiper, spotted	*Actitus macularia*
Sora	*Porzana carolina*
Sparrow, Lincoln's	*Melospiza lincolnii*
Sparrow, savannah	*Passerculus sandwichensis*
Sparrow, song	*Melospiza melodia*
Sparrow, swamp	*Melospiza georgiana*
Sparrow, white-throated	*Zonotrichia albicollis*
Swallow, bank	*Riparia riparia*
Swallow, tree	*Tachycineta bicolor*
Thrush, hermit	*Catharus guttatus*
Thrush, wood	*Hylocichla musteline*
Titmouse, tufted	*Parus bicolor*
Turkey, wild	*Meleagris gallopavo*
Veery	*Catharus fuscescens*
Vireo, red-eyed	*Vireo olivaceus*
Warbler, black-and-white	*Mniotilta varia*
Warbler, black-throated blue	*Dendroica caerulescens*
Warbler, Canada	*Wilsonia canadensis*
Warbler, palm	*Dendroica palmarum*
Warbler, yellow	*Dendroica petechia*
Water thrush, northern	*Seiurus noveboracensis*
Woodcock, American	*Scolopax minor*
Woodpecker, downy	*Dendrocopos pubescens*
Woodpecker, hairy	*Dendrocopos villosus*
Wren, winter	*Troglodytes troglodytes*
Yellowthroat, common	*Geothlypis trichas*

Bat, big brown	*Eptesicus fuscus*
Bear, black	*Ursus americanus*
Beaver	*Castor canadensis*
Bobcat	*Felis rufus*
Chipmunk, eastern	*Tamias striatus*
Cougar (mountain lion, Florida panther)	*Felis concolor*
Coyote, eastern	*Canis latrans*
Deer, white-tailed	*Odocoileus virginianus*
Fisher	*Martes pennanti*
Fox, red	*Vulpes vulpes*
Hare, snowshoe	*Lepus americanus*
Lemming, southern Bog	*Synaptomys cooperi*
Mammoth, woolly	*Mammuthus primigenius*
Mink	*Mustela vison*
Mole, eastern	*Scalopus aquaticus*
Mole, star-nosed	*Condylura cristata*
Moose	*Alces alces*
Muskrat	*Ondatra zibethica*
Opossum, Virginia	*Didelphis virginiana*
Otter, river	*Lutra canadensis*
Raccoon	*Procyon lotor*
Shrew, masked	*Sorex cinereus*
Shrew, water	*Sorex palustris*
Skunk, striped	*Mephitis mephitis*
Vole, meadow	*Microtus pennsylvanicus*
Vole, southern red-backed	*Clethrionomys gapperi*
Weasel, short-tailed (ermine)	*Mustela erminea*
Wolf, red	*Canis rufus*

SELECTED BIBLIOGRAPHY

Bardach, J. 1964. *Downstream: A natural history of the river from its source to the sea.* New York: Grosset and Dunlap.

Borror, D. J., and R. E. White. 1970. *Field guide to the insects of America north of Mexico.* Boston: Houghton Mifflin.

Brown, L. 1979. *Grasses: An identification guide.* Boston: Houghton Mifflin.

Burt, W. H., and R. P. Grossenheider. 1961. *A field guide to the mammals.* Boston: Houghton Mifflin.

Butler, B. O., and T. E. Graham. 1995. Early post-emergent behavior and habitat selection in hatchling Blanding's turtles, *Emydoidea blandingii,* in Massachusetts. *Chelonian Conservation and Biology* 1 (3):187–96.

Caduto, J. M. 1990. *Pond and brook: a guide to nature in freshwater environments.* Hanover, N.H.: University Press of New England.

Carpenter, V. 1991. *Dragonflies and damselflies of Cape Cod.* Brewster, Mass.: Cape Cod Museum of Natural History series, no. 4.

Carr, A. 1952. *Handbook of turtles: The turtles of the United States, Canada, and Baja California.* Ithaca, N. Y.: Cornell University Press.

Carroll, D. M. 1991. *The year of the turtle: a natural history.* New York: St. Martin's Press.

Cobb, B. 1963. *A field guide to ferns and their related families of northeastern and central North America.* Boston: Houghton Mifflin.

Conant, R., and J. T. Collins. 1991. *A field guide to reptiles and amphibians of eastern and central North America,* 3rd. ed. Boston: Houghton Mifflin.

Congdon, J. D., and R. E. Gatten, Jr. 1989. Movements and energetics of nesting *Chrysemys picta. Herpetologica* 45:94–100.

Cowardin, L. M., V. Carter, F. C. Golet, and E. T. La Roe. 1979. *Classification of wetlands and deepwater habitats of the United States.* U.S. Fish and Wildlife Service, Biological Services Program, FWS/OBS-79/31.

Dickerson, M. C. 1969. *The frog book.* New York: Dover Publications (reprint of 1906 edition, Garden City, N.Y.: Doubleday, Page and Co.).

Ernst, C. H., R. W. Barbour, and J. E. Lovich. 1994. *Turtles of the United States and Canada.* Washington, D.C.: Smithsonian Institution Press.

———. 1982. Environmental temperatures and activities in wild spotted turtles, *Clemmys guttata. Journal of Herpetology* 16:112–20.

———. 1977. Biological notes on the bog turtle, *Clemmys Muhlenbergii. Herpetologica* 33:241–46.

Errington, P. 1957. *Of men and marshes.* New York: Macmillan.

Fair, J. 1990. *The great American bear.* Minocqua, Wis.: North Word Press.

Farrell, R. F., and T. E. Graham. 1991. Ecological notes on the turtle *Clemmys insculpta* in northwestern New Jersey. *Journal of Herpetology* 25(1):1–9.

Fasset, N. C. 1969. *A manual of aquatic plants.* Madison, Wis.: University of Wisconsin Press.

Fernald, M. L. 1950. *Gray's manual of botany,* 8th ed. New York: American Book Co.

Finlayson, M., and M. Moser, gen. eds. *Wetlands.* 1991. New York: Facts on File.

Gaffney, E. S. 1990. *Dinosaurs.* New York: Golden Press.

Garber, S. D., and J. Burger. 1995. A twenty-year study documenting the relationship between turtle decline and human recreation. *Ecol. Appl.* 5:1151–62.I

Golet, F. C., A. J. K. Calhoun, W. R. DeRagon, D. J. Lowry, and A. J. Gold. 1993. *Ecology of red maple swamps in the glaciated Northeast: a community profile.* U.S. Fish and Wildlife Service, biological report no. 12.

Harding, J. H. 1990. *Michigan turtles and lizards.* Michigan State University Cooperative Extension Service.

Hellquist, C. E. 1996. A flora and analysis of the bryophyte and vascular plant communities of Little Dollar Lake Peatland: Mackinac County, Michigan. M.S. thesis. University of New Hampshire.

Hitchcock, A. S. 1971. *Manual of the grasses of the United States,* 2 vols. New York: Dover Publications.

Johnson, C. W. 1985. *Bogs of the Northeast.* Hanover, N.H.: University Press of New England.

Kaufmann, J. H. 1992. The social behavior of wood turtles, *Clemmys insculpta,* in central Pennsylvania. *Herpetological Monographs* 6:1–25.

Klemens, M. W. 1993. *Amphibians and reptiles of Connecticut and adjacent regions.* Hartford, Conn.: State Geological and Natural History Survey of Connecticut, bulletin no. 112.

Kricher, J. C., and G. Morrison. 1988. *Ecology of eastern forests.* Boston: Houghton Mifflin.

Lazell, J. D., Jr., and M. Michener. 1976. *This broken archipelago: Cape Cod and the islands, amphibians and reptiles.* New York: Demeter Press.

Mitsch, W. J., and J. G. Gosselink. 1986. *Wetlands.* New York: Van Nostrand Rheinhold.

Morgan, A. H. 1930. *Field book of ponds and streams.* New York: G. P. Putnam's Sons.

Motzkin, G. H., and W. A. Patterson III. 1991. Vegetation patterns and basin morphometry of a New England moat bog. *Rhodora* 93:307–21.

Needham, J. G., and P. R. Needham. 1962. *A guide to the study of fresh water biology,* 5th ed. New York: McGraw Hill.

Niering, W. A. 1985. *Wetlands.* Audubon Society nature guide. New York: Alfred A. Knopf.

———. 1966. *The life of the marsh: the North American wetlands.* New York: McGraw Hill.

Pedevillano, C. 1995. *Habitat values of New England wetlands.* Concord, N.H.: U. S. Fish and Wildlife Service.

Peterson, R. T. 1947. *A field guide to the birds: Eastern land and water birds.* Boston: Houghton Mifflin.

Peterson, R. T., and M. McKenney. 1968. *A field guide to wildflowers.* Boston: Houghton Mifflin.

Petrides, G. 1958. *A field guide to trees and shrubs.* Boston: Houghton Mifflin.

Pielou, E. C. 1991. *After the ice age: The return of life to glaciated North America.* Chicago: University of Chicago Press.

Pough, R. H. 1951. *Audubon water bird guide.* Garden City, N. Y.: Doubleday.

———. 1946. *Eastern land birds.* Audubon bird guide. Garden City, N.Y.: Doubleday.

Rezendes, P., and P. Roy. 1996. *Wetlands: The web of life.* San Francisco: Sierra Club Books.

Reschke, C. 1990. *Ecological communities of New York state.* Latham, N.Y.: New York Natural Heritage Program, New York State Department of Environmental Services.

Scarola, J. F. 1973. *Freshwater fishes of New Hampshire.* Concord, N.H.: New Hampshire Fish and Game Department.

Sperduto, D. 1994. *A classification of the natural communities of New Hampshire,* working draft. Concord, N.H.: New Hampshire Natural Heritage Inventory.

Tiner, R. W. 1998. *In search of swampland: A wetland sourcebook and field guide.* New Brunswick, N.J.: Rutgers University Press.

Tryon, B. W. 1990. Bog turtles (*Clemmys muhlenbergii*) in the South: A question of survival. *Bulletin of the Chicago Herpetological Society* 25:57–66.

Tuttle, S. E. 1996. Ecology and natural history of the wood turtle *Clemmys insculpta* in southern New Hampshire. 1996. M.S. thesis, Antioch/New England.

Tyning, T. F. 1990. *A guide to amphibians and reptiles.* A Stokes field guide. Boston: Little, Brown.

Ultsch, G. R. 1989. Ecology and physiology of hibernation among freshwater fishes, turtles, and snakes. *Biological Review* 64:435–16.

Van de Poll, R. 1996. Common hydrophytic plants of southern New Hampshire. Keene, N.H.: Antioch/New England Ecosystem Management Consultants.

INDEX